Word
Court

BARBARA WALLRAFF

Word Court

Wherein verbal virtue is rewarded,

crimes against the language are punished,

and poetic justice is done

HARCOURT, INC.

New York   San Diego   London

*To all letter writers everywhere,
and especially to the ones who have
written nice letters to me*

Requests for permission to make copies of any part of the work
should be mailed to: Permissions Department, Harcourt, Inc.,
6277 Sea Harbor Drive, Orlando, Florida 32887-6777.

Library of Congress Cataloging-in-Publication Data
Wallraff, Barbara.
Word court: wherein verbal virtue is rewarded, crimes against the language
are punished, and poetic justice is done/Barbara Wallraff.—1st ed.
p.   cm.
ISBN 0-15-100381-5
1. English language—Usage.   I. Title.
PE1460.W225   2000
428—dc21   99-24678

Text set in Sabon
Designed by Linda Lockowitz

Printed in the United States of America
First edition

C E F D

Acknowledgments

Sixteen years ago William Whitworth hired me to work for *The Atlantic Monthly,* and his willingness to take a chance on me then has led to just about every good thing that's ever happened to me professionally. Thank you, Bill. High up on the long list of those good things is this book, which happened because André Bernard was also willing to take a chance. Thank you, André.

Thanks go, as well, to my *Atlantic* colleagues, who cheered me on, wised me up, cut me slack, and helped me in so many other ways. Toby Lester and Wen Stephenson and their new-media posse were invaluable backup in the hunt for "Word Fugitives," also known as America's Most Wanted Words. Time and again Cullen Murphy, Allan Reeder, and Martha Spaulding earned my special gratitude and admiration for their vigilance, which allowed me to seem in the Word Court column, and so here, to be more sagacious than I am. Where I look foolish, of course, it's no one's fault but my own.

In the able-assistance department, Jesse Wegman looms large. Here he is joined by an exaltation of interns whom I shrink from naming for fear of leaving a worthy one out.

Thanks to Professor Steven Pinker for helping me

with my homework. Thanks to Lindy Hess no matter what. Thanks to the *Oxford English Dictionary* people who gave me the keys to their splendiferous online kingdom. Thanks to Clara Glaubman, Joel Hirsch, my favorite polymath Kermit Midthun, and Evelyn B. Wallraff for trying—and, I'm happy to say, largely failing—to find fault. Thanks to Eleanor Gould Packard, who in her gentle and solicitous finding of fault was an inspiration even more than a confederate. Thanks to Francine Prose for her estimable emceeing. Thanks to David Hough, Linda Lockowitz, Meredith Arthur, and all the other people at Harcourt who worked on this book, except the lawyers. Thanks to everyone who has shared a peeve, a tale, a suspicion, a surprise. Don't stop now!

And thanks, finally, to my darling Julian, for encouraging me to take chances and taking a chance on me, too.

Contents

misunderstood grammar-related issues, including split infinitives, why *I feel well* is good grammar and *I feel badly* is not, ending clauses with prepositions, *that* versus *which,* what it is about *hopefully,* whether *Magic* are plural in Orlando and *Jazz* in Utah, what it is about *unique,* let's keep it *between you and me,* please, and possessive puzzlements of all sorts.

Introduction

Barbara Wallraff's *Word Court* is not only instructive and delightful but also immensely reassuring. Its very existence is a comfort to those of us who care about the language, to those of us who write and read and speak, and to those of us who entertain the inchoate, mystical, and probably indefensible notion that the principles of standard English are something like the Bill of Rights, or the Gregorian calendar, or even the law of gravity—the very foundations of order and harmony, the rules that guide our lives, the necessary structure without which the world we know would fly apart.

What's so cheering—especially to those of us who are sick of hearing ourselves complain that our students can't write, our children won't read, our colleagues can't spell, and *no one* has any interest in the proper way to use words or how to string sentences together—is that in fact so many people are *so* interested that, month after month, readers address curious or perplexed or even enraged communications to "Word Court," Barbara Wallraff's regular column in *The Atlantic Monthly*, the magazine where she has worked as an editor for many years. From all over the world, she writes, "they send me letters, they send me e-mail, they send me voice mail, asking and telling and bragging and inveighing about how English is used and how it should be."

It's hard to conceive of a more competent or reliable judge, or one more qualified to resolve these matters of grammar and usage that so many people take—so surprisingly—to heart. And it's equally difficult to imagine an approach, and a literary voice, less like that of our least favorite, most punitive eighth-grade teacher—that paradoxically soporific and terrifying scold with whom so many people seem to associate the whole concept of grammar. Barbara Wallraff believes in addressing these apparently touchy issues with humor and tact, two qualities very much in evidence throughout *Word Court.* Consequently, her book is not at all like the pronouncements of some stodgy or fussy "wordwatcher" but, rather, like the hilarious and helpful ministrations of Miss Manners, keeping a cool and sophisticated eye on the etiquette of language. MsGrammar@theatlantic.com (for that is Barbara Wallraff's much-visited e-mail address) is at once knowledgeable and flexible, intent on maintaining the clarity of our common language and alert to the promptings of "precedent and consensus." At times her rare combination of expertise, patience, bemusement, and wit is oddly reminiscent of Click and Clack, NPR's *Car Talk* brothers—in my view, two of the great educators in America.

Word Court is generous with practical and specific advice. Among its most useful suggestions is that we abandon our struggles with hideously awkward tangles of singular and plural, of pronoun agreement and shattered infinitives, and simply "write around the problems"—that is, rewrite the sentence. And it addresses the complex questions that most often confront us when we sit down at the keyboard, or have a simple conversation. How ready should we be to embrace—or how determined to reject—neologisms? ("It's your choice when you will begin to accept recently adapted words—and which ones. The verbs *to gift, to impact,* and *to parent*...are widely disliked—and who needs them? *To fax* and *to Rollerblade* are almost inevitable coinages, though, because the activities they describe are new, and new language must be found for them.") How do we cope with the fact that our language has so far failed to mirror our enlightened modern ideas about gender, thus forcing us to make many delicate daily decisions involving "sex and the single pronoun" and words such as *freshman* and *chairman*? ("A speaker or writer who is trying simply to express an idea, rather than to pick a fight with listeners or readers, needs to tread carefully. . . . *Freshperson* is obviously impossible—but *chairperson* seems harmless enough.") What are the benign and the improper uses of jargon? What about participles and gerunds, pronoun antecedents, parallel series? And how far must we go to avoid ending a sentence with a preposition? (Not far at all, it seems.)

I've said that *Word Court* is delightful and informative, but I should also add a slight caveat: it's humbling, as well. My sense of my own superiority and invulnerability in matters of grammar was dismantled, bit by bit, as I read along.

One of the book's most beneficial chapters, "A Grammarian's Dozen," considers, in order of ascending importance, "thirteen specific grammatical issues that aren't well mapped in many people's heads and are therefore widely misunderstood." By the time the dozen reached its double crescendo, "Case of personal pronouns" followed shortly by "Possessives," I had learned the answers to all sorts of questions that somewhere along the line I had lost the courage to ask. For example: What exactly are restrictive and nonrestrictive clauses, and how does the comma figure into all this? Foolishly, I had come to think that it was too late for me to admit that I didn't know the rule, and so was operating on instinct rather than knowledge—in other words, faking it—always hoping that some saintly, attentive copy editor would save me from my own mistakes.

Another chapter, "Say No More," offers an "eccentric little usage dictionary," a lexicon of commonly misused or troublesome words and phrases. This made me realize how dauntingly severe and frequent my own mistakes were. For weeks I'd been complaining about a copy editor who, I was claiming, had introduced grammatical errors into a recently published review of mine; he'd made it sound as if I didn't know how to use the word *comprise*. Well, thanks to *Word Court,* I now know that I *didn't* know how to use *comprise*—my apologies to the maligned copy editor. Nor, for that matter, did I have any idea about the real meaning of *fulsome* and *officious,* or the proper spelling of *liaison.* It's spiritually beneficial to find out that we can still make mistakes—and pragmatically valuable to have them corrected.

And yet, for all her welcome help with the specific words and phrases, Barbara Wallraff never loses sight of why we might want that help—of what the larger issues are. "Our ability to communicate will break down if we don't work together at maintaining our language," she writes, and she provides numerous hilarious and scary examples of the mangled prose that indicates a break-down of this sort has occurred. She's quick to recognize cases in which what seems to be a linguistic problem is merely a symptom of a more serious social disorder: "An expression like *women's work* is demeaning only if women are already demeaned. The important thing, therefore, rather than changing the wording, is to change the low status of women—or whatever group is at issue." She resists the dehumanizing ways in which language is being deployed: "I wince when I hear some-one say to a supermarket cashier who seems idle, 'Are you open?' What's wrong with 'May I check out here?' or 'Is your register open?' "

Word Court convinces us—as our eighth-grade teacher perhaps failed to—that the purpose of grammar is not to suppress our precious individuality but, rather, to let us express it more clearly and comprehensibly, to protect ourselves (insofar as we can) from being misun-derstood:

"What language describes can be all over the map, and yet language itself is relentlessly linear: words must be expressed, and understood, one at a time. Anyone trying to tell a complicated story, in which various things happen at once, or make a complicated argu-ment, in which there are multiple relationships among ideas to be explored, has to wrestle the words into some sequence or other. And language can be as detailed or as loftily distant as we please: I can lead you in a slow, meticulous, attentive sweep of a given patch of concep-tual territory, examining and analyzing many of its par-ticulars as we go, or together we can skim over it, noting little more than its boundaries."

Barbara Wallraff writes beautifully and helps us to

do the same. Reading *Word Court* is rather like discovering, or being reminded of, how our voices can soar once we are able to read the notes—the language of music—and learn to sing on key.

—FRANCINE PROSE

Word
Court

Judge not, that ye be not judged.
—MATTHEW, VII, I

CHAPTER ONE

Who Cares

. . . or should that be "Who Cares?"

Or should *that* be " 'Who Cares?'?"

Do you care? But I bring up these questions merely as rough and ready examples of the sort of thing that my mail has taught me many people care deeply about, not as a topic into which I hope to plunge immediately, if you don't mind. (If you do mind, then please turn to Chapter Five and read the item on question marks in the section "Unquestioned Answers.") Nearly every day for years people who care about our language have been in touch with me, in my capacity as the World Wide Web's MsGrammar@theatlantic.com and the judge in *The Atlantic Monthly*'s Word Court column. From all over the country—really, all over the world—they send me letters, they send me e-mail, they send me voice mail, asking and telling and bragging and inveighing about how English is used and how it should be.

My correspondents are chemistry professors and fifth-graders, bureaucrats and amateur genealogists, secretaries and lawyers, copywriters and ministers and radio-show producers, recent immigrants and concerned parents and university presidents and builders of birdhouses. Some of them are wise and charming and witty; some of them are choleric; some are erudite, some clueless, and some completely nuts. They write from big corner offices and kitchen tables, dorm rooms and Army posts, from Canada and Mexico and Finland and Japan and Australia, from Alaska and Texas and Washington State and Washington, D.C.—all limning their fascination or frustration with American English.

I am not an academic linguist or an etymologist. Linguistics and what I do stand in something like the relation between anthropology and cooking ethnic food, or between the history of art and art restoration. As for etymology, I second the psycholinguist Steven Pinker, who, in his book *The Language Instinct,* concludes a laugh-out-loud-funny section about people who make a hobby of word origins, or "wordwatchers," with the confession "For me, wordwatching for its own sake has all the intellectual excitement of stamp collecting, with the added twist that an undetermined number of your stamps are counterfeit."

What I know about language derives chiefly from my having edited, line by line and word by word, other people's writing over the past two decades. For the last sixteen of those years, as an editor on the staff of *The Atlantic Monthly,* I have read and approved every editorial word scheduled to appear in that magazine. It's been my duty to check over the work of great prose stylists like Roy Blount Jr., Anthony Burgess, Ian Frazier, Cynthia Ozick, E. Annie Proulx, and John Updike—to pluck half a dozen examples out of sixteen years filled with great prose stylists of widely divergent kinds—and make sure that everything in their stories and articles is just as it should be. If it isn't, I suggest improvements. I have learned a great deal simply from observing how writers like these achieve the effects they do.

The Atlantic also publishes lots of articles by specialists, who may be used to writing for others in their fields. Members of this group craft sentences like "Confronted with the lack of sure knowledge, many assume that they are being manipulated for devious political reasons" and "The release of interim numbers to the scientific community and the press has given rise to a variety of inconsistent but often-cited figures." They haven't minded being prompted to say instead "Uncertainty makes many people mistrustful" and "The figures cited by scientists and the press are provisional and inconsistent"—and I'm sure the magazine's readers also didn't mind that they were.

Then, too, *The Atlantic* is proud to publish young, up-and-coming writers. I try to be especially solicitous toward this group. They are in their formative years with respect to editing, and if editing is as much like mothering as it sometimes seems to be, I don't want to be responsible for anyone's lifelong neurosis.

Regardless of who the writer is, in most articles and stories I find things that are definitely, indisputably wrong. I also suggest many changes that are matters of taste, and often my suggestions are possible solutions to problems that have a range of other possible solutions. I can't hope to present—to *The Atlantic*'s writers or to you—every option for writing, or speaking, well. All I can do is offer at least one solution to every problem that writers or my correspondents raise. I can't tell you everything that is good English, but in virtually any situation I can tell you *something* that is. Your dictionary or your spouse or the wise old fellow who taught you grammar in high school may well disagree with my advice—and why not? In this book I am expressing my opinions, not promulgating laws. I would only add that *The Atlantic Monthly* regularly gets called things like "one of the two or three best-edited magazines in the world" *(The Washingtonian)* and wins praise for its "respect for language, reasonableness and careful thought, ...and a capacity to surprise and entertain" (National Magazine Award citation); you could do worse than follow my advice.

Thank heaven, I do not stand alone as I fight my heroic battles against incorrect language! *The Atlantic* has a corps of crack word troops on duty at all times. There's even a fellow I refer to as my secret weapon—an elderly polymath in Sharpsburg, Maryland, whose subscription I quietly underwrite, because he reads every issue from cover to cover and reports to me (and only me!) any mistakes he's found.

Sure enough, despite everyone's best efforts, the wrong word or bad grammar sometimes sneaks through the lines into the magazine. When it happens, I hear about it. Believe me. When something even just suspect appears, I hear about that, too. What with seeing letters that come in about the contents of *The Atlantic* and soliciting word disputes for Word Court, I think I must have heard at least once about every cranky little punctilio that bothers anybody. Silly me: I consider it a proud accomplishment that when an irate reader wrote in to object to the grammar of the article title "How Many Is Too Many?" (he thought it should be "How Many Are Too Many?" and if you also think so, please see Chapter Three, No. 4, "Agreement in number"), I was able to explain so persuasively why he was wrong that he signed up by return mail for a three-year renewal of his subscription.

Most of my Word Court correspondents, as well, write to me about specific words or phrases, and a large portion of this book will be given over to their questions and the answers to them—including a few exchanges that have appeared in the column in somewhat different form and many that have never been published at all. Before we start on all that, though, I'd like to take a moment to reflect on the usual tone of my correspondents' remarks.

I have a pet peeve.

It annoys me very much when I see ———

I wince every time I hear ———

——— *seems cloyingly sweet with a hidden agenda of arrogance.*

Such usage when I was in grade school would have merited a rap on the knuckles by the presiding nun.

Have we gotten so timid in our speech that we are willing to torture our grammar, or is this usage proper?

It is an ugly word that, to me, has no meaning and, worse, clangs in my ears.

It is sort of like a squeaky hinge or having a kitten sharpen its claws on your head; at first it is only mildly annoying, but with repetition it becomes almost unbearable.

...this egregious solecism...

This somewhat gross solecism…

Imagine my consternation.

I can't stand it anymore.

These are some of the little signs, omens and portents that signal our approaching demise.

Such reactions occur, and word disputes erupt, in all kinds of settings.

My co-worker and I have had a grammatical disagreement for at least ten years.

Can you straighten out the argument my boss and I are having?

In a recent meeting with our company president, a colleague of mine used the phrase ———. The president scoffed at his poor use of English…. My chastised colleague felt suitably humbled until…

My wife and I have a dispute about the meaning of ———

My friends and I have pondered and debated ———

A friendship of more than fifty years hinges on your expertise.

My partner and I play cribbage together. When we count our respective hands…

My father and my aunt, both wise, well-informed, and mature adults, are engaged in an intense discussion about ———

How can I inculcate proper sentence structure in my children if…

Since children place a great deal of confidence in what they hear and see on television, I am bothered by the grammatical inconsistencies they pick up on the evening news.

Help! People in my choir are arguing over this one, and it's driving me crazy!

Well may you wonder whether the usages these people dislike so much are part of *your* vocabulary—and if so, whether their complaints are justified. But, again, for the time being the point is simply that many people care about how we express ourselves, and that they judge us by our language. One letter I received reads:

I love language/linguistics too much, perhaps—so much so that I'd be proud to be called a philologist wanna-be (as opposed to a dilettante, I hope!).

My significant other (same age: 44) could care less. This baffles and worries me. Should she care? She maintains that because she is not in a position that requires it, good grammar is a personal preference only—that she can take it or leave it without consequence!

Is grammatical accuracy necessarily a sign of intelligence? What does it say, if anything, about a person who doesn't worry in the least about whether she says was *or* were, went *or* gone, ran *or* run? *She is otherwise responsible (has raised three law-abiding children, is not a barfly or a motorcycle mama, is a very conscientious worker, a loyal employee, and a good housekeeper).*

She works for a county welfare office, but I recently had a boss in manufacturing who was the same. In addition, he couldn't spell the word spell *if his life depended on it! But he could communicate ideas for projects quite well, gave presentations in a calm and thorough manner, was fairly well organized in directing the daily operations of a small department, and was very good at implementing decisions made by upper management and employee groups. I eventually found it impossible to take orders from a man who could not even spell basic words and, for other reasons as well, agreed on a separation package from the company.*

Both of these people are high-energy "doers," joining school boards, etc., so I find it hard to believe that it's just intellectual laziness. In contrast, I have perhaps three or four times the vocabulary of both of them put together, have excellent grammar, and can spell words that they don't even know exist—but I'm so organizationally challenged that I have to write out the route to the bathroom to make sure that I get there and back!

As you can tell, I'm having a good deal of cognitive dissonance over the dilemma of trusting someone with my life who doesn't see any significance in the difference between was *and* were.

Hmm. Some of the issues raised here just might be outside the scope of this book. All the same, the man has brought up important points. Are people who care about grammar superior in some way to people who don't? I wouldn't go that far. But certainly our language is a valuable possession that we hold in common. And I believe that people who treat it cavalierly are doing it harm.

If a group of us were setting out to develop a brand-new, perfect language—a system of symbols by which we could communicate with one another completely and exactly, in a way that admitted of no misunderstandings—we would want to come up with just one word for each meaning that we might need, and assign just one meaning to each word. Alas, it's too late for English to be quite so precise. Standard American English—the English of our dictionaries and grammar books—is a great, messy deluge of words, some of which overlap in meaning, many of which have multiple meanings, and many of which can be used as various parts of speech. So even if we follow the rules of standard English, there's no guarantee that our meaning will be clear. The same goes double if we fail to follow the rules.

Along with this drawback comes an advantage: standard English gives us a range of choices about how to communicate almost any thought, allowing us to express our individuality as we make our points. Note, for example, the varying ways above in which my correspondents have communicated displeasure.

Some people will object that *their* individuality is best expressed by breaking the rules. This idea has a certain appeal as it applies to, say, music or clothes or cooking—all aesthetic matters in which conformity doesn't necessarily win compliments. But, as you may have inferred even from the content-free form of what my caviling correspondents have to say, deviations from standard English, or what people take to be deviations, are more likely to arouse fury, pity, or scorn than admiration for the deviator's individuality.

And English is not just an aesthetic form or a cultural signifier, like music or cooking, but, again, a system of communication. Our ability to communicate will break down if we don't work together at maintaining our language. You can prove this to yourself by visiting a part of the world where for some time English has developed in ways independent of the American variety's development, and trying to figure out what the local people are talking about. To give just two marvelous examples, drawn from *The New Englishes,* by John Platt, Heidi Weber, and Ho Mian Lian: in Nigeria a person who *declares surplus* is planning to host a party, and throughout Anglophone West Africa the word *wonderful* expresses pure amazement and would not be out of place as a response to the news that someone had just died.

Another problem we encounter if we wander off from standard English is that we will progressively lose touch with our past. Here is a snippet of Chaucer:

> *Whoso shal telle a tale after a man,*
> *He moot reherce as ny as evere he kan*
> *Everich a word, if it be in his charge,*
> *Al speke he never so rudeliche and large,*
> *Or ellis he moot telle his tale untrewe,*
> *Or feyne thing, or finde wordes new.*

It's not so easy anymore to tell what was on his mind, is it? In order to continue to understand Chaucer and Shakespeare and the King James Bible at all, and Gibbon and Jefferson and Austen and Dickens in rich detail, we should embrace standard English, and do what we can to ensure that it changes as slowly as possible.

We may hope that future generations, too, will want to understand us. Not that our casual conversations around the breakfast table are likely to interest them particularly, or even our favorite sit-coms, except as evidence of what our era was like. For such contexts, as will be discussed in Chapter Two, the relatively free, transient, and idiosyncratic stylings of informal English will do fine.

Sometimes, though, we may want to make a serious point to people outside our own immediate circles—people living in the present or the future. We may wish to communicate with members of one of America's elites: the people in control of, for example, business or finance or education or scientific research or politics or the law or the media. Whether we belong to such an elite and just want to talk to our peers, or we aspire to belong, or we seek to influence these elites because, after all, they influence our lives, standard English is the tool for the job.

The—well, the elitism of an argument like this will appeal to some people and offend others, as these quotations from my correspondents may suggest.

> *Those who criticize minor blunders of speech are often accused of unearned haughtiness or limp-wrist snobbery. Let them tell that to the Ephraimite who could not pronounce the* h *in* Shibboleth. *And when "he said 'sibboleth' for he could not frame to pronounce it right" he was slain by the Gileadites along with 42,000 others.*

> *I tend to be very liberal about grammar, idioms, and other spoken idiosyncrasies, but get very upset when someone bungles it while trying to sound posh.*

> *I am an Ivy League–educated physician who is not afraid to use bad grammar. I do it all the time and it feels good. My patients understand me, and, I would*

argue, prefer it. My brother, a Midwestern-educated music professor, uses good grammar, and is really snooty about it. What gives?

But standard English is not something handed down from on high. It may seem disingenuous for someone who calls herself the judge of Word Court to say that, and yet I do not just make up my answers, any more than a real judge rules according to whim. Whenever I can, I rely on precedent and consensus. What's more, although the column may give the impression that I have the last word, I don't: I receive plenty of letters disagreeing with my rulings. Rarely do these change my mind on the matter in question, but they often teach me how emphatically some people hold a different view. For example, should it be "*a* historical event" or "*an* historical event"? This surprisingly controversial issue is discussed in Chapter Four. Here suffice it to say that if you find yourself wanting to make a point about such an event without arousing someone's ire or contempt, your best bet will be to call it "an event in history." In this book you will hear from my critics as well as from me on a number of contentious points and so will have the chance to make up your own mind.

Everyone who chooses to use standard English must make an endless series of decisions about the language, and thereby has a say in how it develops. If people habitually use *contact* as a transitive verb—as in "I hope you will *contact* me"—the usage becomes a part of standard English (and, in fact, it has done so). If people insist on calling the establishment where they go to wash their clothes a *laundromat,* then whether the creators of the Laundromat® launderette franchise like it or not, the generic meaning eventually becomes standard English (it, too, has done so). If everyone stops saying *forsooth,* the word is sure to be marked "archaic" in dictionaries (this day has not yet come).

For this reason, and also because the world that words describe keeps changing—hauberks and greaves are, forsooth, rather rarer than they were in Chaucer's day, whereas CD-ROMs and tacos and snowmobiles are infinitely more common—the components and rules of standard English keep changing, too. The challenge to remain simultaneously current and correct is eternal. Oh, well. Many people seem inclined to rise to the challenge, because they care deeply about language. Isn't that why you're here?

I mean it about not insisting on always having the last word, so I'm going to let someone else end this chapter—a correspondent of mine who disagrees with nearly everything I've said. At least, I think he does. And if, having read the foregoing, you find yourself in sympathy with his view, now's the time for you to say "Who cares," close the book, and give it away.

> *What I'm trying to think is whatever it is that you intended to make my writing comprehensive is not necessarily ameliorated for easily digestible audiences. Despite you and your implications for your active nay-saying readership, those readers who want to find no difficulty in getting what I mean closely as if it were their own intention to formulate language as my words' embody. Sometimes when your rough in your meaning it is far better to wield an imprecision blade which must be handled with ever more carefully in the hands of him who wishes no error occured in the accurate diffusing of one's wisdom. Let me bring these*

flailings of my own accord to an end: let us alone
making those poorly conceived "mistakes" of yours,
and we likely will look in an opposing manner as you
dispense with those ill-begotten grammatical habits.

AN ASIDE

Warning

"Warning" may be hyperbole, but if this were called "Procedural Notes," who would read it?

With a few exceptions (they will be apparent), throughout this book I have lightly edited my correspondents' letters, cleaning up typos, errors, and inconsistencies that distract from the points the writers want to make, or sometimes homing in on one point when they have written me about two or three. When I refer to a correspondent as "he" or "she," it's because I have seen the signature on the letter the person sent and know his or her sex. (For current thinking on what to do when you don't know someone's sex, please see the section titled "Sex and the Single Pronoun," in Chapter Two.)

Flattered though I am when mail seeking my advice arrives from distant countries, I've tried not to let it go to my head. I'm not the world's expert on anything. My expertise is specifically American—by which I mean that it has to do with English as English is spoken and written in the United States. (If this meaning of the word *American* troubles you, please see "Something for Everyone," also in Chapter Two.)

I cite many books in this one. Because language is always changing, language-reference books change, too. Some that continue to be popular for years may go through a number of editions; other highly respected ones may nevertheless fail to sell well and will go out of print or be heavily revised—for good or for ill. Because my focus is on enduring usage, I have not felt it important to cite the latest edition of each book I refer to, nor have I even wanted to do so. And because this is not a work of historical scholarship, I haven't made it a point of honor to track down the first edition of a book in which a given citation appears. When I've cited another book, I've simply referred to the edition I have, the date and publisher of which can be found in "Shelf Life," the aside at the end of Chapter Four. If I have more than one edition and the differences between the editions are significant, this is pointed out.

Thinking is not linear, but words are: organizing a book like this one inevitably involves a number of decisions that others may find arbitrary, misguided, or even woeful. Sorry! Questions that seem to me to point up various changes now roiling our language appear in Chapter Two. Questions that clarify consequential aspects of grammar appear in Chapter Three, in a completely subjective ascending order of importance. Chapter Four treats questions about specific words and phrases: where two or more words are discussed together, the discussion will be found under the alphabetically first word that my correspondent asked about. (Thus a letter about *procrastinate* versus *prevaricate*, into the discussion of which I drag *equivocate*, appears under "Prevaricate," as it also would if a later reader of the first letter had been the one to bring up *equivocate*.) Chapter Five is a miscellany. It begins with matters that are like those in Chapter Four except that no one has asked me about them, and it continues with ideas for words that someone wishes existed, with pronunciation questions, and with complaints and observations about redundancies, pleonasms, and wastes of words. Chapter Six, finally, is meant to put all of the foregoing in perspective and to encourage you, the reader, to step back and admire what a piece of work is the language that we share.

CHAPTER TWO

❧

The Elements of Fashion

Fashions fade, style is eternal.
—Yves Saint Laurent

Certain of my correspondents object to *medaling* athletes and *fax* machines, *freshmen* and *women writers,* *Alaskan villages* and *rigorous learning.* Others, meanwhile, seek my blessing for *genericticity, housemember,* and *repurposing.* They may scruple at *Enjoy!* and *could care less* and *problem solve,* or complain about people who complain about *niggardly.* In various ways, these words and expressions reflect current trends in the language—trends that have surely already come to your attention. Like all swift-flowing rivers of change, these trends contain swirls and eddies whose effects are short-lived, and also powerful currents to bear us far from where we are and have been.

Past Masters

The spread of education adds to the writer's burdens by multiplying that pestilent fellow the critical reader. No longer can we depend on an audience that will be satisfied with catching the general drift & obvious

*intention of a sentence & not trouble itself to pick
holes in our wording; the words used must nowadays
actually yield on scrutiny the desired sense; to plead
that anyone could see what you meant, or so to write
as to need that plea, is not now permissible; all our
pet illogicalities will have to be cleared away by degrees.*

May I say that we take the point—regardless of who
is making it? As it happens, who is making the point is
the wonderful H. W. Fowler, perhaps the person in all
history most beloved in English-usage circles. Linguists
can be patronizing about him, and yet it inspires me to
remember that he was an artist more than a scientist of
language.

Fowler is beloved in part because he follows his own
advice, and writes persuasively and elegantly, in a way
appropriate to his time and place and purpose. So many
of his opinions have struck so many people as authoritative for so long that we may be inclined to give him the
benefit of any doubt and go along with the opinions we
don't fully understand, or agree with. Still, when he
writes something like

*A curious & regrettable change has come about in
the last twenty or thirty years. Whereas we used, except on formal occasions, to talk & write of Lord
Salisbury, Lord Derby, Lord Palmerston, & to be
very sparing of the prefixes Marquis, Earl, & Viscount, the newspapers are now full of Marquis Cur-
zon, Earl Beatty, Viscount Rothermere, & similarly
Marchioness this & Countess that have replaced the
Lady that used to be good enough for ordinary wear.
We have taken a leaf in this as in other matters from*

> *the Japanese book; it was when Japan took to Euro-*
> *pean titles that such combinations as* Marquis Ito *first*
> *became familiar to us, & our adoption of the fashion*
> *is more remarkable than pleasing*

we have to admit that he seems a wee bit remote from our time and place. How could he not? Fowler's great work, *Modern English Usage,* from which both of the quotations above were taken, was published in 1926, in England. The wonder is that so many of his pronouncements do continue to apply, and in the United States at that. Even where Fowler protests such "superstitions" of his time as the importance of avoiding split infinitives and "the dread of a preposition at end," he is relevant, for those superstitions continue to be handed down through the generations, along with his strictures against them.

Theodore M. Bernstein, an American—a *New York Times* editor—whose usage guides were published in the 1950s and 1960s, and whose 1965 book *The Careful Writer* remains widely used and respected, is another worthy adviser, and one closer to us, but at times even he sounds out of touch.

> *"Publicist Found Dead." The man referred to in the*
> *headline was a press agent.* Publicist *originally re-*
> *ferred to an expert on public law, and then was more*
> *loosely applied to those who wrote on public issues.*
> *Despite the dictionary, need we debase the word still*
> *further to gratify those who strive to make the poorer*
> *seem the better?*

Well, we mustn't believe everything we read. Whether or not a given cause seems lost, we can appreciate the thinking according to which it was worth standing up for in its day. In fact, much of what we read the authorities for is the thought behind their words.

Here's a lovely demonstration of how Fowler's mind works:

> *Those who presumably do know what split infinitives are, & condemn them, are not so easily identified, since they include all who neither commit the sin nor flounder about in saving themselves from it, all who combine with acceptance of conventional rules a reasonable dexterity. But when the dexterity is lacking, disaster follows. It does not add to a writer's readableness if readers are pulled up now & again to wonder—Why this distortion? Ah, to be sure, a non-split die-hard! That is the mental dialogue occasioned by each of the adverbs in the examples below. It is of no avail merely to fling oneself desperately out of temptation; one must so do it that no traces of the struggle remain; that is, sentences must be thoroughly remodelled instead of having a word lifted from its original place & dumped elsewhere....*

And Bernstein's:

> Whether or not. *Usually the* or not *is a space waster; e.g.,* "Whether the terrorist statement was true or not was not known." *When, however, the intention is to give equal stress to the alternatives, the* or not *is mandatory:* "The game will be played whether it is fair or not." *The following sentence fairly cries out for the* or not: "The union feels that the shortcomings of the machinery the law provides for dealing with major strikes have already become so clear that Congress is likely to consider alternative remedies, whether the law is upheld in the Supreme Court."

One way to test whether the or not is necessary is to substitute if *for* whether. *If the change to* if *produces a different meaning—and it would do so in the second and third of the foregoing examples—the or not must be supplied.*

As we take in not only the decisions that our wise old advisers have made but also how and why they made them, we refine our own ability to reach conclusions about the new language issues that life is forever thrusting at us. New issues arise from a range of sources.

From Birthing to Funeralized

The most obvious of these sources are the new things, new ideas, and new activities that English is continually being called upon to describe. Each year some thousands of new words are coined. (Estimates of the number of thousands vary, according to the extent of the rummaging that the estimator has seen fit to do in specialized lingoes and ephemera.) Neologisms come up in every possible context, and relate to every possible stage of human existence. I've picked out a few representative ones to discuss here.

I'm perturbed about the adoption of the word birthing—*as in* birthing suite—*to denote a room where childbirth and recovery take place (so that mothers do not have to give birth in a labor and delivery area and then be moved to a maternity area). Mind you, I don't object to the idea, only to the name, considering that its original popularity (as I understand it) comes from a character in Margaret Mitchell's* Gone With the Wind—*a character whose illiteracy was apparently being offered as a subject for amusement. Why would modern hospitals even consider adopting this name for their new, high-tech facilities?*

It does seem silly to derive *birthing* from the verb *birth,* that verb having in turn been derived from the much better-established noun *birth,* just in order to do a job that the noun could have done in the first place. (*Birth suite* sounds all right to me, at any rate.) But this sort of thing happens all the time in English, and not only among illiterates. In fact, in *Gone With the Wind,* Scarlett, as well as her maid, Prissy, talks about *birthing,* and both women were employing a preexisting Southern colloquialism. Given that this colloquialism does exist, and given also that the point of the *birthing suite* is to allow women to give birth in settings where *hospital* and *hospitable* have more than an etymological relationship, it's not surprising that the informal form is winning out. All the same, you needn't use it if you don't like it.

I've received complaints not only about athletes who have *medaled* in the Olympics but also about high-school guidance counselors who talk about *transitioning* young people, art shows that are *juried* or *curated,* books that are *authored.* This letter makes the general point.

My critics tell me that because I was born in 1914, I am old-fashioned and not in tune with current usage. But how can I be complacent when reporters and talk-show hosts seem unable to differentiate between nouns and verbs? For example, "a good read*" or "*your *take* on this."*

English has always allowed verbs to be pressed into service as nouns, and nouns as verbs. The linguist Otto Jespersen, in his seminal *Growth and Structure of the English Language* (published nine years before you were born), called the "freedom with which a form which was originally a verb is used unchanged as a substantive" a "characteristic peculiarity" of our language, and he even gave some instances of words exhibiting a "curious oscillation... between noun and verb." *Frame,* for example, was initially a verb, meaning "to form"; then it became a noun meaning "border," as in *picture frame*; and from there the verb acquired the new meaning "to put a frame around."

Nonetheless, it's your choice when you will begin to accept recently adapted words—and which ones. The verbs *to gift, to impact,* and *to parent,* notably, as well as the nouns *take* and *read,* are widely disliked—and who needs them? *To fax* and *to Rollerblade* are almost inevitable coinages, though, because the activities they describe are new, and new language must be found for them. Beyond such practical considerations lie matters of taste. With language we all communicate not only what we're trying to say but also how trendy or traditional we are.

After that last exchange was published, a reader weighed in.

I respectfully disagree with your answer. Obviously, the person should properly have said "This is a good reading material." I am also surprised that you consider our American language "English." But I am the most surprised about it that you consider the word fax *to be a word at all!!! This is an abbreviation. I have seen letterheads from many companies that use the full expression:* telefacsimile. *If we want to use this as a verb, we should tell our secretary, "Please send a* telefacsimile *to General Electric Company." Just violating the rules of the language does not make the language change.*

P.S. The fact that I myself use on my letterhead the abbreviation fax *does not change the facts.*

Duly noted.

And here we have a specific point that could stand in for many other specific points about neologisms:

A friend and I sat on my balcony one night just talking, and at one point I attempted to say that I was a fan of genericness—*that's the word that came out of my mouth. It seems to me that some such term—* genericness *or* genericity *or* genericticity—*should exist. Is there one? If not, I hereby dub* genericticity *the all-encompassing noun form of* generic.

Some people like to have a gadget for every purpose in their kitchens; others would rather make do with basic, versatile tools, particularly if they only rarely need, say, a vol-au-vent template or a cake saw. By the same token, maybe you often find yourself discussing generic things or generic qualities and will use your word a lot. (If so, do note that *-ness* and *-ity,* but not *-ticity,* appear in dictionaries as suffixes meaning "quality" or "state.") Or maybe you don't, and won't (in which case you could have said you're a fan of *the generic*). Of course, coining a word is only the first step toward introducing it into the language, just as patenting a gadget only begins to make a place for it in our culture. It's up to people in the aggregate to decide whether there's a need for the invention and whether it will endure.

A surprising proportion of the words that people suppose to be recent creations, however, are in fact well established—or, at least, they once were. Farsighted Harry S. Truman said, "There is nothing new in the world except the history you do not know."

> *My ears have become sadly tolerant of the increasing misuse of the word* disrespect *as a verb, as in "I won't* disrespect *you." I assumed it was just a colloquialism popular with the younger generation. But in the movie* Good Will Hunting *the sagacious psychologist, played by Robin Williams, turns on his impudent patient with "Don't you ever* disrespect *my wife." Ouch! Although the prefix* dis- *converts many of our words to antonyms, don't you agree that the application here is incorrect? Or am I just disrespecting new and diverse styles of expression?*

And another letter:

> *The weather channel has put a spin on the very respectable word* tornado—*namely,* tornadic. *I put the word through my spell-checker; the computer reported, "Questionable." I agree. What do you say?*

I have a little 1836 American dictionary that doesn't sanction either of these usages, but my copy of *Webster's New International Dictionary, Second Edition, Unabridged,* from the 1950s, contains them both. It says that *disrespect* as a verb means "show disrespect to," so this appears to be one of those things, like Ray-Ban sunglasses, that were all but forgotten yet came back into style. And *tornadic* is just an adjectival form of *tornado*—the only one our language has. I'd never heard it before, but I don't know what we can object to about it.

Again, neologisms, or what people take to be neologisms, relate to every stage of our existence.

I am writing to express dismay and bafflement over some terms I have encountered recently in the obituary columns of local newspapers. I do not find them in any of the dictionaries I own. One obituary listed the date of the memorial service and then gave a later date as the time of inurnment. *Since this event was to be held in a cemetery, I presume that the body had been cremated and the ashes were to be buried or interred after being placed in an urn. It seems to me the word* interment *would have been sufficient.*

 The next shocker was an obituary that stated that the cremains *would be shipped to another state for disposition. I suppose some people find the term* ashes *distasteful, but whoever dreamed up* cremains?

 And then, the last straw! The paper announced that Mrs. So and So would be funeralized *on such and such a date.*

 What are your thoughts?

I think it might be time for you to buy a new dictionary. Each of these words is in at least three of the five recent dictionaries that I most regularly consult, and has been in use for decades. Certainly, you don't have to use these words, or like them, no matter what dictionaries say (and you might even consider reducing the offending dictionary to cremains). But your not unreasonable protest is more a matter of what you find tasteful than what is acceptable English.

Words that are indeed startlingly new today may by tomorrow be ordinary, or have become tatty clichés (as *good bones* with reference to architecture and *poster boy* and *rocket scientist* and *Been there, done that* are as I write this). Or they may disappear without a trace. In this way, language *is* like clothes. If you want fashionable prose of the moment, then by all means assemble it out of the latest words; if you want stylish prose that is likely to last for many seasons, choose pieces that are more traditional.

Sex and the Single Pronoun

Another important source of questions about language has been a growing consensus that men and women should be treated evenhandedly. To what extent our language needs to change to reflect this consensus is a matter of sometimes heated debate. The question is no doubt part of a larger one, having to do with equal treatment for all human beings, no matter how we categorize them—and we'll turn to this larger question in the next section. I'd like to focus on the male-female issue first, though, because I receive more letters about it than about all other aspects of egalitarianism combined.

> *We are wrestling with the term* freshman *here at Michigan Technological University. Some prefer* first-year student; *others contend that* freshman *is necessary, because of confusion introduced by international students, transfers, and so on. What do you think?*

I am bothered by the increasing use of the word chair-person, *instead of* chairman. *Even more unsettling is the new custom of referring to human beings as* chairs. *A few years ago the American Association of Parliamentarians ruled that* chairman *is correct for both sexes, pointing out that* madame chairman *has been in use for years to indicate the feminine. What's the story?*

I find a deep and disturbing clash between the grammar my demanding English teachers taught me and the current almost universal use of they *as a pronoun for the singular word* person *and its synonyms. If a person was taught that this is the wrong way to say it, what are they to do about it?*

Sigh. I sometimes wonder whether the true purpose of all such issues isn't to sort readers by mental age. I've noticed three groups. The mentally elderly read something like "A *freshman* might decide that someday *he* wants to be the *chairman* of a big corporation" and assume that the person in question must be male—not so much because of the wording as because society used to be that way. Those of us who are a bit younger mentally can read that sentence without feeling that it excludes women. We learned in school that one of the meanings of *man* is "humankind": a *freshman* or a *chairman* can be a member of either sex. We also learned that there is such a thing as the "generic *he*"—a *he* that refers to any person, in a context where no particular person is present as an antecedent for the pronoun. People of my mental age group therefore wonder what all the fuss is about. Those who are mentally still younger make the fuss. When they read the *freshman* sentence, they, like the mentally elderly, suppose that it applies only to men—but they are enraged by the sexism they perceive. Unfortunately, their solutions to the problem, such as "*A first-year student ... s/he*" or "*...they,*" tend to annoy us fogies. The former lacks grace and can't be pronounced; the latter is more grievous, for it compromises such logic as English syntax has.

A speaker or writer who is trying simply to express an idea, rather than to pick a fight with listeners or readers, needs to tread carefully. Changing *freshman* to *first-year student* is probably treading too far: women have been freshmen in great numbers for decades, and so the word carries no particular connotation of male privilege, or of masculinity at all. *Freshperson* is obviously impossible—but *chairperson* seems harmless enough. So does "A chairman [or 'chairperson']...*he or she*" or, when the need to keep using both pronouns results in something overelaborate, "Chairmen...*they.*" Another possibility is to try to leave the contentious words out: "A freshman might hope to lead a big corporation someday."

After those three letters and my reply to them were published, I was taken to task as follows:

While backing away from sexist and gender-bound language, you have bumped into ageist language. I assume that by "mentally younger" as compared with the "mentally elderly," you were referring to a cohort group born later as compared with those born earlier, rather than to chronological age groups.

With luck, you may not hear from others of my cohort who are exulting in the wisdom that comes with age and do not choose to scare the later-born with negative predictions related to age.

Oh, dear. Sorry! I certainly didn't mean chronological age. I was working on the theory that we are all as old or young as we think we are, and which group we belong to is purely a matter of choice.

And another objection:

Person *used in combinations has got to be the ugliest locution yet invented for any language. Though the word may be a perfectly acceptable singular noun, I refuse to use the combining form, nor will I allow an editor to insert it into anything I've written. I will go along with* congresswomen; *but discussing a mixed group that includes both* congressmen *and* -women, *I will refer to a few members of* Congress *if the phrase must be neutered. But* congresspersons *is an insult to the ear, as is* chairperson(s), *a term you refer to as "harmless enough."*

I just don't think you're allowing yourself to get into the spirit of the trend. It's more fun than you think. For example, I call my friends the Wallmans "the *Wallpersons.*" (Though the word *people* tends to be used to refer to more than one *person* [about which, please see the entry under "People" in Chapter Four], -*persons* is the usual plural for -*person* in combinations—a peculiarity that may be contributing to your dislike.) Jim Wallman is a *Wallman,* naturally; but his wife, Bonnie, is a *Wallwoman.* They take a *ropersontic* approach to life, and love both the ocean and animals; they have crusaded to save the poor Florida *personatee,* which motorboats often *persongle.*

See? If everyone were as *personiacal* as this, I like to think, soon even the most earnest of egalitarians would be rolling their eyes, and we could put political correctness behind us and move on to the next social excess.

I dislike using their *instead of* his or her *in a sentence, but it sounds so much better. Example: "Each student should bring* their *woolen socks." Is this usage of* their *acceptable? What are some alternatives?*

There are still people who hope to ignore this whole controversy and simply stick with *he* and *his* whenever they are writing about an unspecified person ("Each student should bring *his* socks"). I used to be one of them. I assumed that some word had to be able to refer to everyone, and I didn't take it personally that the choice wasn't *she*. And so I felt included—in the whole Western tradition's worth of writing. The tradition of the generic *he* seemed possibly fuddy-duddy, but not hostile.

While teaching a class about language a few years ago, however, I was denounced by a student for my support of the generic *he*. The student was a young man, and when he was finished speaking, a number of young women in the class loudly applauded him for putting me, a successful professional woman, in my place.

I had various thoughts about this. Among them was that there is great depth of feeling on this issue today. It no longer seems possible to be a well-intentioned and sensitive person without explicitly including those of us who are *she*s.

Now back to your example of the mess all this has gotten us into. Technically speaking, the problem with

"Each student should bring *their* woolen socks" is, of course, that *each student* is singular and *their,* referring back to it, is plural. Practically speaking, the problem is that "*his or her* woolen socks" does sound worse, and not just to you. Both the technical problem and the practical one are heading toward big trouble down the road if they're left unsolved.

Not far down the first road, on which plural pronouns (like *their*) are allowed to have singular antecedents (like *everyone*), it begins to be hard to tell what a writer is trying to say. Have a look at "Each topic in the self-esteem curriculum is covered in detail, so that the children may be aware of *their* importance." Is that the topic's importance or the children's? The distinction between singular and plural helps readers keep things straight, as long as they can trust it. At the same time, down the "*his or her* socks" road lurk sentences like "A person who thinks that *he or she* is important rarely stops to ask *himself or herself* who else holds this opinion of *him or her.*" Yikes!

The solution is to write around the problems. Admittedly, this does mean that we must think about what we're writing, but finding solutions is rarely hard. Sometimes a troublesome noun that was singular can be made plural: "*All students* should bring *their* woolen socks." And sometimes the pronouns can be lopped off: "Each student should bring woolen socks." Don't both of these sound even better than your ungrammatical version?

A beef I have with National Public Radio: they misuse the words sex *and* gender. *I was taught that*

"nouns in romance languages have gender; *people, bless their little hearts, have* sex.*"*

I myself have been taken to task for allowing the word *gender* to refer to the difference between males and females—and also for allowing the word *sex* to do so. The distinction you make in such a humorous way is the traditional one. Nonetheless, set phrases like *gender gap* and *gender bender* now appear in reputable dictionaries, suggesting that tradition is not universally upheld. Call me radical and reckless, but I just can't see changing the phrase *gender gap* to *sex gap.*

The very suggestiveness of your wording suggests something else as well: one reason the word *gender* is catching on may be that *sex* sometimes conveys something—well, sexier than the speaker or writer intends.

HELP!! Aging geezer is struggling to stay politically correct—needs assistance.

What is the currently acceptable salutation for a business letter written to an organization when no individual within the organization is known and the gender of the letter receptor is also unknown?

The conventional salutations I learned in school, Dear Sir *and* Gentlemen, *are no longer apropos. An ardent feminist opening my letter with this kind of language may deep-six it or at least be offended and unfavorably disposed toward my requests.*

With no wish to offend anyone and every desire to get along peacefully in the world, I am stumped. Any light you can shed on this problem would be appreciated.

Bless you for being so considerate, and indeed you will be blessed if the people you write to respond in kind. I myself use *Dear Sir or Madam* or *To Whom It May Concern* or, if I think the organization or employee is quite informal, *Hello.*

Recently I have noticed a trend afoot toward *Greetings,* but I am resisting it. I can't forget that the word was once closely associated with U.S. Army draft notices, on which it appeared.

❧

I object to women writers. *No, not to the authors themselves but to calling them that. Expressions such as* woman golfer *and* woman politician *are all too common in modern idiomatic English. The corresponding usage to describe a man in a stereotypically female role is always the adjective* male: *for instance,* male nurse. *This will surely be a better world when we no longer need to qualify nouns with gender. Until then we could improve the world slightly by using adjectives where adjectives are needed* (female author, female golfer) *and letting nouns refer to people, places, and things.*

I'm sure most of us feel that this is already a better world, now that women and men have more choices about their roles in it. Having some choice about what to call ourselves is also nice. English generally does offer its users more than one way to say something—more than one correct way, for a choice that boils down to a matter of taste. Few find the likes of *lady writer* or of *authoress* tasteful these days, so *woman writer* is pretty much the only extant alternative to *female writer*—assuming that the context is not one like "Jane Austen was a writer," in which no purpose is served by specifying sex.

While it's true that the noun *man* is rarely used as an adjective, or "attributively," many other nouns are: think of *bull rider, sperm bank, king crab*. In fact, *woman* (unlike *man*) often appears in dictionaries either as an adjective in addition to a noun or with the notation that the noun is often used attributively. At least, that's what is in dictionaries belonging to this woman writer.

I was happy to see the letter complaining of the use of women *in* women writers, *but the complainant's complaint was not the same as mine.*

My distaste for the term stems not from the use of woman *in this sense but from the pluralization. We do not refer to* children prodigies *or* babies brothers— *so why not* woman writers, *just like* child prodigies *and* baby brothers?

You're right about what is traditional in English. However, as R. W. Burchfield notes in *The New Fowler's Modern English Usage,* "Plural attributive nouns, once relatively rare, are now commonplace (*appointments book, customs duty, narcotics dealer, procedures manual*)." Although the first of his four examples doesn't pass muster in American English, the others serve to make the general point. As for the specific one: having searched a database of newspaper and magazine articles for you, I can say confidently that *women* is seen much more often than *woman* before plural nouns.

❧

*In the town of Cortland, New York, a waterfront
park on the Hudson River will be opening soon. The
central purpose of the park is to provide access to
the river for people interested in fishing. The name of
the park—the subject of our dispute—is intended to
reflect this fact.*

The first name suggested was Annsville Fishermen's Point. *This name was rejected for its sexist connotations, and* Fishermen's *was changed to* Fishers.
*The question is, Should the possessive form be used,
making it* Annsville Fishers' Point? *The park does not
belong to fishers, nor will it be used solely by fishers.*

*If you respond quickly enough, we will incorpo-
rate your decision into the actual name of the park,
and the form you prefer will appear on the plaque
upon dedication. Please help us out.*

I can't talk you into *Annsville Fishing Point,* can I? It
isn't clear what *Fishers* means. *Fishermen's* is clear,
and in my opinion a bit too much is being renounced
as sexist these days—but people *will* object, and it
does you credit that you are taking everyone's feelings
into account. *Fishers,* though, could be…lustrous
dark-brown cousins of the weasel? People with that
surname? Who knows?

If you must have *Fishers*: On the one hand, the
apostrophe (after the *s,* as you have it) is appropriate,
because the meaning is the same as with *Fishermen's.*
Possessives don't necessarily signal what we'd think of
as ownership: think of *a day's journey* or *for pity's
sake.* The relationship between the people fishing and
the park will be possessive in a grammatical sense. On
the other hand, the official U.S. entity in charge of geographic names strongly discourages apostrophes in

place-names. And here—where, again, it isn't clear what the word *Fishers* means—the apostrophe probably does serve little purpose. I would leave it out.

I got a lot of feedback on this exchange. Most correspondents had things like these to say:

> *That man's problem in piscatorial political correctness could be readily remedied with an assist from Izaak Walton:* Annsville Anglers' Point.
> *If that is too classical in this iconoclastic age, one could always borrow—and pluralize—the title of Xaviera Hollander's opus* The Happy Hooker. *That'll put those darned males in their place. Glad I could be of help.*

> *Persons concerned with such trivia as the possible sexism of* fishermen *should be dropped into the nearest personhole.*

Ah! A personiac!

Kidding aside: A search I recently conducted on the World Wide Web tallied 125,071 documents said to contain the word *fisherman,* 527 containing *fisherwoman,* 848 *fisherperson*—and 103,631 *angler.* (About half a million documents contained *Fisher,* but the vast majority of those had to do with other things, such as Fisher-Price toys or Eddie Fisher.) I found 76,751 documents containing *policeman,* 4,156 *policewoman,* 616 *policeperson* or *police person*—and 270,397 *police officer.* The results I got for other sets of words tended to follow some such pattern. Although it is evident that people dislike substituting *-person* for *-man* (or *-woman*), the objection may be more aesthetic than political. (The fellow I introduced to the "Wallpersons" a few pages back is surely a

good spokes...er, spokesbeing for this point of view.)
Where unassuming sex-neutral alternatives exist,
many are happy to make use of them.

Something for Everyone

Unsurprisingly, people have sensitivities about a number
of issues besides sex and sexism. Can anyone blame
nonwhites and the disabled and foreigners and all other
groups for wanting equal treatment? And yet how those
sensitivities ought to be reflected in our language isn't always clear.

> *Reading a recent book by Noam Chomsky, I discov-*
> *ered that he had no problem using the word* niggardly
> *(meaning "stingy"). Although I always knew that ety-*
> *mologically the word has no racist overtones whatso-*
> *ever, I was nevertheless reluctant to use it because I*
> *felt that it could be misinterpreted. But lately, after*
> *some thought—and after seeing that Chomsky (no*
> *slouch when it comes to matters of our language) uses*
> *the word freely—I decided, screw all these unedu-*
> *cated self-righteous PC word-police types; I have*
> *grown to like the word, and will use it as I please. I*
> *feel that to do otherwise is to acquiesce in the degen-*
> *eration of our common English language, to the bene-*
> *fit of no one, save perhaps the PC word-police types.*
> *Am I justified?*

Whether or not you should use the word depends on
your audience. If you hope to be persuasive to a
group of "uneducated self-righteous PC word-police
types," as you put it, then perhaps *niggardly* isn't
your best word choice. If, though, you are addressing
a learned convention of etymologists...

Some months after the foregoing exchange was published in the Word Court column, I was forced to recognize that, for good or for ill, *niggardly* is more widely reviled than I had supposed. Early in 1999, Mayor Anthony Williams, of Washington, D.C., accepted the resignation of David Howard, his recently appointed ombudsman, because Howard had said to two co-workers, one of whom was black, "I will have to be *niggardly* with this fund." Only after the media howled in protest and derision was Howard reinstated. *The Economist* wrote:

> *The dictionary assures us that* [niggardly] *has nothing to do with the Latin* niger, *black, meaning only "miserly" in Old Norse; but as a former head of the National Bar Association asked the* New York Times, *"Do we really know where the Norwegians got the word?" Good point. They'd already discovered America, hadn't they? Straight off the longship on to the Bronx Expressway, and who knows what they heard through those horns on their helmets. "But it turns up in Middle English, too," you protest, "as* nig *and* nog, *meaning miser." Right: so racism was alive and well in the era of Sir Gawain.*

> *At the university where I work, the head of services for students with disabilities informed me that* HANDICAPPED PARKING *was misused to refer to parking reserved for those with handicaps, since the term "obviously" meant that the parking space had a disability. I claimed that English formed compounds like this all the time. She said not. Naturally, in the heat of the moment I was not able to think of examples. Can you give me some?*

Black colleges? An *Italian neighborhood?* The *poor-house? Handicapped* is an adjective that is regularly used as a substantive, or noun—a completely normal practice. Think of the adjectives in "Give me your *tired,* your *poor*..." But when you put this noun-with-the-form-of-an-adjective in front of another substantive *(parking),* it starts looking like an adjective again. This is a quirk inherent in how our language goes together, but you're quite right that the phrase isn't wrong. Actually, I was relieved to see that your head of services wasn't agitating for signs that read PHYSICALLY CHALLENGED PARKING. Perhaps the tide of political correctness has turned.

When that exchange appeared in the column, oh, my goodness, what a lot of mail it generated!

I was dismayed to see your use of the term political correctness *in the common and inaccurate way popularized in this country to describe a perceived invasion of silliness in language modification so as not to offend various groups. Political correctness is neither political nor correct in this country, where liberal, conservative, and nonpartisan groups alike all strive for the cherished* politically incorrect *label. The cynicism in a sneering term like* politically correct *is a cheap way to make a joke out of legitimate concerns about the easy use of language as a damaging tool against the less powerful. While terms like* physically challenged *may seem awkward when spray-painted in a parking space, the notion of using a powerful tool like language to effect social change ultimately stems from certain "politically correct" groups not wanting to be called* nigger *or* fag. *Another charming politically incorrect term that comes to mind is* women's work, *used to keep the "scribbling women" writers of the nineteenth century in their place.*

It seems to me that the opprobrium works the other way around from the way you say. That is, an expression like *women's work* is demeaning only if women are already demeaned. The important thing, therefore, rather than changing the wording, is to change the low status of women—or whatever group is at issue. Otherwise, any new wording will ultimately come to seem like a slur, too. After all, what has been gained by the transition from *crippled* to *handicapped* to *physically challenged* and so on?

A letter was brought to my attention that had been written to The Atlantic Monthly. *The letter alleges that I had a poor grasp of the English language because as the "head of services for students with disabilities," I had informed its author that the words* handicapped parking *were "misused." In fact what I told him was that* handicapped parking *was not the preferred term used by individuals with disabilities. I had the civility to inform him of this preference directly rather than censuring him in a national magazine where no possibility for direct dialogue existed.*

The intent of my statement to the letter's author was to show respect for people with disabilities and at the same time clearly identify the nature *of the parking space. The preferred way to refer to people with disabilities is not to call them* handicapped people. *And the appropriate, clearer way to denote a space as an* accessible *parking space is to denote it as such. The parking spot, in fact, is not handicapped; it is accessible to those people who require specialized parking. Informed, observant individuals are increasingly using the denotation* accessible parking *as one way to show respect for people with disabilities.*

The author of the letter clearly understood the intent of my statement, and I am offended that he would take issue with me on such a trivial matter while portraying me as ignorant in the use of English. He knows me to be an effective, articulate advocate for the rights of people with disabilities. I would never use the words physically challenged *when referring to people or parking, and am offended I have been portrayed as a possible agitator by you.*

I wrote the foregoing correspondent back to say that it was never my intent to offend her, which is true. I began to add that I didn't think she'd come off badly at all—but I deleted that before sending the letter, because it was a self-serving lie.

At the end of the item about handicapped parking *you stated, understandably, that you were relieved that the head of services for students with disabilities was not agitating for signs that read* PHYSICALLY CHALLENGED PARKING. *I say "understandably" because as a recently disabled young woman, I find the term facile and patronizing, and everyone else I have met with a disability concurs. And don't get me started on the bizarre terms* differently abled *and* handicapable.

I wonder where these terms originated. I suspect well-meaning nondisabled people created them. I can imagine a teacher telling able-bodied students not to say that Mary has a disability, *because that makes it seem as if her situation is negative and we should help people feel positive.*

But having a disability is a problem. It is annoying

and time-consuming. It is not the end of the world, and you can have a great life regardless of whether you have a disability. This is the message that ought to be sent, not that disability *is a bad word.* Disability *is an honest word. It is honest because a person with a disability is "not able" to do certain things. For example, I cannot run, and I cannot walk without a crutch and a leg brace. Even so, I just graduated from law school and will soon be a practicing attorney. I can still do so much—both to benefit society and to realize my own dreams. But the disability may cause difficulties along the way. Trying to sugarcoat the situation with facile terms does not do anyone any favors.*

You may have noticed that I have not used the term handicap. *Years ago I was told that in seventeenth-century England this was a term for people who are "handy with their caps for begging." Could you find out whether this is true?*

P.S. If you decide to print this, could you please edit it so that my comments do not hurt the feelings of the creators of the term physically challenged? *I am only interested in learning who the arbiters of political correctness are and how their concepts fall into everyday conversation, not in hurting their hypersensitive feelings.*

Thanks for your thoughtful letter. Etymology isn't really my field. But those whose field it is tell me that *handicap* derives from a gambling game in which the bets were put into a cap—so a golfer's *handicap,* say, or a racehorse's, is truer to the origins of the word than a disability is. Does that make you like the word a little bit better?

There is a tendency for the media to encourage Americans to believe that the world is encompassed by the Pacific and Atlantic oceans with the use of expressions like the World Boxing Champion, *the* World Series, *and so on.*

Now that you mention it, these phrases do seem grandiose, and yet, according to Stuart Berg Flexner's *Listening to America,* they began innocently enough. America's first heavyweight *world* champion of boxing, Paddy Ryan, won that title by beating an Englishman, in 1880. As for baseball's *World* Series and basketball's *World* Championships, when these contests began, in the 1880s and in 1905, the teams that played in them represented the world's only professional leagues for their sports. The fact that baseball and basketball caught on in other countries, too, can't have seemed like a very good reason to change the championships' titles to something humbler, and so the anachronistic titles remain. More recently instituted contests, like the Super Bowl, hockey's Stanley Cup, and the Final Four in college basketball, tend to lack such global pretensions.

The word America *appears in print and is heard in conversation and song. I mentally insert* United States of *in front of it, hoping that the user isn't referring to South, Central, or another part of North America.*

My dictionary, Webster's Ninth New Collegiate, *does not list the word. However, its definition of the word* American *is "of or relating to America"—hmm!*

Is it correct to use the word by itself? Is there really such a place?

Some dictionaries, including *Webster's Ninth* and the current—tenth—edition, isolate most proper names in appendixes, listing only words derived from them in the main body of the text. You'll note that the main body of *Webster's* under *United States* doesn't say anything about a specific country but gives only a generic meaning ("a federation of states..."). It does, however, mention our country in the definition of *American.*

Having lived in Mexico and traveled in Canada and South America, I can confirm that people who live somewhere on the American continents outside the United States can be touchy about it when we say that we're *Americans.* But what else are we supposed to call ourselves? *U.S. citizens?* Call yourself that if you like—it's too bureaucratic for my taste. Besides, there are those songs you mention, such as "*America* the Beautiful" and "God Bless *America.*" And our country came into being with the *American* Revolution, and many organizations bear names like *American* Airlines, the *American* Civil Liberties Union, and the *ASPCA,* and on and on.

The etiquette involved may be questionable when U.S. residents refer to themselves as *Americans* in front of Canadians, Mexicans, or South or Central Americans—a bit as it would be if Protestants were trying to distinguish themselves from Catholics by asserting that they were Christians. Nonetheless, both *American* and *America* itself are well established internationally as pertaining to the United States, and

there's no reason we should deny ourselves the use of
these words when talking either with our fellow
Americans or with people who live on other
continents.

When that exchange appeared in the column, I was
surprised at how controversial it turned out to be. Here
are two letters that illustrate the poles of opinion, and a
third that highlights a different possible source of irrita-
tion. The first letter came from a Canadian who lives in
the United States, the second from a resident of Mexico,
and the third from an, um, American in America.

*Too often I read the work (if you can call it that) of
American journalists that live under the inept impression that they can speak for every other culture on the
planet. I found myself considerably irritated by the
fact that this particular article intimated that Canadians have some sort of complex about being called*
Americans. *Trust me, it is the last thing in the world
we want to be called. I think you would find (if you
did any research at all) that most people in the Ameri-
cas (North, South, and Central, not just the U.S.) do
not want to be called* Americans. *People in Mexico
are* Mexicans, *people in Brazil* Brazilians, *people in
Peru* Peruvians—*are you getting it now?*

*Word Court raised an issue sensitive to the residents
of thirty-two nations of the Western Hemisphere, and
treated it patronizingly and dismissively. That is the
usurpation of the proper noun* America *and the adjective* American *by the people of the USA.*
The absurdities created by the misuse of America
are endless. In soccer: Team America *vs. Argentina.
On the Larry King show, to a Canadian: "When did*

you come to America?*" And then, we have* Cuban-Americans, *the equivalent of* Belgian-Europeans.

Granted, there is a problem of national nomenclature. There is not the United States of America. *Both* Brasil (with an s) *and Mexico include the title* United States *in their official designations. Yet they have clearly identified names, endemic to themselves.*

So, what is the proper name for the richest, most powerful nation upon the face of the earth? I guess if you've got that much money and that much power, you have your pick.

In the course of your discussion, you stepped right into another terminological morass. American Catholics, who tend to be the Roman kind, have attempted over the years to appropriate the Catholic label, but let me tell you there are many other sorts: Anglicans, Eastern Orthodox, Russian Orthodox, and probably others.

Furthermore, some of these groups are Protestant, in that they do not pledge allegiance to the Church of Rome. The Protestant Episcopal Church in America, for example, is clearly Protestant, and it also calls itself Catholic.

Please rename this ENGLISH WORD COURT, unless you are prepared to deal with words in all 3,000+ languages in use today.

I'll do so as soon as I start getting letters, and publishing replies, in any of the 2,999+ others.

For several years now I have noticed increasing reference to people as inanimate objects, as in "Are you

the one that borrowed my dictionary?" Is this more
than a passing trend? What do you make of it?

I'm as touchy as anyone, I like to think, when it
comes to issues of dehumanization. For example, I
wince when I hear someone say to a supermarket
cashier who seems idle, "Are you open?" What's
wrong with "May I check out here?" or "Is your register open?"

I hope you will trust me, therefore, when I tell you
that the word *that* has a long history of referring to
people as well as things. This usage may in some contexts sound a bit crude, but it is not ungrammatical,
and it can sometimes offer a writer a graceful way
out, as in "Did she say it was a man or a book *that*
she curled up with last night?"

As these letters show, it upsets many people when we
are, or seem to be, insensitive to others. Then again, we
mustn't be foolishly oversensitive—in part because we
don't like to be foolish and in part because if we go too
far, we'll just end up upsetting someone else.

The Wrong, Wrong, WRONG! Approach

Are we chameleons, trying to fit in everywhere? No. But
if we want people to focus on what we are trying to say,
rather than on messages we're sending inadvertently, we
need to show some subtlety. And while we are being careful not to trample on others' sensitivities, we'll
do well to cultivate tolerance in ourselves—not only
tolerance of other sexes and colors and persuasions of
people but tolerance, period. For one thing, it is a virtue to attend to what others are trying to say, instead

of seizing gleefully on their inadvertences and shrieking "Gotcha!" For another, our own intolerance isn't likely to bring out the best in others: they can be expected to be intolerant of our intolerance—and off we go.

> *Many times we all encounter people who make errors in spelling, language or useage. Usually I just ignore the error and go on. Sometimes I want to correct the speaker or writer. For instance the former president of a major university here in Oklahoma often uses the word* irregardless, *and the local TV station has a local service entitled* BULLETIN BOARD. *Question: How do you tell these good people they are making errors without embarrasing them?*

My job is a bit like being a police officer in that I don't really have to worry about whether the performance of my duties embarrasses people or not.

Maybe that particular simile came to mind because the late, lamented *New England Monthly* magazine at one point, for fun, printed up "Grammar Citations," which looked like traffic tickets. Instead of phrases like *Failure to observe stop sign* and *Illegal left turn*, phrases like *Misused 'unique,'* *Dangling modifier*, and *Ambiguous antecedent* appeared next to the little boxes to be checked. That's one nice way to handle these things—with humor.

Of course, tact is important, too. I hope you won't mind if I use you as an example here. It is obvious that you care about correct usage and spelling, so perhaps you will be grateful if I point out that *usage* is spelled without an *e* after the *s*, and that *embarrassing* has one more *s* than you typed in your letter. I could suggest some little stylistic improvements to your letter as well, if you'd like.

But I mention these things only because they relate to your subject: I don't think ill of you or anyone for making typos. And we all need an editor. I'm glad we do; otherwise, I'd be out of a job.

I have no idea what bothered that man about *Bulletin Board*—and you'll notice I didn't ask.

I just heard a presumably well-paid TV personality refer to himself as "persona non gratis." I thought it was very funny under the circumstances, but when he repeated it, I was embarrassed for him. What should one do? If improper usage were crooked seams on stockings or spinach in the teeth of a lunchmate, a real friend would say something. If it were a physical handicap, it would be too personal for a mere acquaintance to address. But what if it's a professional handicap? Is it worse to embarrass someone once or let them do it repeatedly for themselves?

Someone who has already embarrassed himself will not thank you for pointing it out. And yet you might prefer that the other person at least heard the right form, and so had the chance to learn by example. The trick is to work it into what you have to say as if you hadn't noticed anything wrong with the other person's version. Maybe you should send your television personality a letter that says something like "I want you to know you're hardly *persona non grata* in this household!"

After reading about the "persona non gratis" I recalled an incident in which a well-educated leader of an honorable organization of women took as her motto for the year "If you see a person without a

smile, give them *one of yours." I hesitated to correct
her because she'd had three hundred yearbooks
printed with the mistake in them.*

*My language dispute is with the sentence "Is it worse
to embarrass someone once or let them do it repeatedly for themselves?"*

    *Someone is singular. Shouldn't the pronouns then
be* him *and* himself? *What is Word Court's ruling on
this?*

May I ask you to read a second time my response to
the letter you're asking about?

Lots of expressions irritate people without being incorrect in any sense. Whether to use them is a matter of
taste.

*After a waiter sets a plate of food before me at a
restaurant, the last word to leave his mouth before he
walks away is "Enjoy!" This seems to be catching on
everywhere. I went to the doctor for a pulled tendon.
Handing me a prescription and my bill, he said,
"Enjoy!" Isn't* enjoy, *when used in the imperative, a
reflexive verb requiring a pronoun or noun, as in*
Enjoy yourself?

What if the waiter said *"Enjoy your meal"*? This perfectly correct sentence establishes that *enjoy* can be
used transitively (with a direct object), as well as in
the reflexive way (with a direct object that is the same
as the subject) that you note. The *Oxford English
Dictionary* gives several citations for intransitive uses
besides, including an evocative one from 1549 that
reads, "Yet he neuer *enioied* after, but in conclusyon

pitifully wasted his painful lyfe," and American dictionaries confirm its opinion that the verb needn't have an object.

Grammar, then, isn't the problem. Could the problem be that the waiter is telling you what to do? And that you consider it the restaurant's job to provide an enjoyable experience and your prerogative to decide whether the restaurant has succeeded? And that it therefore seems presumptuous for an employee to be commanding you, *"Enjoy!"*? As for your doctor, could the problem be that you really would have been interested to know which he expected you to enjoy: the pulled tendon or paying the bill? But now we have strayed into the realm of psychology, and that's not my department.

I'm a teacher. "Have a successful learning day" is what the assistant principal says over the intercom every other morning or so. There's something about the phrase that grates on my nerves. Am I being needlessly critical?

The magic of language is that it enables us to see into the minds of others: the form in which we express our thoughts is as much a part of the communication as the content is. There is nothing ungrammatical about your assistant principal's exhortation. And yet it does amount to a cliché *(Have a nice day)* that has been retrofitted with bureaucratic-sounding piffle *(successful learning day)*. No wonder it grates. To rise above that feeling, try imagining what it would be like to *be* someone who habitually says such a thing, instead of someone who only has to listen to it two or three times a week.

Then, too, there are expressions whose meaning people know perfectly well. They just wish that pigs had wings, or wore perfume, or something like that.

> *Please help with a language question. The phrase* French bath *always meant to me covering body odor with perfume, rather than actually bathing. Obviously, it means something else to others, for the entry in the* Random House Historical Dictionary of American Slang *reads, "An erotic act consisting of extensive licking of the partner's body."*
>
> *I would like my version to become more accepted.*

I didn't know *what* to say to that. Finally I wrote back:

Bonne chance!

Now here are a few letters that I hope will, collectively, vaccinate you, as it were, against intolerance. All of them are about small things. But notice how worked up the letter writers get. In a sense, the source of all these questions—or, in some cases, rants—is the dangerous, if very human, impulse to see things in black and white.

> *According to* Webster's, *the word* methodology *is defined as "the science of methods, rules, procedures, etc., as it is applied by a science or an art." It seems that this word is often misused when the author really means* method, *defined as "mode or manner of procedure, or principle of classification, etc." It seems that many people use* methodology *because it sounds more learned than the simple word* method. *I have categorically purged this word from any of my students' papers.*

I'm with you as far as wanting to put an end to the abuse of *methodology,* which is indeed rife, but I just don't believe in categorically purging words, except maybe racial and religious epithets, from my vocabulary. Rather, I try to see the value in every dear little one of them. Poor *methodology* need not lead a meaningless existence; nor does it deserve to be snuffed out. *Method* and *methodology* stand in something like the relation to each other that *tactics* and *strategy* stand in to each other. A *method* is supposed to be a procedure or technique, while a *methodology* is the underlying principles or system. Thus a person might sensibly say, for instance, "My *methodology* is to try as many *methods* as I can, and see which work."

My special aggravation is with the Japanese word hancho. *First of all, the military personnel who adopted the word, which means "squad leader," thought that, for example,* Pancho *and* poncho *are homonyms. English is probably the only language where the* a *in* father *is pronounced like the* o *in* on. *Second, like Murphy's Law, the meaning changed from "a minor leader" to "a very important person." Third, the suffix* -cho *in Japanese means the very top person in an organization:* gakucho, *"the dean of a school";* incho, *"the head of a hospital";* hancho, *"the sergeant in charge of a squad"; etc.* Head honcho *is at once an anomaly, a redundancy, and a misspelling.*

I think you're overlooking the fact that the Japanese don't use our alphabet. *Honcho* is nothing more than a phonetic rendering of what English-speakers have heard Japanese-speakers say.

You might enjoy knowing that your example word *poncho* stems from a mishearing: the original Araucanian (South American Indian) word is pronounced "pontho." The full history of the misunderstandings and mishearings involved as foreign words have been incorporated into English would probably be uproarious.

I realize that the meanings of words can change with time, but what if the meaning is fixed in a formal, unchanging document? I refer to the U.S. Constitution. It is almost universal at even the highest levels of news reporting (for example, TV networks and major newsmagazines) to refer to members of the House of Representatives as congressmen *or* congresswomen. *I want to cry out, "That's wrong, Wrong,* WRONG!*"* Congress, *according to the Constitution, consists of both the House and the Senate. Thus a senator is also a member of Congress.*

Certainly, representative, *with fourteen letters and five syllables, takes more space to print and is harder to pronounce than the eleven-letter, three-syllable* congressman. *But the latter term is simply incorrect.*

I have a solution: housemember. *It has no more letters or syllables than* congressman, *slides off the tongue easily, and has the advantage of being gender-neutral.*

What do you think?

It's true that a *congressman* may be a member of either house of Congress. But dictionaries do specify that he is more likely to be a member of the House. Oops, I mean the lower house, the House of Representatives. Our language includes many eccentricities and evident illogicalities. Right there in Congress, for example, can be found *sergeants-at-arms* who carry no weapons. Maybe you should consider this in that light.

I grit my teeth when I hear Alaskan *used as an adjective. In my opinion, an* Alaskan *is a person from Alaska. One would never refer to* Californian wine *or* Texan grapefruit, *so why would one assume it's okay to say* Alaskan village?

Well, but you wouldn't say *France wine, Italy food,* or *Hawaii village.* Where to use noun-adjectives (like those place-names) and where to use regular adjectives (like *French, Italian,* and, yes, *Alaskan*) can't easily be decided in the abstract. In fact authorities' objections in this general area tend to be the opposite of yours. A construction like "Alaska state education curriculum subcommittee decision"—noun piled on noun piled on noun—is considered poor form. Obviously, the solution to this problem isn't just to change *Alaska* to *Alaskan* and *education* to *educational* and so on but to start fresh. "A decision by the curriculum subcommittee of Alaska's department of education," or something like that, will be much easier to read for everyone except native speakers of German, who are used to seeing towering stacks of nouns.

I would like to comment on a short story by John Barth that appeared in The Atlantic. *Thumbnailed to the first page of the story was an excerpt including this: "a quarrel currently* truced." *There is no such word.*

*I refuse to read this story! I'm only a reader,
not a writer, but I know when the language is being
garbaged!*

Do you, now? In fact the verb *truce*—along with the
verb *garbage*—appears in *Webster's Second,
Unabridged,* which as far as many linguistically conservative readers and writers are concerned is the gold
standard for American usage. Inasmuch as it has been
out of print since 1961, no one today accuses it of
being unpleasantly avant-garde. Your verb *thumbnail*
is absent, though this one, too, appears in *Webster's
Third*.

I have reproduced the following, final letter exactly,
because I find it fascinating that someone so adamant
about one fine point should be so oblivious of others.

*I am constantly 'Put Down', by Grammarians—and
more especially by Editors—for my intransigent insis-
tence upon writing:* "INFACT" BUT, IN FACT *is, indeed,*
"INFACT"*! that is the way that it is commonly used;
and, is no more grammatically incorrect than:* "IN-
DEED", "INTO", "CANNOT", OR ANY OTHER SUCH
CONSTRUCT*!*
    Certainly, it is—at the least—as correct as: "<u>EACH
AND EVERY</u>"*?* EACH MEANS EVERY; EVERY MEANS EACH*!*
ONE MAY AS WELL SAY: "EACH AND EACH"; OR: "EVERY
AND EVERY"*!*

Dear reader, has the vaccination taken yet? When you
simply must object, will you try not to be hot-tempered
about it? And will you try never to make a fuss unless you
are certain you are right? As Benjamin Disraeli said, "It is
much easier to be critical than to be correct."

I Was Like "Huh?"

It may be that snappishness is just one aspect of a larger trend toward informality; when we're on our best behavior, we don't tend to snap, shout, and carp at others. Everything from home design to office dress codes and on to English as it is used every day is undeniably growing more and more casual. Granted that people have been informal in private since they were Neanderthals. And granted that at, say, the turn of the century, when the country was largely rural and comparatively poor, and educational levels were low, the average American was still more informal than he or she is now. (I mean that a much smaller proportion of the population owned dress shoes, or knew which fork to use for the salad.) But in our public culture—what we tell the world we want to be—few of us aspire anymore toward Victorian decorum and gentility. We often call people by their first names on first meeting and borrow our modes of expression from sportscasters (*Yesss!*) and computer marketers (*user-friendly*).

In fact, many new words entering standard English these days are arriving from such unceremonious subcultures as sports and computers or have managed to shake off downright jokey connotations. Examples of such words that are well on their way to joining standard English, because people find them useful, are *factoid*; *old-boy network*; *stun gun*; *to bond* as an intransitive verb meaning "to form a close personal relationship"; the verb *massage* in the sense of manipulating data; and *serious* meaning "considerable" or "of professional quality."

Still, most of us, if we walked into a room full of

strangers and were introduced around, would make conversation in standard English. Curiously, we would probably loosen up our language if we came upon the same strangers in an online chat room, just as we do when we are talking with our family or old friends. This freer kind of language is known as informal English—a name that unfortunately sounds a bit as if someone were holding the subject at a distance, with tongs. I prefer to call informal English "house English," for to me this name seems more in keeping with what is being described. House English dresses down, as it were, the way we ourselves do at home.

Standard English continues to buck the trend. I hear frequently from those doing the bucking—people asking disdainfully whether some phrase or other has become acceptable, or deploring an expression that sounds naïve or ignorant or overfamiliar to them. Some complaints have more justification than others. When people object, for example, to idioms that their spouses use at the breakfast table, my first reaction tends to be that forgiveness ought to be granted automatically for any lapse of grammar committed in a bathrobe, before the coffee is ready. But it may be that the letter writers are expressing the question in those terms because their spouses also use those expressions in more public settings, and they are hoping to put a stop to that politely—in other words, privately, over the breakfast table.

A kind of complaint regularly made about house English is that it's unclear. Sometimes this charge seems to me trumped up—but not always. As a frightening article in *The New York Times* explained not long ago, under the headline "TRAIL OF AMBIGUOUS E-MAIL IN A

STUDENT'S TORTURE TRIAL," the English used by a young man and a young woman in months of e-mail messages to each other, leading to a highly regrettable meeting, was unclear in a very important way. The article said:

> *Unlike most sexual assault cases, which rely heavily on testimony and physical evidence, the case of People v. Jovanovic includes exacting records of communications before and after the incident.*
>
> *But because of the hybrid nature of the e-mail messages—lacking the intonation and nuance of speech, as well as the clarity of carefully written letters—the prosecution and defense have reached opposite conclusions about nearly every passage.*

The conclusion to be reached here is that house English has definite limitations. Often it flies in the face of the time-honored standard-English way of saying the same thing. Or it may imply more intimacy with the reader or listener than is suitable for general-purpose language. Advertising copy composed of sentence fragments ("You and a book. No telephones. No televisions. Just the sound of the ocean") tends to do both those things at once—it breaks rules self-consciously and reaches for intimacy—and in the process irritates some people. Certain house-English expressions are perennials, but others are bound to be short-lived. Here is a smattering of questions about house English, old and new:

> *We gave my father-in-law a set of napkins, and said they might be appropriate if he was throwing a small dinner party. He said, "I only throw small parties anymore." Putting aside the trump-all grammar rule that says your father-in-law is always right, I wonder*

if anymore *is correct when used in a positive statement.*

The *Dictionary of American Regional English* convincingly demonstrates that *anymore* has been used in colloquial affirmative contexts at least since the 1930s. It isn't standard English, but the usage can now be found all over the country (most rarely in New England), in casual speech and writing by people of all educational levels. When you do hear it, you'll notice that it tends to come up in contexts where, though the form is affirmative, the meaning is negative. What your father-in-law said, for example, is roughly equivalent to "I *don't* throw large parties *anymore.*"

Just by the way, if the position of *only* in the quotation from the father-in-law bothers you, as it did a few of my correspondents, you may wish to look up the entry for that word in Chapter Four.

My wife and I have a dispute: When I use the expression I could care less, *she contends that the literal meaning is* I care somewhat *and that if I want to show a total lack of interest, I should say* I couldn't care less. *I say that* I could care less *is idiomatic usage, with the same meaning as* I couldn't care less. *Can you resolve this for us?*

Could care less has been with us since about the 1960s, and has been driving some people bonkers all the while. It's not considered appropriate for formal speech or writing, and, of course, it's illogical. But English doesn't behave any more logically than people tend to do. Two analogous examples: How did *Tell me about it* come to mean "I know"? How did *You can't be serious!* come to mean "I know you *are* serious, and I am surprised"? Etymologists have answers to these questions. The answer to yours is that *I could care less* is by now indeed an informal idiom that means what you say it does.

I would like to offer this comment to your note that "could care less has been with us since about the 1960s."

When I was in seventh grade (1962 or so), I came somehow upon the writing of Will Cuppy, who cracked me up with his silly mock-formal essays, complete with footnotes. One sentence that has stuck in my mind to this day related to fish diseases, and ran (approximately): "The common or everyday ten-cent goldfish has xanthochroism and could care less."

Cuppy's heyday—if he ever had one—can't have been later than the 1940s. Was he more of a pioneer than I knew?

I was sorry to see you knuckle under in the matter of could care less. *Or did you? Can your response also be read two ways?*

The writer's wife is right. I could care less *does not mean the same thing as* I could not care less. *Words have meaning and changing the meaning should not be undertaken lightly.*

When a Roman emperor misspoke himself, a brown-noser in the audience said, "Aha, the word now has a new meaning." But there was also a lover of beauty and a seeker after truth in the audience. He objected, at the risk of his life. "No way," he said. "The Emperor can confer citizenship on aliens and

*change them into Romans, but he cannot change the
meaning of words." He, too, is on the wife's side.*

*Having said that, I must agree that there is much
in the world that is irrational. If this were a logical
world, women would straddle a horse and men would
ride sidesaddle.*

My boss and I have a recurring battle over the use of
try and, *which she insists should be* try to. *She contends that* to try and *do something means to achieve
the goal, and is therefore incorrect; but* to try to *do
something doesn't predict success and is therefore
proper. I argue that* to try and *do something clearly
indicates one's hope for success, and is therefore
proper. Who is right?*

Try and is widely considered colloquial, so you probably shouldn't use it in writing at work. Nonetheless—
as you may enjoy casually remarking to your boss one
of these days—*try and do better* and the like are examples of hendiadys, a device that was used as a poetic ornament in Greek and Latin. Hendiadys, as
H. W. Fowler explains it, is "the expressing of a compound notion by giving its two constituents as though
they were independent and connecting them with a
conjunction instead of subordinating one to the
other." *Nice and warm* (as against *nicely warm*) is another example Fowler gives of the device as it crops
up in English.

*Have you ever gone into a restaurant in mixed com-
pany and been greeted with "Hi, guys, I'm Muriel and*

I'll be your waitress today"? And then when you're finished, been hit with "Can I get you guys anything else?" Where does this multisex term guys come from? Webster's *clearly defines a guy as a "fellow (male)" in the slang definition and as "a grotesque effigy of Guy Fawkes who was a source of ridicule." Neither of these definitions is uplifting for the male or appropriate for the female. How do these sayings get started, and more important, how are they squelched?*

What would you like Muriel to say? All of us English-speakers regularly find ourselves searching for ways to make *you* unmistakably plural. In theory, of course, *you* by itself can mean just what *you guys* does, and it has a long and honorable tradition of being neutral with respect to sex. But in a context like the one in which Muriel is using it, the word cries out for some accompaniment, because her listeners can't tell whether it refers to everyone at the table or the person at whom she's looking, and it's rarely possible to include each person by making eye contact with them all.

Muriel doesn't have many alternatives available to her. "Hi, *y'all*" will pass muster only in the South. "Hi, *guys and gals*" and "Hi, *folks*" are corny. "Hi, *people*" is not bad, though it's a bit eccentric and Muriel would have to be careful with "Can I get *you people* anything else?" This has become an epithet when it refers to members of any group that feels harassed or oppressed or different. "Hi, *everybody*.... Can I get *anybody* anything else?" may be the safest and best choice.

Be all that as it may, I don't know any way of getting Muriel to cease and desist with *you guys* other than saying something like, "Tell me, Muriel, do you think of yourself as a *guy*?" This is a trick question, since it's generally only in the plural that the word is used to mean a member of either sex.

Then again, you could avoid the problem by patronizing restaurants that are more pretentious.

If my eleven-year-old, David, is a bellwether, the venerable verb to say *is on its way out. The word* like, *as in "I was* like *'Huh?'" is one source of the erosion. Another source is* to go, *as in "He* goes *'What?' and I* go *'Whatever.'" I've explained that cows go "moo" and dogs go "bow-wow," while people say "Howdy do." To no avail. I've been tempted to make fun by prompting with "Tell me what she* went *next," and "And then what was he* like*?"—but I shy from becoming a Torquemada. What does Ms. Grammar think I should do?*

"When I was a child, I spake as a child," Saint Paul wrote. I see no harm in it if kids use the current kid dialect when talking with other kids, or even in casual conversation with you, as long as they can also demonstrate a command of standard English when, say, lunching with Grandmother. David ought to be able to manage that relatively minor attainment. Children's capacity for language is awesome. When Charles Berlitz, of Berlitz Publishing and what is now known as the Berlitz Language Center, was a small boy, his father spoke to him in English, his mother in French, his grandfather in German, and his aunts and cousins in Spanish—and he learned to converse with everyone. All the same, imagine little Charles's relief on his first day of school when he realized that he wasn't going to have to learn a new language to communicate with each of the other children in his class. He was also, according to later reports, full of pity when he discovered that most of those other children spoke nothing but English.

These exchanges might give the impression that the real distinction to be made is not between house English and standard English but between the spoken and the written word. Not so! It *is* true that spoken English is increasingly influential, because today radio and television allow people to speak, unmediated by print, to millions at once. But listeners become irritated when influential speakers in more or less formal contexts fail to use standard English, and a staple of my column is complaints about the language used on air by newscasters and meteorologists. Here's a case in point: an exchange that appeared in Word Court, plus a small sampling of the many letters I subsequently received.

> *I'm not sure that I can adequately describe what's bothering me. What it* is *is—that's it! I call it the "double* is," *and I hear it almost daily. Perhaps the worst offender is the political commentator Cokie Roberts. How did this weird construction ever gain ascendancy over the simple declarative sentence?*

Cokie Roberts told Word Court, "I have no notion of what I say! In live broadcasting you just talk. The main thing is to get the point across." In the course of a ten-minute conversation she did not say *is is* once—and I'll bet you haven't heard her say it recently, either. When people are told about their idiosyncrasies, they usually retrain themselves.

That's too bad—at least, in this case. "What it *is*

is..." is nothing worse than an idiosyncrasy, and it can be useful for adding emphasis. Furthermore, speakers deserve more leeway than writers, who have had the opportunity to revise. Now, *you* need never say "What it *is is*"—but will you try to tolerate its use by others? You might like it better if you think of it as a near relative, grammatically speaking, of the classic line, from *Cool Hand Luke,* "What we've *got* here *is* a failure to communicate."

I am just as much offended by the "double is*" as the letter writer. But oddly, he failed to cite an actual example. Here are two frequent offenders:*
    "The thing of it is, is *that..."*
    "The fact of the matter is, is *that..."*
    In each case the speaker sees the cliché preceding the comma as equivalent to a single-word subject, and follows it with a verb. Catch half a dozen newscasts or talk shows and you can't miss it.

I was disappointed both in the letter concerning the use of is is *and in your response. You* are *correct that "What it* is is*..." is not in itself incorrect and can be useful. The problem is that so many people, having heard someone respectable say "What it* is is*..." (or a comparable construction), use the "double* is*" when it is unnecessary and grammatically wrong—when, for example, they start sentences like this: "The problem* is is *that..."*
    Like Cokie Roberts, most of us "just talk" to get the point across. However, we sense that our point is made more forcefully if we impress the listener with our knowledge of how to talk—a knowledge gained chiefly by listening and (we hope) correctly imitating. Such usages often become habits where we have no

notion of what we say. Blatant examples are the millions every day who incorrectly say I *in place of* me *because of all the times they were told as kids that they should, even though they didn't understand why.*

Some very intelligent and productive people I work with routinely say is is *when* is *suffices. (It's easy to get away with, because, said rapidly enough, it sounds like a hesitation or stammer.) Others, including President Clinton, have made the same error in recorded statements I've heard on National Public Radio, and Cokie Roberts herself did so this morning on* Morning Edition. *Let's at least try to make them aware of it.*

I was going to let someone else straighten out that letter writer's difficulty with is is; *he has a valid complaint but gives the wrong example. Today, however, I heard the accused Cokie Roberts incriminate herself again: about forty-six minutes into the David Brinkley show she said, "The truth of the matter* is, is *that the President can't be irrelevant."*

I firmly believe is is *to be the most egregious current misuse of the English language, as it has crept into the conversation of even educated people without their knowledge.*

If you remain unconvinced that people ask as much of speakers as they do of writers, please turn to "No Blunders Aloud," about pronunciation, in Chapter Five. Not only professionals who are being well paid for their words, and not only people speaking publicly, but all of us are judged by how we speak.

———

Good Jargon, Bad Jargon

One other trend in our lives worth mentioning here is toward the specialization of knowledge, and therefore specialization of language. There are today great, broad realms of English not meant to be understood by the ordinary person. When jargon is serving its highest purpose, it is obscure to the uninitiated only as a side effect of being clear to specialists, because it packs a lot of knowledge into a few words. Paradoxically, if the speaker or writer did all the explaining that would allow nonspecialists to understand what was being said, the language would become virtually impenetrable to everyone. Imagine, for example, recasting "He played the lute," with the help of *The American Heritage Dictionary,* to read "He played a stringed instrument having a body shaped like a pear sliced lengthwise and a neck with a fretted fingerboard that is usually bent just below the tuning pegs." Do you find that clearer? Never mind that it's thirty words instead of four.

Or what about an article title that appeared in the table of contents of a recent issue of the medical journal *Neurology*: "Erythropoietin-associated hypertensive posterior leukoencephalopathy"? I asked a neurologist to translate this into standard English for me, and I won't even try to improve on the job he did: "A disease state affecting the back of the brain—in particular, those areas involved in the transmission of electrochemical impulses—which is associated with the use of a drug that is prescribed for patients with chronic anemia and that stimulates the production of red blood cells but can have the side effect of raising blood pressure to unhealthy levels." Not only does that turn four words into fifty-nine but if we were as familiar with *leukoen-cephalopathy* as we are with *lute,* we'd surely find it maddening.

Professional jargons thus belong in the category of things that consenting adults do and say in private: there the rules of standard English apply only to the extent that the participants want them to. Certainly, if people want to bring the insights of a professional field to outsiders, they must translate the jargon into standard English. They may hope to achieve a more pleasing result than our revisions above, but in order to do so they will probably have to find a better, more accessible starting point.

So much for the benign uses of jargon. It can also be misused. Sometimes people try to dress up mundane ideas as if they were too special for the ordinary person to understand. This rarely works. The most embarrassing attempts seem to turn up in bureaucratic and corporate prose discussing something that isn't at all far removed from everyday life. The fancy language serves only to make us wonder what the speaker or writer is trying to get away with. Woeful pseudojargon deserves to be relegated to a level of language all its own, which I call "Englishese." Here are some letters about jargons and Englishese:

> *My engineering co-workers assault my eyes and ears with bureaucratic jargon, such as* functionality, utilize, parametrics, *and* documentation *when they really mean* function, use, parameter, *and* document. *What can I do about this?*

Not much beyond saying mildly, over and over, like a record that you can expect will remain broken for the rest of your professional life, "I'm afraid I don't understand what you mean by that. Isn't there a simpler way to say it?"

I am an interior designer, and I understand that the correct term for fabric window coverings is draperies, *not* drapes, *as they are so often called. I understand that* drapes *is a verb and not a noun. Am I right?*

But interior design is *your* field. Of course, my field involves looking up words in dictionaries. I can show you dictionaries that insist that *quote* is a verb, not a noun, but I am unable to find any that make the same case for *drape*. If your colleagues and, more important, your clients use *drapes* as a noun, feel free to do so, too.

I'm confused. As a health-care *professional, I read information from organizations with national scope of responsibility—e.g., the Institute for* Healthcare Improvement, *the Joint Commission on Accreditation of* Healthcare Organizations—*addressing issues related to* health care. *An article in a recent issue of* The Wall Street Journal *contained references to* healthcare, health care, *and* health-care. *What is the current standard term for the provision of medical services to patients?*

There's no particular reason to treat *health care* differently from *medical care* or *managed care,* and you never see those pairs of words jammed together. At least, that's the point to keep in mind about *health care* as a noun. When such a term is used as an adjective, it ought to be hyphenated ("a *health-care* initiative"), to make clear that the two words are functioning as a unit.

Institutes and commissions and corporations, however, hate having hyphens in their names. I suspect that this prejudice is the source of your problem; when people reject the standard way of doing things, what they will decide to do instead can be hard to predict. Browsing a few hundred health-related Web sites for you, I found *Health Care, HealthCare,* or *Healthcare* in about a dozen proper names, and the hyphenated term in none.

Obviously, it's not up to you to decide how organizations should spell their names, any more than it would be appropriate for you to start spelling the names of your friends and colleagues however you pleased. But you can see to it in your own writing that no matter what they call themselves, you have them providing *health care* or undertaking *health-care* initiatives, and so forth.

Help! I am a harried copy editor currently working on several college-level textbooks in the fields of general education and special education. I am beset with clunky verb-phrase constructions that the authors insist have become common parlance in their fields. The worst of these is the use of the phrase problem solve *as a verb, as in "when you* problem solve *with parents and colleagues" or "The dilemma can be avoided if more effort is made to identify a shared need to* problem solve.*" Authors insist that my initial inclination to change these phrases to read* solve problems *skews their meaning, since* problem solve *(verb) carries very specific connotations.*

Another common usage employs the noun transi-tion *as a verb, as in "A structured classroom routine will help students* transition *from one activity to an-other." After dutifully changing this faux-verb to* move, switch, *or* make the transition, *I was informed by the authors that* transition *is the common, and pre-ferred, verb in this context.*

What do you think about these two usages? Am I just being anal-retentive with regard to language (as has been known to happen)? Bear in mind that these folks are teaching the people who will be teaching our children.

On the one hand, specialized fields need specialized jargons for their specialized ideas. On the other, it's not as if the idea of solving problems and the idea of making a transition were particularly specialized.

Have you tried telling your authors that *problem solve* as a unit and *transition* as a verb aren't in the dictionary? *Transition* as a verb does appear in the permissive unabridged *Random House*, but neither word is found in *The American Heritage Dictionary*, which is relatively current and makes a point of in-cluding and commenting on disputed usages. Pre-sumably, your mandate is to ensure that the texts are in standard English, so the dictionary test is im-portant.

Then again, I can understand the position that "when you *problem solve* with parents and col-leagues" isn't identical in meaning to "when you solve problems." Maybe that one should be "when you work with parents and colleagues to solve problems"? This is the level on which to try to engage your au-thors: get them to propose the best way to change what they've written so as to say what they mean in standard English.

I work with a person who insists that cash flow *is one word even after being shown the dictionary entry, which clearly spells it as two words. He believes that by making it one word, he is starting a trend, similar to the joining of the words* health care *into one word. I find it particularly frustrating because neither of the bankers in the office where he works corrects his mistake. Since we are investment bankers, I think that writing* cash flow *as one word looks as if even though we're supposedly experts in finance, we don't know how to spell.*

Why does he want to start a trend, do you suppose? I imagine that if you ask him, he will say that *cashflow* looks better to him than *cash flow* does. But *cash flow* obviously looks better to most people. This is the only form that dictionaries give for the noun, and they're duty-bound to mention it if there's widespread dissent.

At the magazine where I work, I've been frequently hearing the word repurposing—*as in "repurposing information" (taking material that was designed for print media and converting it to a Web-based format). A colleague wants it banned from our magazine; I insist it is used universally and is here to stay. What's your thinking on this neologism?*

I'd never seen the word myself until you wrote, so you can't persuade me it's used universally. However, *The Atlantic*'s new-media people assure me that they're quite familiar with the word. What's more, they say they can't give me any exact synonyms for it—the fundamental test for whether a neologism deserves houseroom or not. The most nearly synonymous word they could think of was *recycling,* but *recycling* carries unfortunate connotations of garbage.

Repurposing is jargon, but I don't mean that pejoratively. Within a specialized field, jargon like this serves as shorthand, so that, for example, you and your colleagues don't need to keep saying "converting print material to a World Wide Web format"; *repurposing* allows much more economical phrasing. I'm not eager to see it turn up in nontechnical contexts (say, "Courtney Love, once thought of as a singer, has sought to *repurpose* herself as an actress and a model"), but I agree with you that the word has its place.

I was appalled by your response to the question about repurposing. *As* purposing *is not a verb,* repurposing *is not a verb twice over! What's more, taking information that was designed for one medium and converting it to another does not change the purpose of the data itself, only its method of delivery. For English-language synonyms, try* reformatting, transferring, *or simply* converting *data to the Web.*

Repurpose??? You must have been asleep when you replied to that letter. What about recast? *It has the advantage of being quite a lot more graceful, and it's in the dictionary.*

My correspondents may not always agree with me on what allowances ought to be made for specialized fields, but please note how strongly they tend to feel that whenever possible, business and professional English should be standard English.

A recent front-page article in the San Diego Daily Transcript, *a business daily, caught my eye. It was titled "Engineer Fights Web Spamming." What? I had to read the article, of course. It was about a man who started a Web site featuring live photos of San Diego Bay and local attractions. Others started using his site as a return address for live-sex services and tarot-card reading, however, which he was not pleased about. The article referred to "spammers" who used his site as the return address for junk e-mail.*

A rule of thumb is that as long as the writer, or editor, of an article feels the need to define a term like *spamming,* it's jargon. It becomes part of our common language only when the writer is able to trust that readers can find the word, if they need to, in nonspecialized dictionaries. This means, ironically, that new words, or new meanings for words, tend to turn up in the dictionary just when people don't need to look them up anymore. When no one who reads the headline says "What?" the word will then be standard English.

As the self-appointed grammar policeman in my university department, I have banned the word proactive. *It is an ugly word that, to me, has no meaning. "I want a* proactive *response to this request." Why not simply and more clearly say "I want an* energetic *response" or "I want a* decisive *response"?*
My research assistants, particularly one who was

*an English major, think I'm hopelessly mired in an-
cient and irrelevant efforts to preserve the King's
English. They're wrong, of course?*

Language, like clothing and food, has its fashions,
and in certain circles *proactive* is fashionable. Those
who like the word find it forward-thinking and alert,
and they may be tempted to use it where they want to
convey that feeling—whether its actual meaning,
which is "pre-emptive" or "anticipatory," applies or
not. When the word crops up, perhaps you should
begin saying, or writing in margins, "Do you mean
anticipatory?" Until then, there's no point in being—
well, proactive. It's best to judge a word case by case.

These next two letters are about one of the most thank-
less tasks known to humankind: writing mission statements.

*Our school system recently undertook the project of
rewriting its mission statement. It was a collaborative
effort of the staff, community, administrators, and
board of education. Among other things, the final
statement included the following: "The school district
will provide rigorous learning." There has been considerable discussion as to what rigorous learning
would be. I would appreciate your thoughts.*

On the one hand, people say *rigorous training* and *a
rigorous education,* and your phrase isn't much different from either of those. But on the other, do you
know what dictionaries say about *rigorous?* "Characterized by rigor," yes, but the word has traditionally
been pejorative, for the most part—or, at least, the
synonyms given are along the lines of *harsh* and
trying. I hope those aren't the words you'd use to

characterize the kind of education you want your students to have. Maybe, *solid learning*?

Another problem here has to do with whether your group really believes that learning is something that can be *provided*. It seems to me that what you're providing is teaching, and that about all you can do with respect to learning is to *seek to enable* or *encourage* it.

Last week, in a meeting, the question came up of whether our mission statement should be revised. It reads as follows: "The mission of the steering committee is to foster employee involvement to achieve continuous improvement through communication, recognition, and commitment of both individual and team efforts." *I volunteered right away to revise it, stating that the sentence is too long, has two infinitives, doesn't make sense, and is just not good English. The response from the department heads was that they had all worked long and hard composing it and it should stay as is. Later my department head came to me and said that if I wanted to, I should take a shot at revising it.*

The statement seems to me to be a collection of worthwhile words randomly thrown together. Is it bad English or just an awkward sentence?

No one has told you? Mission statements exist for two reasons only: so that the committee working on one can have a catered lunch brought in, and so that any employee who wants to have a little nap at the office can just get out the mission statement and read it over. Run the other way! Never think about this again!

Higher English

Whether we like it or not, our language is never going to stop changing. Some of the changes are nothing more than ephemeral matters of fashion, bound to be supplanted by further such ephemeral matters; others seem certain to endure. While we try to sort them out, it will behoove us to question all our rules and punctilios, to ensure that each of them still serves a purpose. Many do, as my sharp-eyed, quick-tempered correspondents are forever pointing out.

Since we've been naming types of English, let's give the name of "higher English" to the sort of standard English that we'll be discussing in the remainder of the book: the sort with all bells and whistles attached and all punctilios observed, useful in non-ephemeral settings and in any place where our audience consists of strangers whom we hope to impress with our views and our verve.

AN ASIDE

House Style

Should you write the phrase *the president of the United States and the British prime minister* or *the President of the United States and the British Prime Minister* or *the President of the United States and the British prime minister*? *Decisionmaking* or *decision-making* or *decision making*? *Number One* or *No. 1* or *#1*? *10:00* or *ten o'clock* or *10 A.M.* or *10:00 a.m.* or...? *A, B, and C* or *A, B and C*? And what about such things as italics and exclamation points—does "the more the merrier" apply, or is less more?

These are just a few of the decisions that together make up a publication's or an organization's or a writer's "house style." If "language is the dress of thought," as Samuel Johnson had it, matters of house style amount to something like accessories. Though none of the possibilities given above is wrong, opinions will vary about which choices are more tasteful or appropriate for certain purposes.

Capital letters tend to show respect. Propagandists know this instinctively, and they invariably capitalize the name of their philosophy, the title of their leader, the term for the group's adherents, and so on. Some mainstream American publications capitalize the title of our nation's leader and not the titles of the leaders of other countries. But doesn't a juxtaposition like "The *President* met with the *prime minister*" look ethnocentric? When considered from this point of view, even "The *President* and the *people* are at odds on this matter" might seem slightly skewed.

Numerals and quotation marks and symbols are not particularly respectful, but they are attention-getting and emphatic, and a lot of them together has the potential to look nerdy and brusque: compare *10%* and *ten percent,* for example, or *10 A.M.* and *ten o'clock.*

What any given style decision manages to convey is likely to be subtle; it's the cumulative effect that counts. Note how different in appearance are the two quotations in what follows. Of course, appearance is hardly the only difference between them, even though they are discussing the same thing. Certain style decisions tend to reflect fanatical—or, at best, peculiar—points of view. The first quotation is from the Web site of the Heaven's

Gate cult, thirty-nine of whose members committed suicide together in Rancho Santa Fe, California, in 1997. Even at a glance, it looks just plain crazy, doesn't it? The second is from an article in *The New York Times* explaining the cult's philosophy.

> *Whether Hale-Bopp has a "companion" or not is irrelevant from our perspective. However, its arrival is joyously very significant to us at "Heaven's Gate." The* joy *is that our Older Member in the Evolutionary Level Above Human (the "Kingdom of Heaven") has made it clear to us that Hale-Bopp's approach is the "marker" we've been waiting for—the time for the arrival of the spacecraft from the Level Above Human to take us home to "Their World"—in the literal Heavens. Our 22 years of classroom here on planet Earth is finally coming to conclusion—"graduation" from the Human Evolutionary Level. We are happily prepared to leave "this world" and go with Ti's crew.*

> *In its documents, the group described a world view on the furthest fringes of millennialism, with disconnected elements of Christianity interpreted through a thick lens of science fiction.*

> *In essence, its teachings boiled down to a belief in exalted purpose for a few, combined with an exceptionally grim view of life on an Earth where evil was in control—a heady mixture of profound hope amidst utter isolation.*

> *Heaven's Gate left no shortage of clues as to its negative thinking about the value of this-worldly life. The group subscribed to a gnostic religious view of the soul as a separate and superior being, temporarily inhabiting a physical form.*

Some people protest that house-style questions are beneath their notice, but these questions simply can't be evaded to any good effect. Almost any choices people make—short of choosing to commit suicide so as to be beamed up to a heaven on a comet—will leave them looking more rational and thoughtful than a failure to make choices. Of course, the choices must be followed consistently—or, at least, exceptions to them must be made consistently. If you write *20 percent,* for example, you should put the next percentage in the same format (say, *80 percent*), unless it appears at the beginning of a sentence, where the tendency is to spell numbers out *(Eighty percent),* or unless the number has just one digit, for most house styles spell out most single-digit numbers *(eight percent).*

A range of books, the most popular of which are probably *The Chicago Manual of Style, Words Into Type,* and *The Associated Press Stylebook,* contain detailed recommendations about house style. Using a book can come as a great relief, whether or not you are delighted with the particular recommendations it makes, because doing so will free you from having to make choice after choice and to try to remember every one of them. See the aside at the end of Chapter Four for suggestions about how to choose a style manual.

❧

CHAPTER THREE

A Grammarian's Dozen

You know more than you think you do.
—Dr. Benjamin Spock

Here we will consider the happy idea that our command of grammar is already impressive, mingled with the deflating idea that it's no wonder we have such command, since grammar is just meant to map what's in our heads. And we'll delve into thirteen specific grammatical issues that aren't well mapped in many people's heads and are therefore widely misunderstood.

A Speech of Parts

Most of us learned something about grammar at some point, just as many of us learned a bit of a foreign language and maybe the highlights of calculus. But good luck making use of that knowledge today! People often ask me questions that they could easily answer for themselves if they only remembered what they'd been taught about parts of speech and how the parts fit together, or don't. And yet the differences among adjectives, adverbs, conjunctions, nouns, prepositions, and all the rest, and the purposes each part of speech serves, are hardly a subject for the kind of habitual conversation that would keep everything fresh in a person's mind. Who can blame anyone for being hazy about grammar? Here are two cases in point:

> *Is it just me, or are we rapidly losing the adverb—or should I say, are we losing the adverb* fast? *I'm not sure if it's the inclination of people to speak in shorter "sound bites" or just lazier speech habits, but there seems to be a definite inclination to use an adjective in place of an adverb. Television and newspaper ads shout "Hurry, they're going* fast!" *when there's a sale, or the weatherman discusses the latest cold front forming in "northeast Montana."*

Ah, but *fast* has long been an adverb as well as an adjective. (In fact, it can be any of five parts of speech: adverb ["She runs *fast*"], adjective ["She's a *fast* woman"], noun ["She broke her *fast* today"], verb ["She doesn't *fast* every year"], and, according to *Webster's,* though not the *Oxford English Dictionary,* interjection ["*Fast!*"—used in the sport of archery as a warning].) In this, it's like a number of other words that have been part of English ever since the language was Anglo-Saxon: *free, quick, short, slow, well,* and *wild* are a few examples that come to mind. As for "*northeast* Montana": *northeast* here is modifying a noun, so it's not supposed to be an adverb; adjectives do that job. Nonetheless, *northeast* (think of "The storm is heading *northeast*") is another of those old words that can be either part of speech.

> *I have a thesis to turn in soon, and there is a word I'm using that the word processor says is incorrect.*

After researching this word in Merriam-Webster's Collegiate Dictionary, Intermediate Dictionary, *and the* Columbia Concise Dictionary, *I noticed the word is used in the past tense plus as an adjective but not in the present. This word is* authoritate. *The research showed it to be* au-thor-i-ta-tive, au-thor-i-ta-tively, au-thor-i-ta-tive-ness *only. What's with this?*

The past tense? I don't think so. *Authoritative* is an adjective derived from the noun *authority,* and the adverb *authoritatively* and the noun *authoritativeness* take it from there. The word you're hoping for would be a "back-formation"—a shorter word derived from a longer one but looking as if the longer word were derived from it. Back-formations that meet a need are coined as a matter of course: *diagnose* from *diagnosis, reminisce* from *reminiscence, donate* from *donation.* But *authoritate* has not been coined, probably because other words exist to serve the purpose you have in mind. *Be authoritative* is an obvious possibility. Or *decide,* perhaps? Or *command,* or *determine,* or *direct,* or *dominate,* or *ensure,* or *judge,* or *lecture,* or *order,* or *rule?*

To make matters worse, grammar is generally taught (when it's taught at all) as if it inhered in the words being studied, rather than in the minds of those of us who are using them—as if it were like physics, rather than like a branch of psychology. It isn't. If you throw a pebble, the distance it travels will be equal to the product of its velocity and the time it spends aloft—a fact about that pebble in the natural universe which will remain true whether or not anyone cares to calculate the pebble's velocity, or even hears the pebble fall. But the "fact" that *pebble* is a noun is a mental construct from start to finish. Furthermore, this fact is not true except among those of us who speak English, nor is it the whole truth even in English: *pebble* is also a verb that means "pave or pelt with pebbles" or "impart a pebbly texture to."

Such grammatical slipperiness is a quality of a large proportion of English words, including many of the ones we use most often. (When people use a word a lot, they tend to play with it.) *Fast* is a good example. Not only can it be any of five parts of speech, but as most of those it has multiple meanings and usages. As an adjective, *fast* can mean "rapid" or "immovable" or "staunch" or "wild and promiscuous." Then, too, the noun form of it that means "abstention from food" (one of two separately derived noun forms) can be used as an adjective, as in the phrase *fast day*.

To add to the confusion about parts of speech, some adjectives that do not appear in the dictionary as nouns may be used as nouns:

> *I have a severe grammatical affliction. You see, nowhere in my dictionaries is* afflicted *defined as a noun, but I constantly see it used in print—and, of course, also hear it in that lazy form of communication called speech. Example: "The pope has dedicated his life to helping the* afflicted." *So, please tell me, are people who use this word as a noun among those afflicted with poor grammar?*

In your example sentence, *afflicted* is perfectly correct; it is being used as an "absolute adjective." "Absolute," denoting a word or phrase that is standing in an unusual relation to the rest of the sentence, has a lot of different applications, because a lot of unusual relations exist in English. Here the peculiarity is that an adjective is serving as a noun.

Although this is a somewhat unusual position for *afflicted* to find itself in, it's not an especially unusual role for adjectives in general. Think of "For ye have the *poor* always with you...." In fact, *poor* has been used this way so often that dictionaries consider it a noun as well as an adjective. Such conversion is the route by which many other established nouns, among them *classic, intellectual,* and *unemployed,* have found their way into our language.

There are even words that are hybrids of nouns and adjectives, as I tried to explain in the Word Court column to the fifth-grade class that wrote me this letter.

Our local newspaper used the words "fun ideas" *recently. We have learned that* fun *is not a descriptive, but we see it used that way all the time. And* "everyone" *says* fun vacation, fun movie, *and lots of other things. Is this correct usage now?*

Not that he's made a scientific study of it, but the psycholinguist Steven Pinker says he can tell whether people are under or over thirty years old by whether they're willing to accept *fun* as a full-fledged adjective, or what you call a descriptive. Let me guess: you are all under thirty. Regardless, you are quite right to question whether standard English allows *fun* to be used as an adjective. It doesn't, really. *Fun* may exhibit some adjective-like qualities at times, but it is a noun. And I'm not telling you how old I am.

If you'll promise not to say "I had the *funnest* time" or "That was *so fun,*" though, I'll tell you why *fun ideas, fun vacation,* and *fun movie* really aren't so bad. Lots of nouns are used "attributively," or as adjectives in front of other nouns. Think of *science-project ideas* and *Christmas vacation* and *action movie.* You won't find *science* or *project* or *Christmas* or *action* in the dictionary as an adjective; each is a noun, like *fun.* But all these words—and, indeed, most nouns—can be used attributively.

Being clear about this point of grammar has its pluses and its minuses. Sticklers are likely to assume that you're misusing *fun* where it's not obviously a noun, so maybe you should steer clear of attributive uses when you want to make a good impression on people over thirty.

As Pinker had warned me, in truth it's a little more complicated than that, though I didn't have space to say so in the column. He wrote me:

> *"We were at a* fun *party," which is acceptable even to us geezers, doesn't seem to fit the patterns of a genuine attributive-noun construction, as in "We were at a* dance *party." First, the stress pattern is different: "fun PARty" vs. "DANCE party."*
>
> *Second, so are the modifiers: "That was a really* fun *party," with an adverb modifying* fun, *is fine, whereas no one would say "That was a really dance party" (that is, a good example of one). Conversely, "a great dance party" is good, whereas "a great fun party" is weird.*
>
> *Finally, the meanings are different—a dance party is a genre of party (cf. costume party, Christmas party, etc.), whereas a fun party can be any kind of party as long as it turned out to be fun. Fun really does look like an adjective here.*

The basic problem is that not all adjectives exercise the full set of adjective options. For example, for-mer is an adjective, as in "former wife," but you can't say "That wife is former"; conversely, you can say "The man is afraid" but not "the afraid man."

The distinction, then, is not that boomers use fun as an attributive noun and slackers use it as an adjective but that boomers allow fun to have a few adjective privileges, and slackers allow it to have most or all of them, including modification by so and comparative -er and -est forms.

Not only are individual words and their parts of speech slippery, but syntax, or how the words go together, is, too. Think of the sentence "Live fast and have fun." Is that two commands—two exhortations to do things—or a prediction that if you live fast, you will have fun (comparable to "Drive fast and you'll get there on time")? Then again, what about "Go fast and say your prayers"? Is that a warning, on the same pattern as the "Drive fast" sentence, or is it a two-pronged exhortation to a monk?

When slippery words appear together, the number of ways the parts of the sentence could theoretically fit together expands out of all proportion. I learned this lesson in the mid-1980s when I looked into computers' ability to process and correct English. At the time, researchers in the field of artificial intelligence were struggling to program computers so that they could respond to commands in "natural language"—that is, a human language like English, as opposed to then-current computer languages like COBOL and C. In one particularly advanced project the researchers programmed their computer with certain words, the parts of speech that each of those words could be, and the legitimate ways that the parts of speech could go together, and then asked the computer to "parse" test sentences—to determine the parts of speech of which they were made. Some perfectly ordinary sentences, they found, could be parsed in many potentially legitimate ways. It might be hard to know what certain renditions of a given sentence were supposed to mean, but, of course, this was supposed to be a step toward enabling the computer to compute meaning; a computer doesn't "know" what anything means.

A team of experts had devoted years to the project, but accurately parsing the sentence "Test results show that sand filters produce more even results" remained well beyond the computer's abilities. This sentence really is a doozy, because not a single word in it is invariably one part of speech. As far as the computer could tell, the main verb might be *test,* and the sentence might be a command, like "Test batteries." (That, in fact, was its first guess.) Or the verb might be *results* or *sand* or *filters* or *produce*—or the final *results.* This sentence, as it happens, has literally hundreds of legitimate parses. The record-holder, though, among the sentences that the researchers had tried was "In as much as allocating costs is a tough job I would like to have the total costs related to each product," which, believe it or not, has 958 possible parses. We should consider it a minor miracle that virtually all of us human beings who can read that sentence, or the "Test results" sentence, will make sense of it in the same way.

English grammar is rife with little curiosities, anomalies, and seemingly arbitrary rules. If *doze in the sunshine* is a verb followed by a prepositional phrase, then why is *breathe in the fragrance* a compound verb and its object? The difference in meaning supplies the answer to this puzzle. Similarly, why is the final word in "They are *married*" an adjectival complement if in "They were *married* last Saturday" the same word is part of a passive verb? Again, the forms are similar, the meanings different. If you believe you are ignorant of grammar, do note that you recognize such differences, whether or not the terminology for them is ready on the tip of your tongue. Whether or not you have the vocabulary to express everything you know, you have quite a sophisticated understanding of grammar.

As for seemingly arbitrary rules: The grammar of "I want to ask her" is correct, is it not? And isn't the word *whom* in the same, objective case as *her*? So which is correct: "I want to ask *whom* she is" or "I want to ask *who* she is"? And then, would it be "She is *whom* I want to ask" or "She is *who* I want to ask"?

Perhaps your seventh-grade English teacher told you, as if the whole thing were obvious, that what comes after *ask* is an objective complement, in the objective case; and what comes after *is* is a subjective complement (also known as a predicate nominative), in the same case as the subject of the verb. A whole clause (that is, a grammatical unit with its own subject and verb, and probably some other parts besides) may serve as either an objective or a subjective complement, and its internal grammar remains unaffected by its subordinate position in the larger sentence. This rule trumps, as it were, the rules according to which objective and subjective complements are to be treated differently. Thus the right answers are "I want to ask *who* she is" (the subordinate clause is "she is *who* [subjective]") and "She is *whom* I want to ask" ("I want to ask *whom* [objective]"). Obviously!

All this is hallowed by time, having been derived from classical languages and the way they were parsed. Nonetheless, to someone who doesn't know ancient Latin or Greek, it may well be counterintuitive. Here's another, minor point on which the correct grammar is mysterious to many people, because the rule that's intuitive to them is the wrong rule:

> *In a recent Word Court you wrote the sentence "I suspect this is one of the many things that aren't being taught in high school anymore." The proper grammar is "One (of the many things [prepositional phrase]) that isn't...," no? Is that not being taught in eighth grade anymore?*

> "*One* of the many things I admire about Word Court's readers *is* that they say what they think." This sentence and the high-school sentence, you'll notice, are constructed along different lines. This one fits together conceptually so: "Of the many things I admire...*one is* that..." But "Of the many *things* that *aren't* being taught...this is one" is how the other one works. The version you propose, therefore, would not be correct.

Having explained that—tersely, I admit—I got many letters from people who simply refused to believe it. I was grateful to this man for writing a letter that I could photocopy and send to his skeptical peers.

> *I fully agree that the matter is a problem for a great many people. But it hasn't been a problem for me*

since I was a sophomore or junior in college (I am seventy-three now), when a Spanish professor gave us all a quick and easy solution. Your answer did include an example of the professor's suggestion, but without your giving a rule or a clear bit of instruction, which I'll do now: Start with the of. *Once you do that, regardless of the sentence, the answer becomes obvious.*

"One of the many things that isn't/aren't..." (which?) is vexing because one *is clearly singular and* the many things *clearly plural, and people lose track of what it is they are talking about—what the subject is or should be. So they gamble and just hope nobody challenges their English. Start with the* of: *"Of the many things that...," well, obviously, it has to be the plural form, "aren't."*

"This is one of the men who truly owns and operates our system"—actual quote, and dead wrong. Start with the of: *"Of the* men *who truly* own *and operate our system, this is* one." *I don't think anyone could seriously consider plunking down* owns *and operates if he or she had started with the* of.

Don't get me wrong. I'm not saying you have to stick with a construction that starts with of. *I am simply asking you to try it out, to determine quickly whether you need to use a singular or a plural. The beauty of it is that you don't have to be well educated, don't have to know (or claim to know) the rules of grammar. Prepositional phrase? You don't even have to know what that means.*

Of the various possible ways to be sure a person has it right, yours is one I very much like. Thanks!

Reading the Map

Our grammar has no objective reality; the lanes and by-ways of it are often tortuous and counterintuitive—it's enough to make us swear off the whole idea of grammar and just suit ourselves. Yet traditional English grammar is meant, for the most part, to map forms and structures already in our minds. For example, long, long ago, well before there was an English language, someone noticed that sentences tend to have subjects and verbs. (Not until fairly recently has it become clear that this is true of sentences in every known language.) The rule that sentences *should* have subjects and verbs simply recognizes this fact. It is in this sense that all of us know quite a lot of English grammar, having learned it as children, in the course of learning to speak.

To someone trained in the science of linguistics, that is almost a tautology. Linguists are fond of explaining that "grammar" is the rules in people's heads, not the rules printed in so-called grammar books. As Steven Pinker puts it in his book *The Language Instinct*:

> *The way language works...is that each person's brain contains a lexicon of words and the concepts they stand for (a mental dictionary) and a set of rules that combine the words to convey relationships among concepts (a mental grammar).*

Of course, unless each person's brain contains pretty much the same lexicon and the same set of rules as each other person's, we won't have a language in common; all the important rules for English are in many people's brains. Furthermore, the rules printed in grammar books—the good grammar books, anyway—reflect particular people's brains, in order to show how the more able and widely admired speakers and writers use language. Here we leave behind pure description and science, and enter the realms of subjectivity and taste and art.

People do sometimes argue that it is possible to write and speak well without knowing anything about traditional grammar—and certainly someone can be articulate without knowing traditional grammatical *terminology*. But we wouldn't say that a person lacked a mental grammar, in Pinker's sense, just because he was unfamiliar with linguistics, nor would we say that a fine singer knew nothing of music just because she had never learned to read musical notation. By the same token, some of the strengths of a good writer's work are bound to be explicable in terms of traditional grammar, whether the writer can explain them that way or not. Truly, the most remarkable thing about grammar is how many niceties of it virtually no one ever gets wrong. For instance, no one who means "The spirit is willing" says "The willing is spirit" or "Spirit is the willing" or any of various other combinations.

Indeed, there are a tremendous number of niceties that we could get wrong but don't. We all know a huge number of rules without having to think about them. You may say or write a simple sentence ("The spirit is willing"); you may say or write a compound sentence ("The spirit is willing, but the flesh is weak"); you may write a complex sentence ("Though the spirit is willing, the flesh is weak"); you may write a compound complex sentence ("The flesh may be weak whether or not the spirit is willing, and the spirit may be willing whether or not the flesh is weak"); you may put your dependent clauses before the main clause ("Whether or not the spirit is willing, the flesh is weak"), at certain points in the midst of it ("The flesh, whether or not the spirit..."), or after it; you may add adjectival or adverbial elements in various places, modifying various words ("The spirit, that indefinable something..."); you may add absolute elements, such as adverbs, that modify entire clauses ("Fortunately, the spirit is willing"); you may elide some clauses, leaving out the verb ("The spirit is willing, the flesh weak"); you may command, leaving out the subject of the sentence ("Be willing in spirit"); you may inquire ("Is the spirit willing?"); you may exclaim ("How willing is the spirit!"); you may wax metaphorical (as in the punch line of an old joke about computer translation, in which the sentence we've been manhandling becomes "The wine is fine, but the meat is spoiled").

You may not, though, write run-on sentences ("The spirit is willing, the flesh is weak"); you may not mismatch the parts of series ("The spirit is ready, willing, and feels able"); you may not mismatch the number of your subject or subjects with the number of your verb or verbs ("The spirit are willing"); you may not place dependent elements where they will attach themselves to the wrong things ("Rapidly tiring of this example, the spirit is willing but the flesh is weak, we still suppose"); you may not use a single possessive to indicate separate possession by more than one thing ("Here we observe the spirit and flesh's willingness and weakness"). If you're hazy on any of these rules, this book can serve as a refresher. But, terminology aside, you probably know them all.

In my experience, people are likeliest to garble their

grammar through inattention. The odds are that when they do and their mistakes are pointed out, they will immediately see what's wrong and be grateful for the help. Or people may come upon a situation in which two different rules seem applicable and will pick the one that tradition does not sanction—as in our "She is whom I want to ask" puzzle, a few pages back.

Linguists may be tempted to argue that such situations only highlight how artificial traditional grammar is. Indeed, many little distinctions—such as between *who* and *whom*—aren't universally observed for exactly the reason that they aren't now intuitive and probably are, even I will admit, on a path to extinction. But this is one reason why such little distinctions count for something in higher English. If everyone observed them more or less on instinct, there would be less virtue in knowing about them.

Thirteen to a Dozen

Now let's look at a few niceties of grammar that, evidently, not everyone does know about. I have the no doubt fanciful idea that if everyone just had a good grasp of the following issues, it would eliminate the majority of embarrassing grammar-related mistakes that are now made—or, at any rate, the majority of mistakes that could conceivably be made by anyone reading this book. And if that goal for this list is too ambitious, then at least the questions and answers on it will serve to illustrate how very useful a familiarity with grammatical terminology is in resolving language questions. All the questions here can scarcely be asked, let alone answered, except in terms of grammar.

By the way, the list covers six out of ten usages that were most disliked by British listeners to a 1986 BBC program about language, according to the letters that listeners wrote in response to a request by the program to share their peeves and preferences. (The top ten appear in David Crystal's lively and wide-ranging *The Cambridge Encyclopedia of the English Language.*) Note, though, that the peevish British listeners and I disagree about three of the six points: split infinitives, prepositions at the ends of clauses, and the number of *none.*

Grammar is not fully separate from other aspects of language, and questions pertaining to grammar do appear elsewhere in this book. The grammarian's dozen here are basics or classics or matters at any rate worth taking trouble over; some are specific points and some are general issues, according to the breadth of what it seems to me many people don't know. My list begins with relatively subtle matters that I admire others for knowing, and builds inexorably toward points that a person may be thought of as a dingbat for not knowing.

13) Split infinitives

Is it just my reluctance to get with it or have the rules on splitting infinitives been repealed? I recently received a missive from the headmaster of my daughter's primary school in which he managed to split two different infinitives in one sentence! And I note that The Wall Street Journal, *which I took to be more careful than most, now splits 'em with alarming frequency. What gives?*

"*To go* boldly where no man has gone before" sounds perfectly idiomatic to me. But I say that only to establish my bona fides, for I don't have anything against split infinitives—in their proper place. We shouldn't go out of our way to split infinitives, certainly. And it's always good to know what we're doing, so I wouldn't say we should be splitting them unawares. However, authorities at least since H. W. Fowler, in his *Modern English Usage,* have been gently pointing out that splitting an infinitive is preferable both to jamming an adverb between two verbs, where everyone must puzzle out which verb it modifies ("They *refused* boldly *to go* so far away"), and to "correcting" a split in a way that gives an ostentatiously artificial result ("They wanted *to shorten greatly* the length of the trip"). Sometimes those are the only choices we have, except for rewriting the sentence, and my point is that we needn't rewrite.

In fact, it's a natural tendency to follow the pattern established by the likes of "If you're going to put up with the inconveniences of living in outer space, you *must* definitely *want* to be there" with "*To* definitely *want* to be there is important." And what are the alternatives? "Definitely *to want*" changes the meaning. "*To want* definitely to be there"? I think we definitely don't want that version, either.

Furthermore, note how "I want *to travel* far from our solar system and *meet* extraterrestrials" is constructed: one *to,* two infinitives. When the actions described by two or more verbs are being thought of as one process or sequence, it is contrary to normal practice to use a separate *to* for each of them—that is, "I want *to travel* far from our solar system and *to meet* extraterrestrials" is a bit peculiar. Grammarians will tell you that the missing *to* is in ellipsis, but a person could be forgiven for imagining that the *to* that is present is serving both infinitives and the second of them is split wide. And what about "I want *to* but he doesn't"? Here's a *to* with the verb in ellipsis. These aren't split infinitives as such, but they do demonstrate that we are quite used to seeing infinitives and their *to*s at arm's length.

No more than we should go out of our way to split infinitives should we go out of our way not to if splitting the infinitive will yield a clearer or more natural result. To go boldly where the hidebound fear to timidly set foot does everyone a favor.

12) Gerunds or participles?

Everywhere I look, I see the following and wonder if it can be correct: "I was so excited about him having that job," "I wonder what he thought of us going," "I appreciate you doing that."

Are we excited about *him* or about his *having* the job? Words ending in *-ing* are either gerunds, which function as nouns, or present participles, which can modify nouns. The trick with sentences like your examples is to decide which of these a given *-ing* word ought to be. Surely in your first example we're excited about the *having* of the job, and therefore that word should be a gerund and the pronoun should be a modifier for it—that is, not *him* but the possessive *his*.

Similar-looking instances can be conceptually different. In "I was so excited to see *him working* again," the point is less that we're excited to see the *working* than that we're excited to see *him* in that situation. Your second and third examples could follow this pattern—or the other one. They are awkward as is, though, aren't they? Which brings us to the general rule: Treat the *-ing* word as a gerund and make the other substantive possessive unless there's a reason to think and do otherwise.

11) Copulative verbs

People tend to be aware that the verb *is* has some special quality, such that "It *is I*" and so on are correct (distinct from "It *taught me*," "It *frightens me*," and so on). But they are less likely to know that a number of other verbs may work the same way, or may work either way, according to context.

> *When I am sick, I often say "I do not* feel *well." My husband always corrects me, saying that I must be talking about my tactile senses, and tells me to say "I do not* feel *good." I tell him that I have yet to see a "Get Good Soon" sympathy card at the card shop. Am I wrong?*

No, you're not. *Feel* confuses people because it can serve either as a garden-variety transitive or intransitive verb or as a slightly more rarefied "copula," or linking verb. Consider the difference between "When I check the dog for ticks, I *feel carefully* behind his ears" and "When I check the dog for ticks, I feel like a responsible person: I *feel careful*." In the first case, *feel* is being modified by an adverb *(carefully)*. In the second case, it is linking the subject to an adjective *(careful)*, which is modifying not the verb but the subject itself. (To confirm our grasp of this point, let's ponder what "I *feel badly*" means. Despite what most people seem to think, *badly* is an adverb only, and therefore it must be modifying *feel*. This sentence, then, does have to do with a deficient tactile sense. "I *feel bad*" is the way to signify discomfiture.)

Well, too, confuses people, and for a similar reason: it can serve either as an adverb, modifying a verb ("He swims *well*, now that he has taken lessons"), or as an adjective, modifying a noun or pronoun ("He is *well*, now that he has taken his medicine"). As you can see, the two constructions can look quite a lot alike; the difference is in what they mean.

Indeed, "I *feel well*" could be referring to your tactile abilities—just as "Time flies when you're having fun" could be a command. The only thing is, it's not. "I *feel well*" is a perfectly good way to describe your state of health. "I *feel good*" would also work well—although it is perhaps more descriptive of a mental state.

In response to the foregoing exchange in the column, by the way, this letter arrived:

> *Is there any reason to use the more exotic-sounding* discomfiture—*primary meaning:* "overthrow; defeat; disarray; rout"—*instead of the familiar and more accurate* discomfort? *If not, perhaps you should reconsider your comment that saying* "I feel bad" *signifies* discomfiture.

It is true that Fowler warned against confusing *discomfit* with *discomfort,* on the grounds you cite. But reputable dictionaries have been giving *discomfit* the additional meaning of "disconcert; embarrass; discomfort" since at least the 1960s, and by now this meaning is the more common one. In fact, the word in the older sense tends to sound archaic; *The*

American Heritage Dictionary even designates it as such. Would you really say "In 1999, NATO forces *discomfited* Serbia in Kosovo"?

10) Diverging parallels

Something I have wondered about for a long time is what I call nonparallel series. I seem to recall learning long ago that if one writes a phrase of the type "A, B, and C," *then each of* A, B, *and* C *should be of the same grammatical form—*"I came, I saw, I conquered," *for example. A recent issue of* The New York Review of Books *(no doubt an unimpeachable source of good style) contains the sentence* "Zoologists specializing in lizards and snakes are notorious for being rather slow-moving, fond of the hot sun, and rising late, *like the reptiles that they study.*" *When I read that sentence, my mind looks for adjective phrases that will modify "notorious for being." I think,* notorious for being rather slow-moving, notorious for being fond of the hot sun, notorious for being rising late. *This last phrase jars me. My question is: (1) Have I misunderstood the rules all along, or (2) have the rules changed, or (3) are there no rules governing this situation, or (4) have things just gotten lax, or (5) none of the above?*

The sad truth is (4). It has never been easy to keep series running smoothly on track, but we're all supposed to try. The author of your example wasn't trying hard enough. Nor were the authors of these sentences that I've come upon lately: "Do not take this product if you are allergic to aspirin or if you have *asthma, bleeding problems or on a sodium restricted diet,*" "There are more persons being baptized, received, confirmed, and restored from inactive status than there are losses by *death, transfer out or removed for other reasons,*" and "The link you followed is either *outdated, inaccurate, or the server has been instructed not to let you have it.*"

The solution, of course, is to add words until elements that look parallel really are parallel, one way or another. For example, "Zoologists...are notorious for *being* rather slow-moving, *being* fond of the hot sun, and *rising* late" or else "Zoologists...are notorious *for being* rather slow-moving *and* fond of the hot sun, and *for rising* late."

"More Americans get their news from ABC News than from any other source." The pronouncement at the end of the ABC network newscast bothers me, but I'm not sure exactly why. Can you help me to understand why it might sound awkward?

The problem is that a bit too much is in ellipsis—has been left out, for the listener to infer. "More Americans watch TV than read newspapers" sounds fine, no? That's because *watch TV* and *read newspapers* are parallel constructions. But *get their news from ABC News* isn't parallel to *from any other source.* Ellipsis isn't inherently wrong, but it is always worth wondering about.

Continuing to wonder, however, we'll soon come to the question of whether "More Americans *get their news* from ABC News than *get it* from any other source" sounds better. This version might be what the Germans would call a *Schlimmbesserung,* as the term is defined in *They Have a Word for It,* an entertaining book by Howard Rheingold: "a so-called improvement that makes things worse."

I do sympathize with the people who wrote the sentence we're scrutinizing, for I'm sure they were trying to make a factual claim that didn't sound puffy or vacuous. The vaguer nature of the most succinct version of the claim which I can concoct—"ABC News is America's most popular news source"—means that this is probably a *Schlimmbesserung,* too. The sentence you heard is not out-and-out wrong. All the same, ellipsis is supposed to speed listeners or readers on their way, not distract and delay them.

9) Prepositions at the end of clauses

Shame on you. When I turned to Word Court in this month's Atlantic, *I was shocked to read the sentence "This isn't something that we can blame President Clinton for" in your response to one of the questions. Unless you like to leave participles dangling, the sentence would have been more properly worded "This isn't something for which we can blame President Clinton."*

Please be more careful of your own writing and the editing of your column. You do set an example for proper English usage in this grammatically challenged society of which we are all a part.

Now, hold on. "Shame on you" is considered polite discourse where you come from?

Oops. I mean, Now, on hold. "Shame on you" is considered polite discourse from where you come?

What's more (sorry, but you started this), that's no dangling participle; aren't you, rather, objecting to my having ended the sentence with a preposition? If so, kindly have a look at H. W. Fowler's *Modern English Usage* (any of the three editions), or Theodore Bernstein's *The Careful Writer,* or *The American Heritage Dictionary,* or pretty much any reputable usage guide, under "preposition at end" or just "preposition," and see if this doesn't change your point of view. Good writers throughout the history of English—from Chaucer and Shakespeare to Alison Lurie and David Lodge—have not shrunk from ending clauses or sentences with prepositions. It isn't something that we should go out of our way to do, but if the alternatives that come readily to mind seem stilted, there's no reason for us to go out of our way to avoid doing it, either.

Your reply about the suspect nature of the "preposition at end" rule had me cheering, but then you lost me with your appeal to the example of "good" writers. Pointing to the habits of exceptional writers seems less likely to sway etiquette-obsessed types like the writer of that letter than does an acknowledgment of the utterly artificial nature of the rule in question. That John Dryden appropriated this rule from Latin, a language in which it did indeed apply, and that he then inflicted it upon English, is surely the clearest invalidation of this not-so-old chestnut. Out of his overweening admiration for Latin, Dryden clumsily grafted a Latinate trait onto English, which is a Germanic language. But what is necessary for Latin is unnecessary, and often silly, for English. It is a sham rule that flies in the face of centuries of natural language development, and its uncritical perpetuation by the socially anxious should be laughed down once and for all.

Thank you. That's another good reason not to worry about a preposition at the end of a sentence.

Now, hold on yourself. By doing hold on → on hold *are you saying that that* on *is a preposition? Are you sure about that?*

You caught me. I didn't have space to get into it in the column, so I was being sneaky. A grammarian would tell us that *on* is an adverb here or a "particle" that's part of a compound verb. A linguist might go into it a bit more deeply, explaining that the relationship between this sort of particle and a preposition is much like that between an intransitive verb and a transitive one. In other words, though the *on* is not a preposition as such, it is, in effect, a preposition that lacks an object.

The same, in fact, goes for the *up* in Winston Churchill's famous rebuke to his secretary (or an editor or a proofreader, depending on the version of the anecdote) upon finding that a preposition at the end of one of his sentences had been tinkered with: "This is the sort of English [or "arrant nonsense" or "impertinence"] *up* with which I will not put." If we restore that particle to its rightful place and banish from the end of the sentence only what everyone would call a preposition, we get: "This is the sort of English with which I will not put *up*." Does that sound better to you?

8) Antecedents

Supplying pronouns that need antecedents with the proper ones is an entire minor art form—like matching beverages to food or setting an inviting table. The general rules do admit of exceptions, but they're worth bearing in mind all the same: Most pronouns ought to have antecedents that are real, honest-to-goodness nouns, not noun-adjectives or possessives. (Sample problems: "A marble wine cooler only works if *it* is already chilled" doesn't work if by *it* the speaker means the wine, and "A wine's bouquet is sometimes more appealing than *it* is" doesn't manage to say that *it* is the wine.) A possessive pronoun, however, may have a possessive antecedent. (There's nothing wrong with "A wine's bouquet is sometimes more appealing than *its* flavor.") The antecedent should be where no one will have trouble finding it or telling it apart from other nouns in the vicinity, and in the best of all possible worlds it should be the subject or the object of a verb. Objects of prepositions, in particular, tend to make weak antecedents. (Sample problem: "Would you like a glass of wine? *It* is twenty years old.") And, of course, a singular antecedent should antecede a singular pronoun, and a plural antecedent a plural one. (Sample problem: "Anyone who doesn't want *their* wine...")

> *Help is needed on the word* which. *You sometimes hear or read a sentence like this: "I'd buy that new car if I were rich,* which *I'm not." This seems clearly wrong;* which *has no antecedent, and* but *would work better, assuming you need the final phrase at all, which you don't. What is bothering me about this? Somehow I think this construction is not rigorous standard English.*

What ought to be bothering you is exactly what you mention: *which,* a relative pronoun, ought to be referring back to an antecedent noun, which in this case doesn't exist. The word is trying to refer back to the adjective *rich* (and in your "*which* you don't" it is trying to refer back to a verb along with its object), but grammatically that's not allowed, except colloquially. As you suggest, though, *but*—or *though* or *as*—would be fine.

A common variant on this problem is the likes of "I really need a new car, *which* annoys me," wherein an entire clause is meant to be the antecedent for *which*. As a general rule, that's not allowed, either. *This, that,* and *it,* however, being demonstrative pronouns, do not need specific antecedents, and may refer back to clauses; one may say "I really need a new car, and *this* [or *that* or *it*] annoys me."

Not even these formulas will work, however, if there's any ambiguity about what *this, that,* or *it* is supposed to be. For example, suppose the previous sentence had begun, "Not even *this* will work if there's any ambiguity…" Readers could be expected to wonder, What's *this*? Where there isn't obviously one and only one answer to the question, a noun referring back (like *formulas*) is probably needed.

I'm not pleased by your blanket approval of using demonstrative pronouns to refer to clauses. We all do this at times for simplicity, but in formal writing I believe the following is better: "I really need a new car, and this problem *annoys me." In other words, say what it is that annoys you.*

When I was teaching English to Peruvian students who wished to obtain the University of Cambridge Certificate of Proficiency in English, I was guided by a book that under the heading "Coordinate Relative

Clauses" gives the example: "It started raining while Sarah was waiting for me outside the Town Hall, which *put her in a bad mood.*" The paragraph continues, "the...*sentence contains a coordinate relative clause;* which *here refers to the whole of the previous clause....* Which *is the only relative pronoun found with coordinate relative clauses.*"

Maybe you'll enjoy it if I lengthen a chain of quotation by quoting from *The Complete Plain Words,* by Sir Ernest Gowers:

> *The* New Yorker *of the 4th December 1948 quoted a question asked of the* Philadelphia Bulletin *by a correspondent:*
>
> > *My class would appreciate a discussion of the wrong use of* which *in sentences like* 'He wrecked the car which was due to his carelessness'.
>
> *and the answer given by that newspaper:*
>
> > *The fault lies in using* which *to refer to the statement* 'He wrecked the car'. *When* which *follows a noun it refers to that noun as its antecedent. Therefore in the foregoing sentence it is stated that the car was due to his carelessness, which is nonsense.*
>
> *What is? Carelessness? is the* New Yorker's *query.*
> *Which shows how dangerous it is to dogmatise about the use of* which *with an an-*

tecedent consisting not of a single word but of
a phrase.

So was I too hasty? Ah, now, there's another good analogy. When we're driving, we're not supposed to speed, and yet at times we all do. Before we floor it, though, we ought to look around, to see if we're likely to get caught, run anyone over, or bring others screeching to a halt in confusion.

7) Negatives

I was musing and snoozing on a train trip from
Boston to New York when the Amtrak conductor
jarred me with the following misplaced negative:
"The station stop is Providence. All *doors will* not
open. Station stop Providence." Of course, he meant
to warn passengers that only some doors would open
at Providence; taken literally, there would be no point
in stopping, as no one would have a fighting chance
of detraining. Since that time, I've been on the alert,
and have noticed this usage is prevalent in excepting
generalities: All *men are* not *tall,* Everyone's *not* a red-
head, etc. Should I take this up as a crusade or go
back to snoozing?

I'll even join you in the crusade. Recently I've come across "*All* sex is *not* sexual harassment" and "The airport is open but *all* its runways are *not*."
    While we're at it, let's also watch out for sentences like "*Not* all doors will open and *will remain open only briefly*." The subject of that second predicate, of course, ought to be not *not all doors* but *doors*. To shake free of the negative's grip, the word needs to be

repeated here: "*Not* all doors will open. *Doors* will remain open only briefly." This mistake of negligently negating the wrong thing along with the right thing has many variations. "*None* of us wants to be trapped on the train but *to get off calmly without panicking and needing to beat on the door and shout.*" None of us wants to get off calmly? "It was *not* so annoying that I *failed* to complain to Amtrak"—really? "*Neither* on the train *nor* at the airport is there any good reason for the confusion but *only inattention and foolishness to blame.*" In neither place is inattention to blame? On the contrary!

6) Restrictive and descriptive elements

It's that damn issue of that *versus* which. *I understand that the choice has something to do with specific versus general reference. But I can't figure out when one should use* which. *Just to be safe, I use* that *exclusively nowadays and never even attempt to use* which, *because I simply don't know what—or* which—*usage would be appropriate. Fowler is no help, for whenever I consult him, I get sidetracked for hours reading and chuckling, and forget why I picked him up in the first place.*

You're going to think that I've gotten things mixed up and answered someone else's question instead—but just give me a moment, please. An error I often see is the inclusion of commas in a sentence like "The philosopher, Karl Jaspers, conceived of an existentialism quite different from that of the author, Albert Camus." I can imagine a few—a very few—contexts in which commas around the names would be wanted; whether or not they're wanted has to do with niceties of meaning. But let's presume that this sentence is the opening sentence of something for a general readership, in which case it's inconceivable that the commas belong there.

That's because what we're trying to say is "*this* philosopher, the philosopher whose name is Karl Jaspers" and "*this* author, the one whose name is Albert Camus." But contrast that with what we're trying to say in "The first President of the United States, George Washington, conceived of a democratic leadership quite different from the despotism of the King who then ruled England, George III." In this sentence, before we get to the names, we have already identified both of the people who are being talked about, and the names are just serving as a reminder; they have appropriately been removed from the main line of the sentence by being tucked between commas. As a matter of fact, we could delete the names entirely from the leadership sentence, and its main clause would still carry the same meaning. But if we deleted the names from the philosophy sentence ("The philosopher conceived of an existentialism quite different from that of the author"), we'd be lost; thus the names need to be part of the main line of the sentence. In grammatical terminology, such names and words are "restrictive," because they restrict the meaning of what they modify; and the words that can be tucked away are "nonrestrictive," or "descriptive."

Now let's think about a sentence like "The existentialism conceived of by Karl Jaspers was quite different from the existentialism propounded by Albert Camus" and consider the situation of *conceived of by Karl Jaspers* and *propounded by Albert Camus*. Those phrases are restrictive—they're part of the main thought—because the sentence wouldn't say the same thing without them. Actually, it wouldn't make any sense at all: "The existentialism was quite different from the existentialism"? Excuse me?

As it happens, those little phrases, about Jaspers and Camus, could be expanded into subordinate clauses. And in that case—listen carefully—*that,* not to be preceded by a comma, is the signal that a restrictive subordinate clause is under way. *Which,* preceded by a comma and with another comma to follow at the end of the clause, would signal nonrestrictiveness. Thus "The existentialism *that* was conceived of by Karl Jaspers was quite different from the existentialism *that* was propounded by Albert Camus." Likewise, "The democratic leadership *that* was conceived of by George Washington was quite different from the despotism *that* George III demonstrated."

What is *which* for, then? Well, we could sensibly assert the general proposition "Democratic leadership is quite different from despotism." And if that is the point we want to make but we would like to flesh it out a bit with illustrations, we can say "Democratic leadership, *which* George Washington sought to supply, is quite different from despotism, *which* was demonstrated by George III." Similarly, we could say "German existentialism, *which* Karl Jaspers conceived of, is quite different from French existentialism, *which* Albert Camus propounded."

This sometimes subtle distinction between restrictive and descriptive elements pervades English. Often it is reflected in nothing more than the presence or absence of a pair of commas around a clause or phrase, or a single comma behind or in front of an element that begins or ends the sentence. For example, consider the quotation "Of what use is a philosopher who doesn't hurt anybody's feelings?"—from Diogenes. No comma separates *philosopher* from *who,* because Diogenes is not asking whether a philosopher, generally speaking, is of use; he's asking whether a philosopher *of this kind*—the kind who doesn't hurt feelings—is; the *who* clause is restrictive.

Contrast "Despotism is unjust to everybody, including the despot, who was probably made for better things"—from Oscar Wilde. Here *everybody* means everybody, and who is included is an additional, descriptive thought—hence the first comma. And then, Wilde does mean to be saying that any old despot is ill-served by despotism. That the despot was made for better things is an amusing additional idea, but it doesn't change the central point here—hence the second comma.

Some caveats: Besides indicating that a given phrase or clause is descriptive, commas may, of course, bracket it for other legitimate reasons. There are also other kinds of *that*s. Here we're discussing the use of the word as a pronoun, but it can be an adverb, a conjunction (aspects of these two uses are covered in Chapter Four), an adjective, and (on rare occasions) a noun. Note, too, that I don't mean to be holding up Diogenes, of all people, or even Oscar Wilde, as a paragon of comma placement as it is practiced in contemporary English. Older texts often use commas in ways that would be considered wrong today. It was Fowler, writing early in the twentieth century, whom we have to thank for codifying the difference between *that* and *which* in particular, and restrictive and descriptive elements more generally. I can't think of a nicer place to be sidetracked, reading and chuckling, than his discussion (under the heading "that, rel. pron.") of *that* and *which*.

Millions of Americans know how to ride bicycles, and millions can reliably tell restrictive and descriptive clauses apart. As someone who can do both, I find these to be comparable accomplishments—both in terms of difficulty and because once you've got it, you'll never forget it.

But unless you have the basic distinction down cold, please don't even read the next exchange.

Able writers, considerate editors, and respectable publishers have long distinguished between the restrictive and the nonrestrictive, by properly using that *for the former and* which *for the latter. But Word Court asks its readers whether they have "had a dispute about language* which *[they] would like this column to resolve." That sounds terrible. Why have you worded it that way?*

Thanks for noticing! *The Atlantic* does use *that* and *which* to distinguish between restrictive and nonrestrictive clauses. But the magazine also subscribes to something called "the exceptional *which*": when another noun (*language,* in the example) intervenes between the noun *(dispute)* being modified by the restrictive clause and the clause itself, and that second noun might be misread as the antecedent, we use *which* without a comma to signal the connection to the first noun. In the example, it's not language that a person might like the column to resolve but a dispute. Thus the exceptional *which,* a device promulgated by

Eleanor Gould, who has been upholding linguistic standards at *The New Yorker* for more than half a century now.

The distinction seems fairly natural once one is used to it. And it solves a real problem, by enabling one to disambiguate, as they say, the likes of "a book about misbehavior *which* I very much enjoy"—or, at least, it would if the distinction were widely known and used. So I am enlisted in your cause; can I enlist you in mine?

Perhaps you'd like to read the story of the genesis of the exceptional *which* as Miss Gould described it to me:

> *No, I didn't invent it, but I'm pretty sure that Mr. Shawn did. He came into my office one day (when? In the fifties? sixties? seventies? I lose all track of time) with a proof bearing a complicated sentence that we'd both struggled with, and suggested the use of* which *for the more distant possible antecedent. We agreed on the spot that it should be used only when a real likelihood of misreading the sentence called for it. As for your "dispute about language" sentence, I don't think it would readily occur to people to read it as being about language in need of resolving, so I'd probably use* that.

I confess that I was trolling for letters with my phrasing. Shortly after the exchange about the exceptional *which* was published, I revised the sentence to read "a language dispute that you would like this column to resolve."

5) Sentence adverbs

That seventh-grade English teacher about whom I've already been supercilious surely told you that adverbs may modify verbs ("He writes *beautifully*"), adjectives ("He made a *beautifully* intelligent argument"), or other adverbs ("He writes *exceptionally* beautifully"). But he or she probably refrained from mentioning that certain adverbs can be used as "sentence adverbs," or "absolute adverbs," to modify entire clauses. In fact, this is all that some adverbs ever seem to do.

> *One evening this week Mr. Peter Jennings, the news-reader, gave forth with a sentence of the form "———— allegedly killed ————." Wouldn't "It is alleged that —— killed ——" be allegedly better?*
>
> *How should one differentiate between politically correct usage and the misuse of legalistic jargon?*

That *allegedly* isn't out-and-out wrong, though I do know why you're looking askance at it. When an adverb comes next to a verb, we tend to perceive it as modifying the verb—the way adverbs so often do. But is being *allegedly* killed really comparable to being *brutally* killed? Was someone killed in an *alleged* manner? Not at all: *allegedly* modifies the entire assertion. (So does *reportedly* in similar constructions.) To make this clear, it's good form to put the adverb at the outset of the clause: "*Allegedly*, —— killed ——." Sometimes that won't work, but then commas, or pauses in speech, can generally do the job: "—— caught up with and, *allegedly*, killed ——."

Having said that, I must admit that certain sentence adverbs can turn up in midsentence, without commas or pauses, and no one gives them a second thought. Think of "The victim was *obviously* killed before the evening news came on" and "The crime *clearly* has yet to be solved." For the most part, this indulgence is granted to a narrow range of words having to do with point of view, which tradition has accustomed us to understanding in this manner. Not everyone is ready to include *allegedly* (or *reportedly*) in the group.

Paying attention to what is certain and what is only alleged—that is, to what the adverb should modify—is the way to avoid the silly blunder committed by the author of this sentence, from the police-blotter column in my local paper: "The director also said he had installed security cameras in the office, and had observed cleaners *allegedly* stealing supplies."

The proper use of *hopefully* is an issue even more contentious.

I hate to admit, in this company of logophiles, that I've never exactly understood why hopefully *shouldn't begin a sentence, but I don't have the temerity to ask that question. Presumably, there are other words, such as the first one in this sentence, that may be used just as incorrectly in the same construction. Is this so?*

The problem with *hopefully* in a sentence like "*Hopefully*, this explanation will be clear" is that it is an adverb modifying no word that appears in the sentence. In the example I just gave, there isn't even anything present that is capable of hoping.

But the problem with considering that a problem is the one you point out. There certainly are other words that may be used in the very same way: "*Presumably*, my best efforts have gone into making this explanation clear"; "*Mercifully*, this explanation will be finished soon"; "*Frankly,* this explanation may *not* be clear." These are known as sentence adverbs, and no one calls them incorrect.

But the problem with considering *hopefully* a sentence adverb like any other is that many people who care about language happen to loathe this usage. And yet using it in the old-fashioned, modifying-the-verb way ("*Hopefully,* I began writing about this topic, eager to share what I know") tends to seem either bizarre or snooty. It's too bad, but the word just isn't very serviceable anymore.

Although various adverbs may be used to modify entire clauses, *hopefully* isn't among them—yet. I only hope I won't have to concede that it is until I'm an old, old woman.

Here are a few words from one of those people who care about language and loathe the sentence adverb *hopefully*:

The real problem with overuse or misuse of the word hopefully *is not whether the grammatical niceties are observed. A deeper problem is that when we say* hopefully *in the sense of "it is to be hoped" we are shirking our responsibility for the subject at hand. Just as we hide behind the passive voice ("Mistakes were made," said Reagan about Irangate, thus clouding the identity of those who made the mistakes), we also use* hopefully *to dodge our responsibility. If I say "Hopefully, we can resolve this problem," I'm off the hook. But if I say "I hope we can solve this problem," the person with whom I'm speaking may rightly ask me, "Well, if that's what you hope, what are you going to do about it?"* Hopefully *in this sense is a weasel word, a way to hide behind language.*

Whether one is a good and forthright person is a separate issue from whether one has a good command of English. Not only that, but a person with a good command of English has always been able either to own up to hoping or to leave vague exactly who is hoping. As you know, an old-fashioned, and still entirely correct, phrase that leaves it vague is *it is to be hoped*—though these days that seems awfully pompous. *Let's hope* does the same job in a more relaxed way. *Hopefully* may be too relaxed, but it's no more weaselly than its better-respected elders.

And here are related concerns about other words:

Your referral of one of your correspondents to the divine Fowler leads me to ask why you didn't take your own advice and look up the Master on kindly. *We no doubt have lost the battle on* hopefully, *but do we have to accept the sometimes condescending, sometimes minatory* kindly *when the simple word* please *is available?*

In the sentence you are protesting, I wrote, " ... *kindly* have a look at H. W. Fowler's *Modern English Usage*." But it is the "you are *kindly* requested..." formula that Fowler objects to, because this seems to be pointing out how kind we are to be making the request—not what the writer or speaker usually has in mind. Fowler has no quarrel with asking people to *kindly* do things. This adverb is unlike the disreputable *hopefully* in that it actually does modify the verb. It needn't always mean quite "in a kind manner"; it can mean "in an obliging manner" as well, and is appropriate wherever "be so kind as to" could be substituted.

❦

The phrase most importantly *appears frequently in newspaper columns and editorials, and I hear it said on TV and radio. It seems wrong to me. But in discussions with friends they claim it is correct.*

Important is an adjective, and it probably modifies the subject that was in the preceding sentence. I try to substitute other adjectives with most *introducing them, and that seems correct. What is your opinion?*

You are, I take it, complaining about the likes of "*Most importantly,* let's make a special effort to be clear." This is where sentence adverbs (or adverbial phrases) begin to be very hard to explain. *Most importantly* does work pretty much the way that other sentence adverbs do, and there are well-regarded dictionaries that sanction it in this sense. But this phrase remains on the defensive relative to *most important.* At least, those who sanction *most importantly* almost always argue that it is acceptable as a substitute for *most important,* and not the other way around—a fact that speaks for itself.

When you argue your point, you'll want to know that the idea you've advanced about the grammar of *most important* can't be right: adjectives (or, for that matter, adverbs) aren't allowed to modify words in any sentence but their own. *Most important* is usually said to be an elliptical form of *what is most important.*

4) Agreement in number

The principle of agreement in grammar is a lot like that of color coordination in interior decorating: various parts that will be seen as a whole should match or go together. A room full of clashing colors will never mislead anyone, though, whereas the results of botched agreement can be baffling as well as unsettling.

The issue of agreement that most often comes up has to do with whether phrases like *the committee of one hundred* and *a crowd of well-wishers* are singular or plural. Fortunately, this is fairly easy to finesse, because such constructions may go either way, depending on meaning. Start by assuming that the main, singular noun *(committee, crowd)* is what should be agreed with. If that results in something illogical or terribly peculiar, switch to agreeing with the plural object of the preposition *(one hundred, well-wishers)*. Having made a choice, stick with it: "The committee of one hundred *were* all lobbying in their home towns, and when *they* returned to Washington, *they were* met by a crowd of well-wishers, which was [or 'who were'] glad to have *them* back."

Here are several related problems:

For decades those of us in the Cleveland area have referred to our Cleveland Indians as the "Tribe": "TRIBE WINS DOUBLEHEADER." "TRIBE TRADES COLAVITO." "TRIBE LOSES 100TH GAME." *It has been a long, painful history.*

Now some modern teams are adopting singular names that are being treated as if they were plural. We see headlines like "MAGIC LOSE TO CELTICS" *and* "HEAT FALL TO HORNETS." *Complicating this issue are teams like the Utah* Jazz *(leaving aside the commonly held belief that there is no jazz in Utah, if there were jazz in Utah, would there be more than one?) and the Barberton* Magics, *a high school's coinage that preceded all these newfangled names and always has been plural. I hate to think of reading* "TRIBE ARE AT HOME TONIGHT."

No doubt sportswriters new to your area can be shamed, if need be, into following local custom and treating *Tribe* as a singular noun. But local custom could just as well have dictated that *Tribe* be plural, and grammar would not have objected, for the word is a "noun of multitude," which may properly be treated as either singular or plural.

In fact, any team name may be regarded as a noun of multitude, and the local custom in the team's home town is as good a guide as any to how to treat a name that is superficially singular. "*Magic lose*" and "*Heat fall*" are indeed the constructions that the sports desks of *The Orlando Sentinel* and *The Miami Herald* say they would use. They do, of course, prefer it when they are able to say "*Magic win*" and "*Heat beat* ———.*"*

When I served as secretary of the organization in question, I had occasion to write the sentence "The Friends of the USS Massachusetts (BB-2) is proud to…" I thought that was perfectly correct, as I was speaking for the organization as a whole and not for individual members. However, others saw it differently and said that are *should have been used instead of* is. *Which is the correct usage? The old battleship is peaceful and harmless, but sometimes the members aren't. Help!*

Two issues are involved in a question like this. First, is the sense of the noun staunchly plural, staunchly singular, or open to either interpretation? Obviously, one wouldn't say *"Friends are* my favorite TV show"— here the word is the name of the show much more than it is a reference to plural persons. But you were a Friend of the USS Massachusetts, weren't you? And weren't at least some of the other Friends friends of yours? So your Friends at least sometimes acted plural.

Second, which construction sounds more natural? This criterion is why the Rolling Stones and the Spice Girls tend to be referred to in the plural, whereas Abba, Pearl Jam, and the Boston Symphony Orchestra tend to be referred to in the singular.

Having made a general decision about how to treat a given name—and in the case of your Friends, I would vote for using the plural—one may yet admit of exceptions. The only thing that is definitely not allowed is for a given instance of *Friends* to be singular and plural at the same time: "I would think the *Friends was* a friendly organization even if *they weren't* in agreement with me."

Could you please resolve a dispute regarding the use of the word none? *A friend of ours has the following message on his telephone answering machine: "Hello, this is ——— and* none *of us is home right now." It is my contention that the proper phrase would be "*none *of us are home," since* us *is a plural form. We wouldn't say* we is *home, would we?*

You're right that *us* is plural no matter what, just as most words are either plural or singular no matter what. But *none*, which does not depend on *us* for its number, is a special case. The Old English word from which it is derived had both singular and plural forms: *nán* and *náne.* Long ago these melded into the one form *none.* Today's word can be either singular or plural, depending on which form makes more sense in context. The singular *none of us is* declares "not a single one of us is," and the plural *none of us are* says "we aren't." The grammar of your friend's message is fine.

I've lost patience with the increasing carelessness that follows what *with a singular verb, and then a plural verb and some plural noun, as in the following: "What bothers* me *are people* who can't get their verbs to agree with their subjects." *Shouldn't both verbs be plural* (bother ... are) *or both be singular* (bothers ... is)?

As an English teacher in both primary and sec-ondary schools, I used to tell students that what *is a pronoun like a big basket that can contain one thing or many things. Whether you put one or many things into it, the basket itself is singular, calling for this: "What bothers* me *is people* who can't get their verbs to agree with their subjects." *What do you say on this one?*

You're quite right that *what* is presumptively singular, but you're not going so far as to say that it must al-ways be singular, are you? You made *what are* valid points in your first paragraph: verbs must agree in number with their subjects, regardless of the number of any complement present; and once one verb de-clares a given instance of a word to be singular, any other verbs governed by that word must fall in line and also treat it as such.

But we part company on your second paragraph. There is certainly a tendency for *what* to be singular, and your analogy to a basket is a good one for explaining the grammar of sentences like your example and like "In ancient times the tribes roamed *what is* now the Carolinas." All the same, *what* may be plural anywhere the singular seems wrongheaded, as it would in "*what are* valid points," in my first paragraph. The rule of thumb is: If a given *what* means "that which" or "the thing that," it's singular; if it means "those which" or "the things that," it's plural.

What rule on noun number applies when the possibilities become messy or even ludicrous, as in the following examples? "They turned their heads to see us better." (How many heads does each have?) "Both men relied heavily on their wives." (Bigamists both?)

Some may find it obvious that if there's a plural subject and something to be paired with the individual entities making up that subject—usually, though not always, after the plural possessive pronoun *their*—this other noun must also be plural: *They* all have heads, and so it must be "They turned their *heads,*" and so on. But let's say a man has his pride, and a woman has her pride, too. "They have their *prides*"? Surely not.

The general rules are these: When the noun in question describes an abstract or uncountable entity, like *pride* or *vitality,* it ought to be singular. Sometimes nouns that one may think of as concrete and countable will turn out to be abstract in context ("They taught *school*"; "They were held *hostage*"). When one is at pains to make clear that the individuals in the subject are to be paired one apiece with the persons, places, or things in question, the number of the noun can't be relied on to make the point, and other clues must be given ("Each of the bigamists relied heavily on his *wives*"). But it is usually either obvious or beside the point how many of the things are to be paired with the individuals in the subject, and then one needn't scruple to use the plural ("Like lightning, the models changed their *dresses* and *stockings* and *shoes*, and, zipping their *zippers* and buttoning their *buttons*, bolted back to the runway"). This is the rule, it seems to me, that really applies to your *wives*—and your *heads*.

People who are focusing on this issue for the first time tend to decide that they will be purists henceforward, and whenever they remember their decision, they will busily "correct" their own writing and the writing of others. But pretty soon they'll forget, and so they'll fail to notice just how common—and in most cases innocuous—number mismatches are. Here are a few examples that would be more confusing if number did match: "*Anthologies* of poetry are usually edited for *one* of three reasons: to produce *a convenient compendium,* to summarize *a movement or a period,* or to prove *a point*"; "It is time finally to welcome *immigrant children* into our society by adding to the *language* they already know a full degree of competency in the common language of their new country"; "They sealed their *bargains* with *a spoken word.*"

Whenever carefully matching number results in ridiculous wording, don't do it. The higher purpose of all our rules is to foster grace and clarity, and these rules on number conflict with grace and clarity more often than most do.

❧

A member of the Friday Night Couples League at the Wenham Country Club, on Boston's North Shore, had a hole in one on the third hole and another on the fifth. Did he have two holes in one or two hole in ones? One of us believes that the pattern should be the same as in attorneys general *and* passersby. *The other disagrees, believing that* holes in one *would indicate that the golfer gained multiple holes in one shot. A Diet Coke has been wagered on this, and we have agreed that Ms. Grammar shall be the final authority.*

I admit I explained to an earlier correspondent that we needn't consider men who rely on their *wives* to be bigamists, and, in fact, if they relied on their *wife,* then she would be one. But sometimes it's just impossible to match all parts of a sentence or a phrase in terms of grammatical or conceptual number. At least, in trying to match them one may run afoul of some other rule, and then, usually, that rule should hold sway. Here the rule is that the main noun itself, and not incidentals attached to it, is pluralized. Even *RBIs,* when it's spelled out, becomes *runs batted in. Holes in one* is correct, at least technically.

All the same, to say "two *holes in one*" is to ask to be misunderstood. There simply must be some other way to say it. How about "a *hole in one* twice"—and two glasses of Coke?

A golfer would most likely say he shot two aces *in the same round. Reminds me of the zoo keeper who wanted to order two animals. He stated he wanted "two* mongooses," *then changed it to "two*

mongeese," *and finally said, "Send me a mongoose...
and while you're at it, send me another."*

And here's one last letter on the topic of grammatical
number, which arrived in my mailbox after *The Atlantic*
ran a cover story titled "How Many Is Too Many?":

> *How much are too much? When too many people is
> on the earth.*
>
> *That seems the point of the article on population
> growth in this month's issue of your magazine. It also
> reflects the article's somewhat unusual views on noun-
> verb agreement. It seems that the word* many, *which
> is usually plural and refers to number rather than
> amount, requires a plural verb form—in this case,* are.
> *Even if* many *is considered an adjective, the implied
> noun in the question "How many is too many?" is*
> people, *a plural noun requiring a plural verb form.
> One would not usually say "How many population is
> too many?" Unless, perhaps, one are using the au-
> thor's rather "singular" definition of number.*
>
> *I would welcome a justification of what seems to
> be an unwarranted suspension of grammatical rules.*

Think of the question "How rich is too rich?" I'm sure
you'll agree that "How rich are too rich?" would not
be better grammar. Likewise with "How many is too
many?" You're quite right that *many* is an adjective
here, but there is no "implied noun" following it, any
more than there is one following the adjective in a sentence like "How *rich* is he?" or "How *rich* are they?"

The adjective *many,* or *many* together with its mod-
ifier, is itself the subject of our sentence. As George
O. Curme points out in *A Grammar of the English
Language,* a subject may be "any... part of speech"

or simply "a group of words," and he gives a range of examples including "*Two times two* is four"—another seeming plural that isn't one.

Note that because "How many is too many?" is a question, it ends, rather than begins, with its subject—the way "How rich is he?" does. This doesn't particularly matter, of course: grammatically speaking, *how many* and *too many,* each an adverb and an adjective, don't offer much to choose between.

3) Incomparable adjectives

Am I correct in deploring the use of a modifier or qualifier preceding the word unique, *which is heard every day on radio? The common expression is* very unique.

Unique has traditionally belonged to the group of adjectives called absolute or incomparable—meaning that the quality the word refers to must, logically, be either fully present or altogether absent, with no gradations possible in between. One can't, for example, be just a little bit *bankrupt,* or a little bit *anonymous* or *pregnant* or *dead.* Quite a few people, though, seem not to have gotten the news that *unique* is numbered among this rarefied company. And so someone reading or hearing *unique* can no longer assume that it was intended to mean "one of a kind"; maybe the writer or speaker meant just "unusual." This is too bad, because *extraordinary* and *exceptional* and *rare* and *curious* and *unwonted* and *strange* and *peculiar* and *abnormal* and other words as well, in their various ways, all mean "unusual," but *unique,* in its true meaning and in the contexts natural to it, is very nearly unique.

Another incomparable that people often fail to recognize as such is *crucial*—the adjective form of *crux*, which has to do with crosses and crossroads and decisive points. And, despite the U.S. Constitution's "*more perfect* Union," *perfect* is generally considered incomparable as well. So are most words that start with *un-* or *in-* meaning "not"—*unthinkable, intractable*, and, of course, *incomparable* itself. Such a word doesn't quite demand that you take it or leave it; you're allowed to say *more nearly crucial* or *all but unthinkable*, for example. The idea is to treat the quality that the word describes as a standard, not a sliding scale.

See also the entry for "Destroy" in the "Double or Nothing" section of Chapter Five.

2) Case of personal pronouns

I, you, he, she, we, they, and *who* are in the subjective, or the nominative, case, and *me, you, him, her, us, them*, and *whom* are in the objective, or the accusative (as direct objects) and the dative (as indirect ones). *Mine, yours, his, hers, ours, theirs*, and *whose* are possessive, or genitive—but let's not worry about the possessive case just now. It doesn't tend to get mixed up with the others.

> *Many of my friends and co-workers use* me *and* I *incorrectly. For example, "Will you go to lunch with Mary and I?" or "Why did you not contact Jerry or I?" I know that in both cases it should be* me *and not* I, *but I have a problem explaining this. My friends all think that I do not know the correct usage, because English is not my first language.*

English-speakers get into trouble surprisingly often with *I* in constructions that include other people ("Mary and *I*," "Jerry or *I*"). But, really, there's no mystery about *I* and *me*: one uses *me* exactly where one would use it if no one else were involved. "Will you go to lunch with..." Who would ever say *I* at that point?

This test, though, won't help with one phrase that people commonly get wrong: *between you and me.* The rule here is that *between you and me* is always right, and *between you and I* is always wrong. This despite one correspondent of mine, who writes, "I have come to believe that *between you and I* is good English. Among well-educated people I have heard *between you and I* much more often than *between you and me.*"

Surely, well-educated people ought to want to demonstrate a familiarity with the rules of grammar. *Between* is a preposition, and the objects of prepositions must be in the form of objects, not subjects. As Theodore Bernstein observes in *The Careful Writer,* most people "would not dream of saying or writing *between him and they* or *between her and we.*" He argues, too, that "an isolated instance or so of bad grammar culled from even the most gifted writers does not constitute a valid authentication for that particular misusage."

After that exchange appeared in the column, I received the following from a professional linguist:

Concerning between Mary and I:
   Your insistence that the problem is simple lack of "familiarity with the rules of grammar" blames speakers of English unfairly. The whole mess would

never have arisen in the first place were it not for pedagogical attempts to impose "rules of grammar" that run contrary to the straightforward, eminently law-abiding principle of pronoun choice that every speaker of English acquired in childhood. That principle is something like the following:

(1) The nominative form of a pronoun is chosen if the verb agrees with the pronoun. Otherwise, the "default form" (accusative) is used.

Since a conjunction of a third-person with a first-person form triggers third-person-plural agreement (not first-person-singular agreement), the nominative form I *is not chosen. That is the reason people produce* "Bill and me are *happy." That's the form dictated by rule (1).*

In contrast, when the subject is the first-person pronoun alone, the verb does agree with the first-person pronoun. Consequently, the nominative form is chosen: "I am *happy" (not* "I is *happy"). Again, the rule is followed.*

Likewise, "I am *here" and "Here* am I*" but "It's* me." *All quite simple and orderly: pronoun choice depends on verb agreement.*

Your time-honored alternative is:

(2) "One uses me *exactly where one would use it if no other person were involved."*

This rule, however, deposits us in an entirely different grammatical system, a system in which pronoun choice in coordination is inherited from the bigger phrase that contains the pronoun. What purpose can this difficult correction possibly serve?

The actual response of English speakers to the legacy of correction makes the point quite clear. Speakers have responded to corrections like "Bill and me" → "*Bill and* I" *by learning not the un-English rule (2) but an entirely different rule that does not require a complete restructuring of their internal grammar:*

(3) I *is a fancy way of saying* me *after* and.

Rule (3) is the rule speakers follow (I suspect) when they produce "*between you and* I." *It too is a rule of grammar—just not the rule teachers thought they were teaching when they corrected* "Bill and me."

The lesson here is not that people should learn to follow rules of grammar but just the opposite: that you meddle with people's grammar at your peril. The results are often not what you think.

When you and I talk about "grammar," we are talking about somewhat different things. And yet each of us is saying, These are the rules of grammar that exist; I'm not making anything up.

For my own part, I'm perfectly happy to admit that if I *were* to make up a grammar for English, I'd come up with something different from what we have. I might even turn the job over to you, in the confidence that you'd create something both rational and intuitive. But as it is, I have hundreds of years of tradition and literature behind me to substantiate my point of view. And behind you are...children? who haven't fully learned the lessons about their language which their parents and teachers are trying to impart? I'm not just being rhetorical. This really is the way it strikes me.

Also please note that as soon as you start allowing objects of prepositions to be in the subjective case, and all sorts of other constructions that seem "natural," you're making it impossible for readers to trust that they're understanding you properly. That is, you're zipping down a slippery slope whereon nobody is quite sure how the various parts of a sentence are meant to be connected.

The traditional rules exist so that we will all know what they are, and can be free to proceed under the assumption that they are being followed. And the rule that *between you and me* reflects is really very simple. Once it has been determined that *between them* and *between us* are correct, it's inevitable that *between you and me* must be, too—unless you want, as you seem to do, to introduce a not-so-simple exception, ahem, to the basic rule.

In a recent editorial, the commentator Molly Ivins wrote, "But that set off a firestorm of protest from Utahans, one of who *announced it was like living in Russia, where the government can just come in and grab your land."*

Wondering if the who *was a typo or correct usage, I consulted three grammarians, one of whom said* who *was incorrect, and one of who said* who *was correct; the other didn't know.*

Please help.

And in my mail the other day came a Gary Larson greeting card with a drawing of some men wearing powdered wigs, captioned "So, then...would that be '*us* the people' or '*we* the people'?" How amusing. Ha-ha! Now, then, will everyone please stop acting as if the difference between the subjective case and the objective case were quantum mechanics, and get it right? It's not complicated at all.

Consider your sentence—or, rather, the relevant part of your sentence: "one of *who* announced it was like living in Russia." If, instead of a choice between *who* and *whom,* you had a choice between *they* and *them*—as in "one of *they* announced it was like living in Russia" or "one of *them* announced…"—you wouldn't hesitate for a second before choosing the latter, would you? As you'll recall, *them* is in the same case as *whom* (and *they* is in the same case as *who*). Therefore, if *them* would be right, *whom* is the word you want.

That's the technique. To vet pronouns in general: As we just did, mentally pluck out of context the phrase or clause immediately related to the pronoun in question and begin substituting other pronouns until you find one that you know is right. Then make sure that the pronoun you are confident of (here, *them*) is in the same case as the one you actually mean to use *(whom).*

Sometimes while doing the mentally plucking out, you'll find you also want to change the word order. I'm thinking of situations like "There was a protest from Utahans *who* she met in Russia." Let's see: "*They* she met in Russia"? "*Them* she met in Russia"? What's to choose from those? But put the words for that little thought-within-a-thought in what would be their natural order if the thought stood alone—"She met *they* in Russia" or "She met *them* in Russia"—and it becomes clear that *them,* not *they,* would be the right choice. So it's *whom* that's wanted here, too.

Another tip: unless *between you and I* sets off loud alarm bells in your head, you'll be well served to look for *one* pronoun that works, by itself, in your temporary version, even if the phrase you're vetting started out with two pronouns or more. That is, if the puzzle before you is "She met the Utahans and *I*" versus "She met the Utahans and *me*," cut straight to "She met *we*" versus "She met *us*." Of course, *us* is right, so *me*, being in the same case as *us*, is what you want: "She met the Utahans and *me*."

For bonus points, try these two, which are about as tricky as this subject ever gets: "Let's listen to the Utahans, *whom* Molly Ivins expects would prefer not to live in Russia" and "Let's listen to the Utahans, *whom* Molly Ivins expects to prefer to remain in Utah." Which is or are right?*

And one more: Did "*us* the people" or "*we* the people" ordain and establish this Constitution? Please tell me you knew the answer to this one already.

1) Possessives

Now let's worry about possessives—and if you're appalled to see that I've ranked this No. 1 on my grammatical-mistakes list, congratulations on your rare degree of sophistication. Somehow apostrophes keep turning up—or going missing—in the strangest places, and never mind that possessives are another subject that really isn't complicated. I don't know what makes a writer look sillier than misplaced or missing apostrophes. Those problems don't arise in speech, thank goodness, though some possessive problems do.

---

*Ms. Ivins expects *they* would prefer not to live in Russia, no? So the first sentence is wrong; it needs *who*. However, she expects *them* to prefer to remain in Utah, so the second sentence, with its *whom*, is right.

I can no longer keep a lid on my confusion over the oft-used word your *in place of what would seem to be the more apropos* you're—*for example, "Your invited." I have seen* your *used in this way more than once, and I would really like to know if it is correct.*

Oh, dear—has it really come to that? Wherever *you are* would also be appropriate, *you're* (which is a contraction of *you are*) is the right form. *Your* is a possessive adjective, like *my, his,* and *their*: "*Your* question is a good one"—that sort of thing.

· The only reason this is confusing to anyone is that the possessives of nouns (unlike those of pronouns) do use apostrophes: "*teacher's* pet," "*mother's* little helper." These look just the same as contractions of nouns and *is*: "The *teacher's* coming!" "Her *mother's* going to be so pleased!"

My friend Henrich believes that truth comes from God and The New York Times. *I suggested he put all his faith in the divine after I saw a* Times *photo caption recently: "The Kennedy's posed for a portrait...." I told Henrich that the* Times *erred, and that using an apostrophe to make a plural is a conspiracy against language which originated with house-sign carvers at flea markets ("*THE BAKER'S. WELCOME*"). Henrich responded that if the* Times *prints "Kennedy's" as a plural, then it is obviously accepted common usage. Your decision, please!*

If Henrich wants infallibility, God is his only option. Too bad God doesn't do copy-editing.

That glib response met with a few demurrals when it appeared in the column. People supposed that I hadn't really taken in the letter writer's comment about "house-sign carvers," and that I'd failed to realize that a possessive might be appropriate to mark a house. One man wrote:

> *Both* The Joneses *and* The Jones's (*or, maybe,* The Jones') *are commonly seen on mailboxes. Depending on the writer's intent, he or she could defend either choice on grammatical grounds. My bet is that an increasing number of people think that they are saying "This is* the Jones's *house." After all, they can write* Tom's *when they mean* Tom's Bar & Grill.

But the thing to note about *The Jones's* is: Tom Jones = *Jones* or *Jones's* (as in "Tom *Jones* has invited me over for dinner. I am going to Tom *Jones's* house"). Tom and Tina Jones = *Joneses,* or *The Joneses,* or *The Joneses'* ("*The Joneses* have invited me. I am going to *the Joneses'* house"). With *the,* in other words, the name has to be a plural, possessive or not. *The Jones's* is the one indefensible form.

Months after the letter about "the *Kennedy's*" appeared in the column, I received the following note from the man who had written it. His surname is Alper.

> *It's over. We lost.*
> *An Op-Ed piece in* The New York Times *today was all about "*WASP's,*" clear through from headline to the last paragraph. And to add insult to injury, although "*WASP's*" appeared throughout the article, in the final paragraph, for no apparent reason other than the* Times *just doesn't give a damn, the word appeared as "*Wasp's.*"*

I surrender. It's over. We've lost. If I can't fight
them, I guess I'll join them. That goes for me as well
as the rest of the Alper's.

There, there. Don't take it that way. There is a convention according to which the plurals of acronyms
are given apostrophes, along with the plurals of symbols and numerals (*x*'s and *the 1990's*, for example).
It's never made sense to me, and *The Atlantic* doesn't
follow it, but the *Times* does.

When the *Times*'s science section or gardening
column covers *"wasp's,"* write me back. Then it *is*
over.

I have been waging a one-man battle for months at
work. I contend that the possessive form of a singular
noun is created by adding 's, *even if the noun already*
ends in s. *For example, the possessive of* Charles *is*
Charles's.

My co-workers all believe that you add only the
apostrophe to any word ending in s, *so they insist the*
proper form is Charles'. *Who is right?*

Your rule is certainly the usual one, though language
authorities recommend some exceptions to it. For the
most part these arise because an 's is supposed to be
audible if the possessive is read aloud (*Carl's* is said
"Carlz"; the possessive of *Charles* is said "Charles-
ez"—thus, *Charles's*), and an *s'* is not supposed to be
(*cars'* is said "carz," the same as *cars*). After certain
kinds of singular nouns, however, it is difficult to pronounce an additional *s*, and so most authorities would
add only an apostrophe to a proper name that ends in
two sibilants, such as *Jesus* or *Texas*. By a similar

rationale, *for conscience' sake* and *for goodness' sake* are also preferred.

But the exceptions are fine points. Be grateful that your co-workers don't think the possessive of *Charles* is *Charle's.*

An issue has arisen on our campus as to whether an inanimate object can have a possessive. For example, although we routinely talk of "the college's *mission statement" some individuals contend proper usage dictates saying "the mission statement of the college." In many instances, following such a rule results in stilted and awkward-sounding prose. Does such a rule truly exist or is it simply the stipulation of an over-zealous teacher of English?*

By ancient tradition, the nouns for many kinds of inanimate objects form their possessives with *of,* not with *'s,* but this is less a matter of grammar than it is of what sounds natural because of the tradition.

I *have* sometimes heard an argument against the *'s* as bad grammar—namely, that the college doesn't own the mission statement, so how can the possessive be appropriate? This is definitely wrongheaded, for what grammarians mean by "possessive" allows for many relations other than ownership: think of *the bee's knees, a year's supply, doctor's orders,* and *a stone's throw,* for example. Besides, *of* is also considered to be a possessive form, so if this problem were a real one, the switch to *of* wouldn't solve it.

Jaunty constructions in which the possessive is inanimate and the relationship between it and the possessed is quite loose (say, *Boston's Ms. Grammar*) are not considered good form even today. But where avoiding the *'s* results in something more artificial than using it, there is no valid basis on which to object to it.

What would be correct in the sentence that follows? "The leader of the transcendentalists, Ralph Waldo Emerson, ideas were extremely liberal." Should Emerson *be* Emerson's, *to show possession of the ideas? But then the appositive would not agree with its nominative antecedent,* leader. *Or would one need to make* leader *possessive? Somehow that sounds too convoluted to be right. Or perhaps one should recast the sentence completely to avoid the problem. What do you say?*

You've got almost, though not quite, a "picnic's grandmother" construction—so called by the editor and writer Harold Taylor (according to the style manual *Words Into Type*), to remind us not to say or write things like "the girl who gave the picnic's grandmother."

There's a subordinate clause instead of an appositive in the "picnic's grandmother" construction, however. An "appositive," as you know, is a noun or noun phrase that restates, defines, or clarifies what immediately precedes it. With a restrictive appositive (see "Restrictive and descriptive elements," at No. 6, above), such as "the transcendentalist *Ralph Waldo Emerson,*" it's standard practice in a case like your example to make the appositive possessive: "The transcendentalist *Ralph Waldo Emerson's* ideas." I find myself wondering whether Emerson's name ought to be restrictive in your sentence, for the transcendentalists had leaders besides Emerson. Context may not allow it—you may have built a conceptual framework in which there are, say, two opposing camps full of followers, and each has a leader, and Emerson is the transcendentalists'. If context does allow, however, you could say, "The transcendentalist leader Ralph Waldo Emerson's ideas were extremely liberal." I wouldn't call that a beautiful sentence, but it is a grammatical one.

That won't work either with descriptive appositives, which involve commas (your phrase is a good example), or with elements of most other kinds (such as "who gave the picnic"). Recast, recast! There's always a way. How about "The ideas of the transcendentalist leader, Ralph Waldo Emerson, were extremely liberal" or "The leader of the transcendentalists, Ralph Waldo Emerson, had extremely liberal ideas"?

A digression: All this goes a long way toward explaining why I believe in rendering names that include *Jr.* without commas. If *Jr.* is going to take a comma, then unless the name appears at the end of a sentence it will need two: "Harry Connick, *Jr.,* has come out with a new CD" would be the right way to write it if you're in favor of commas. But plainly the meaning of the *Jr.* is restrictive—*this* Harry Connick, not one of another generation, is the point of the designation—and a lack of commas is the signal to readers that they're looking at a restrictive element. Besides, with commas possessives seem illogical—even absurd. "Harry Connick, *Jr.'s,* new CD"?

A further digression: You'll notice that I said *Jr.* but not *Sr.* That's because, properly speaking, the only name in which *Sr.* should appear is that of a widow and mother. I can't keep on with the Connick family without falsifying the details of their lives, so let's say there's a *Harry Harrison* whose son is *Harry Harrison Jr.* If *Harry Jr.* fathers a son whom he and his wife want to name Harry, the baby will be *Harry Harrison III* (and no doubt be called Trey)—temporarily. When *Jr.*'s father dies, *Jr.* becomes *Harry Harrison*, *Trey* becomes *Jr.*, and the former *Jr.*'s mother, except that she probably decided years ago to call herself *Ms. Harriet Harrison*, becomes *Mrs. Harry Harrison Sr.*

It's often possible to figure out points of grammar by listening to educated people speak. Not so in the case of multiple possessives. Faced with the prospect of speaking about a boat that belongs both to their father and to themselves, people will invariably lower their voices while mumbling "my dad's and my boat" *or* "my dad and my boat," *thus betraying that if they happened to get it right, it was blind luck.*

Even The Chicago Manual of Style *punts the question, giving the example of* "the Rosses' and the Williamses' lands" *but avoiding the adjacency of the third and first persons.*

The logic of parallel constructions would lead one to think that my dad's and my boat *is correct, but then why does it sound so wrong? And why is there no construction that sounds right?*

I suppose there's always the boat of me and my dad.

Style manuals and usage books that do rule on this question tend to state flatly that joint possession calls for one possessive (*my dad and my boat*), whereas separate possession calls for more than one (*my dad's and my boats*, meaning a boat for me and a boat for him). Nonetheless, I agree with you that *my dad and my boat* doesn't sound very good. The construction could just as well be referring to two distinct entities: your boat and your dad. Worse still would be *him and my boat.* The problem isn't just the mixing of the third and the first person: *him and her boat* is also hopeless. There's nothing wrong with grammatically equivalent *Marshall and Mileta's boat,* though.

Pronouns are what throws the construction off. In *my dad and my boat,* the two *mys* give the impression of being parallel, though in fact it's *dad* that's more nearly parallel to the second *my.* As for *him and my boat,* no listener, and no reader except a mind reader, is going to be able to figure out what *him* is doing there instead of *his.*

As you drolly note, we may evade the problem if we like, and that's what I'd recommend. After you've said once *the boat that my dad and I own,* you'll have clear sailing with *our boat.*

Are you glad or sorry that we've gotten all the way to the end of this chapter without so much as a mention of subjunctives? In fact, there are a lot of grammatical matters I haven't found room to mention: absolute possessives and double passives and perfect infinitives, and on and on. Systematic coverage of the subtleties of grammar is given in several of the books on my bookshelf, whose titles you'll see catalogued in the aside at the end of the next chapter. I'll be satisfied if I've persuaded you in a general way that the structure of higher English makes a good deal of sense, at the same time that it involves many little peculiarities. Do remember their existence, for it's easy to overlook, and even doubt the legitimacy of, whole charming districts of language if you've never happened upon them on the map.

Diagramming Sentences

Many people have a sort of dark fascination with the idea of diagramming sentences. Either they were taught diagramming long ago in school and they dimly recall that there was meant to be some improving purpose in learning diagramming but now they can't remember how to do it, or they grew up too late to have been taught it and have always imagined that they missed out on one of the fundamentals of an exacting education— like hazing or being caned by the schoolmaster.

According to the linguists who participate in the Ask a Linguist panel on the Linguist List Web site (www. linguistlist.org), the diagramming system prevalent today is Noam Chomsky–style "tree diagrams," in which words and phrases are connected as if by a weeping willow or a marionette's strings, and the lines are annotated with parts of speech. This, however, is taught not in elementary school but, more typically, in college linguistics courses. Also used, though less commonly, are things called immediate-constituent diagrams and tagmemic diagrams, both of which have simply a linear appearance, and also stratificational diagrams, which are said to "resemble plates of spaghetti."

The system that nonspecialists tend to remember, for it is the one that was long taught to American schoolchildren, is called Reed-Kellogg diagramming, after its creators, who published the first description of it in 1879. This is the system in which the words are written above horizontal lines, for the most part, with vertical and slanted lines running between them. The Reed-Kellogg system has never been much used by professional linguists, who warn that it lacks the wherewithal to depict various complicated, though perfectly correct, constructions.

The Ask a Linguist linguists also warn:

> *Diagramming was not intended to improve anybody's speaking or writing ability—except insofar as knowing the syntactic structure of one's sentences might cause one to attend a bit more to one's sentences* (Carl Mills, University of Cincinnati).

> *Diagramming sentences, or any other formal parsing system (many of them work much better than the traditional diagramming system), will have almost no effect on speech ability. It may, however, affect writing ability. The point of diagramming (as I will call any visual parsing system) is to get people to think about syntax, by giving them ways to represent it, and maybe making them practice a bit on using them. If you get in the habit of thinking about what you're saying, and how you're saying it, you're ahead of the writing game. At the very least, you're able to compose sentences and revise them consciously, and this is what every writing instructor is after, in part* (John Lawler, University of Michigan).

> *It probably is not the case that parsing sentences has ever helped anyone write or speak better, but some people believe that idea nonetheless. Traditional parsing focuses too much on individual words, and that is why I don't recommend it to teachers or parents. The*

parsing devices that linguists use focus on coherent chunks—phrases—and would be much better suited to helping students see the relationships among sentence parts. However, the "trees" that linguists use may be too complex for youngsters to deal with (Marilyn Silva, California State University, Hayward).

Listening and reading are far more useful for the general educated language-user than knowing how to parse a sentence. I think a little bit of knowledge about formal grammar, sentence structure, etc., can be helpful to such a person, if only because it helps to know consciously what one is doing when one shifts between, say, active and passive voice. But I have a strong suspicion that this can easily be overdone by schoolteachers who are wedded to the insane idea that "proper" grammar lives in a textbook (Steven Schaufele, Soochow University, Taipei).

Darkly fascinating though diagramming sentences may be, if you thought it was just what you needed to improve your grammar, think again.

CHAPTER FOUR

~

Say No More

So patient a doctor to doctor a patient so.
—WHOLE-WORD PALINDROME

Around the Word Court offices, every day is like my birthday. Nifty little word gifts are constantly arriving from all over. Why, look: here in my e-mail is *adversative,* along with a request that I rule on whether it or *adversarial* is to be preferred. And here's a question about whether *bodes well* is properly parallel to *bodes ill.* And a rather testy note from a woman unable to contain herself about the plural of *chattel.* And—oh!—a new, questionable use of *denigrate,* complete with documentation. Thanks, people—or, as yet another correspondent wants to know, should we say *persons*? Sometimes I respond off the top of my head to questions like these, and then, when I have time to look into matters more deeply, I'm sorry I did. Many language issues are more complicated than they may at first appear.

A number of the questions in this chapter are ones to which I once supposed everybody already knew the answer. But then I would get other letters asking the same question—so that told me something. Furthermore, the answers to some language questions have changed in recent years. Because I have no idea how, in the abstract, to tell apart the ones that have from the ones that haven't, I've thought it best to look into them all. Some aspects of our language are perennially counterintuitive, and we English-speakers will need to go over them again and again until, someday, the way that educated users of English deal with those things does change. And some aspects are new, or at least newly puzzling.

A few other questions here I don't suppose have often been asked before, but I was both entertained by them and flattered that someone asked them of *me*. Moreover, questions and answers that are published in Word Court frequently elicit further correspondence, arguing with what I wrote or pointing out special cases, and I've included some of those letters, too.

Herewith, then, an eccentric little usage dictionary. Words treated in other chapters are cross-referenced in the book's index; the cross-references here are generally for words treated in this chapter.

A, An

I seethe when some pompous fool uses the indefinite article an *before* historian, historic, *or* historical. *The rule regarding articles appears to be quite simple and straightforward: one uses* a *before sounded consonants, including the palatalized* y, *as in* a cat, a year, *or* a urologist, *and* an *before vowel sounds or unvoiced consonants, as in* an apple *or* an hour. *So what's with supposedly educated people saying* an historian?

You aren't alone if you consider this construction about on a par with inventing a coat of arms to put on one's stationery. Americans at least since Mark Twain have been deriding the use of *an* before words beginning with an aspirated, or audible, *h*. Nonetheless, traditional British usage did call for it when the *h*-word's initial syllable was unaccented—thus *a* HIS*tory* but *an* his TO*rian*. Even in England the *an* is now considered an affectation, though R. W. Burchfield's *The New Fowler's Modern English Usage* urges readers not to "demur" if *others* employ the construction.

I was disappointed that you sided with your seething correspondent on the issue of the indefinite article an *before words like* historian, hermetic, *and* heretical. *The use derives not from supposedly educated fools acting pompous, as he avers, but because it is easier to say and better-sounding. "Uh historian" requires two contiguous exhalations and bears more resemblance to stuttering than to refined speech. "An historian" is graceful. Similarly, the pronounced "thee" is clearly preferable to "thuh" before vowels. So I would say to your correspondent, Relax, you're having an hysterical reaction. "Thee" option is up to me.*

I won't reproduce letter after letter on this point, but I should note that I did receive quite a few that either deprecated the original letter writer's intemperance or disagreed with him and me—or both.

Acquiesce

My brother and I enjoyed a lengthy debate over the meaning of the verb acquiesce. *Unresolved in our debate—at least lacking explicit, mutual affirmation of the correctness of the other—we have, ironically, acquiesced. Our mother, a retired English professor, is unable to decide this sibling dispute. Please help.*

Brother Tim asserts that acquiesce *means "to agree." I assert that it means "to fall silent." His understanding looks to the practical outcome of acquiescing: someone wins when someone else acquiesces. My understanding looks to the intellectual activity of the contenders, where, though one allows another to win, there is no agreement as to the propriety of the matter.*

Although there's certainly an element of silence, or tacitness, in *acquiesce,* the primary meaning is "go along with"—that is, "agree." You'll see what I mean if I share the example sentence from my 1942 *Webster's Dictionary of Synonyms* (in which *acquiesce* is treated under *assent*): "No organism *acquiesces* in its own destruction." "Falls silent in its own...."? I don't think so. The meaning is "agrees to."

Adversarial, Adversative

My secretary and I are in disagreement over the use of the word adversarial. *My perspective is that the correct transformation of the noun* adversary *into an adjective is to form* adversative *and not* adversarial. *I note that only* adversative *is found in most dictionaries, but both words are found in most computer spell-checking functions and* adversarial *has found its way into widespread use. My secretary's perspective is that word selection should be based on efficient communication skills, even if the word is grammatically suspect. I disagree. Which is the correct word?*

Even two thirds of the way through the twentieth century, *adversarial* was nowhere to be found in dictionaries; the earliest citation for it in the *Oxford English Dictionary* is dated 1970. But now, to judge from recent U.S. newspaper articles in the Nexis database, it is used hundreds of times as often as *adversative*. (Furthermore, these days *adversative* seems to come up almost exclusively in stories about Southern military academies. From *The Augusta* [Georgia] *Chronicle,* for example: "The *adversative* training and Spartan living conditions at The Citadel motivate cadets to finish their studies in four years, the school and the commission said.") This would probably not be the case if everybody literate still read Latin, for we'd all be familiar with the Latin form *adversativus*; and *adversarial,* though its *-ial* ending also derives from Latin, would strike us as a chimerical creature.

Hardly anyone does read Latin anymore, however, and the chimeras swooping through our language are legion—not only such well-domesticated ones as *bureaucracy, coastal, gullible, pacifist,* and *speedometer* (about all of which H. W. Fowler sputtered a bit, calling them "hybrid derivatives") but also younger, wilder ones, like *Iran-contra-gate* and the *Teflon President, RJ-11 jacks* and *R2D2,* and *ibuprofen* and *Advil* and *Motrin*—these last being an odd-looking trio of synonyms if ever there was one. It's not grammar that *adversarial* is assailing but purity of etymology, and our language is so polyglot generally that I can't summon up much indignation about the fact that *adversative* has—let's face it—lost out to *adversarial.*

Affect, Effect, Impact

I assume writers and editors, in a bit of language laziness, have given up on trying to use the words affect *and* effect *correctly, in favor of accepting the word* impact *as a substitute for both, thus diluting the previous meaning of* impact.

Good point. What people want to mean when they use *impact* as a verb (a usage that many revile) might be better expressed by the verb *affect*: A *affects* B. The noun similar in meaning to the noun *impact* is *effect*: A has an *effect* on B. A mnemonic might be: The *action* is *affect*; the *end* result is *effect*.

See also Impact.

All right, Alright

Recently, when I was student-teaching in an eighth-grade classroom, my cooperating teacher and I had a falling-out over the spelling of all right. *I had read that it was okay to use the less formal spelling,* alright, *in works of fiction, and was allowing my students to use this spelling in their short stories. When my cooperating teacher discovered this, she nearly blew a gasket, insisting that there is only one correct spelling:* all right. *Since this incident I have repeatedly seen* alright *in movie titles, headlines, and stories. Is* alright *all right to use informally?*

The last time I looked into it, eighth-graders didn't seem to need any help in expressing themselves informally. But they'll never learn the grown-up, relatively formal, standard modes of expression unless they are taught them. *Alright* is emphatically not standard English.

All told, All tolled

All told *raises my hackles when used in a context such as* "All told, *there were 37 graduates, 16 in engineering," etc. Writers spell it* all told *when they really mean just* "*all included.*" *I think* all tolled *is really what is meant, because that would mean* "*all summed; all included; all added up,*" *whereas* all told *can only mean something such as* "*notwithstanding someone's withholding information, or nothwithstanding the user's desire not to tell everything, everything is being told.*"

Interesting idea. But an ancient meaning of *tell* is "to count." And both the old, revered, prescriptive *Webster's Second* and the new, respected, prescriptive *American Heritage* give *all told* but not *all tolled*—so that's that.

A lot, Alot

See A while, Awhile.

Alright

See All right, Alright.

Alternate, Alternative

For the past few years I've seen alternative *used as an adjective. I thought* alternate *could be used as either a noun or an adjective, but not* alternative. *Few accept this correction when I proofread for them. Did I miss something in English class?*

Perhaps you are misremembering what you learned? The adjective *alternative* has long existed, with the meaning "affording a choice." (Traditionally, the choice was supposed to be between two, though few eyebrows any longer go up when the word refers to more *alternatives* than that.) In fact some dispute the adjectival use of *alternate,* but this usage has become common over the past several decades, deriving from the older noun, which in one of its senses was synonymous with *substitute.* Now we have *alternate jurors, alternate routes,* and *alternate arrangements,* all being replacements or substitutes, whereas *alternative routes* and *alternative arrangements* are simply options that one might choose between (or among!).

Then, too, there are uses and senses of each of these adjectives in which they do not overlap the other—for example, *alternative* meaning "countercultural" or "nontraditional," and *alternate* meaning "happening by turns."

Among, Between

I have seen a distinct decrease in usage of the word among. *I just read an article that states: "The children ended up with $418,002 to split* between *the three of them." Other instances of the (assumed) misuse of* between *occur frequently in casual conversation, from the pulpit, and in the speech of elected officials and journalists. From the recesses of my dim past I remember a rule that* between *is used for comparisons—well,* between *two concepts.* Among *is to be used for comparisons of more than two.*

Was I sold a bill of goods? What is correct?

You have it just right, except that *between* is also correct when discussing pairs of things within groups of more than two. For example, no matter how many acts a play has, the intermissions occur *between* them, not *among* them. By the way, don't try to say that more precisely with "*between each* of the acts";

between each can never be right, except as part of *between each two*.

Amount, Number

I frequently hear educated people talking about "a limited amount *of seats" or "a large* amount *of dollars." An inner voice immediately retorts, "number of..." Am I being haunted by the ghost of usage past?*

If it is a ghost of the past, the past isn't over! Choosing between *amount,* which is to say overall size of pool or heap, and *number,* or how many, can on occasion be tricky: "the *amount* of bacteria in the sample" or "the *number* of bacteria in the sample"? In some contexts either choice can sound wrong. For those occasions it's worth remembering that *quantity* can mean either thing and is a good substitute for both.

An

See A, An.

And, But, Or

Was there a grammatical error in a recent Word Court? The word but *was used as the first word in a sentence: "But now, to judge from recent U.S. newspaper articles..." The improper use of conjunctions has become very commonplace (which I find maddening). I was taught that in order to convey a clear and unambiguous meaning, a sentence should be complete and able to stand alone. This principle is violated by sentences started with conjunctions such as* and *and* or.

But a sentence taken out of context is unlikely to be truly clear and unambiguous, whether or not it starts with a conjunction.

Sorry—I don't mean to torment you. May I urge you to look at some usage guides? *Merriam-Webster's Dictionary of English Usage*: "Part of the folklore of usage is the belief that there is something wrong in beginning a sentence with *but*." Or Fowler: "... piece of nonsense..." No one is going to force you to start sentences with conjunctions against your will. But the tide of usage is against you—and I don't see why having begun this sentence with "The tide of usage, however," would have made it clearer.

Arguably

Journalists have begun using the word arguably *in describing an artist, a writer, an actor, and so forth, who has achieved outstanding success. I have seen this word used in other contexts as well. My dictionary, which confirms my understanding from early school days, defines* argue *as "to give reasons for or against something."*

The current use of the word arguably *is arguable. For instance, "He is* arguably *one of the most talented musicians to reach the stage in years." This indicates to me that the talent of this musician could be disputed, although the article does not argue the point or compare the musician with other musicians.*

If you could resolve this use of the word without too much argument, I would be grateful.

You are not the only person to have written me about *arguably.* It isn't much loved. And it is newer than

many other words, having been part of our language
for merely a century or so. It has a niche to occupy,
however, if we'll let it. While *arguably* concedes that
others might argue against a point, it tends to emphasize that an argument can be made in something's
favor. *Disputably* (which is not a common word)
gives the impression of taking the contrary point of
view; *debatably* shows no preference for either side;
and *possibly, probably,* and so on fail to bring to
mind argument at all. *Arguably* is a valuable word,
because arguably its meaning is unique.

As, Like

*My son's English teacher gives him writing samples
that use* like *as a conjunction. Have I missed something? Is it now acceptable to use* like *in place of* as?
*Or do we no longer follow rules of grammar like we
used to?*

People who remember the flap over a cigarette that
"tastes good *like* a cigarette should," almost fifty
years ago, can consider themselves up to date—at
least, with respect to the grammar of the slogan. The
rule about *like* never did quite ban using it as a conjunction but only forbade using it to introduce a
clause—that is, a group of words containing a subject
and a verb, such as "cigarette should." (It may be
used as a conjunction if one leaves unexpressed the
verb that would come after it: "The Surgeon General
responded *like* a firehorse to a bell.")
     This rule still holds in standard English, but infor-
mal English almost requires one to break it—a distinction those sly ad copywriters surely kept in mind.
Alternatives that are acceptable at both levels of lan-

guage do exist: *As if* sometimes works ("It sounded almost *as if* they were telling the truth"). Where *as if* won't do, *the way* usually will ("It comes in a pack with a warning label, *the way* a cigarette should").

Re "The Surgeon General responded like a firehorse to a bell": according to my concept of diagramming a sentence there are two prepositional phrases in your example.

> like a firehorse *(used adverbially), and*
> to a bell *(adjective modifying* firehorse*)*

I don't accept like *as a conjunction in this example. Please respond.*

Your diagramming of "He responded like a firehorse to a bell" is ingenious, but meaning will not permit "to a bell" to be adjectival. You will see this for yourself if you'll consider the difference in meaning between the original sentence and "He responded like a firehorse wearing a bell." Rather, according to the usual view, *responds* is in ellipsis after *firehorse* and the phrase modifies that.

See also the entries for "As" and "Like" in the "Unquestioned Answers" section of Chapter Five.

As far as, As for

> *I have noticed that* as far as ———— *is concerned is being replaced with the incorrect incomplete* as far as, *as in* "As far as *the economy, it is in good shape."*
> *Can you comment on this and do what can be done to discourage its use? Perhaps you can persuade offenders that* as for *is acceptable, as in* "As for *hats, they are passé." I have even seen this bothersome device in print, where it is unforgivable.*

It's an epidemic. From two pieces I came upon in *The New York Times*: "'*As far as* what the report is going to look like, I haven't the faintest idea,' David P. Schippers, the chief investigative counsel of the House Judiciary Committee, said in an interview on Friday" and "'*As far as* history, there is no history here,' said Doris Fletcher, speaking of the new British Library."

The uncompleted *as far as* has a long history, but it is no less an error for that. Fowler evidently thought that people made the mistake as a sort of twist on perfectly correct prepositional uses such as "He knows algebra *as far as* quadratics" and "I have gone *as far as* collecting statistics." I agree with you, though, that today's offenders give the impression of making a garble of a different *as* construction, like *as for* or *as to*.

Aughts

Here's a question that has been bothering me for several years: What is the name of the first decade of the 2000s? The aughts? The zeros? The zeds? Why hasn't this issue been resolved by the popular media? What was the first decade of the 1900s called?

Historians and linguistic scholars have an assortment of opinions about what the first decade of the twentieth century was called: it went by *the nineteen hundreds, the aughty-aughts,* or simply *the new decade* and other non-names, various personages have assured me. But *the twenty hundreds? The aughty-aughts*? Those precedents don't help us now. Many new coinages have been put forward over the past decade or so, among them *the zilches, the uh-ohs, the naughties,* and *the preteens*. The three proposals that people seem inclined to take seriously, though, are *the ohs, the double 0s* (pronounced "ohs"), and *the aughts.*

Certain arms of the media have been trying to resolve the issue: *The New York Times,* for example, has published at least two editorials in favor of *the ohs.* But this isn't something that can be resolved by any given authority. English is wonderfully democratic: words and phrases enter the standard vocabulary because large numbers of people like them and find them useful. In this case, we may well fail to settle on one choice, and a hundred years from now historians and linguistic scholars will have an assortment of opinions about what we called the first decade of the new millennium. Maybe precedent is telling us something after all.

A while, Awhile

Until recently I indiscriminately wrote awhile *as one word, whether using it as the object of a preposition or as an adverb. But then my error was pointed out to me. When using the expression as a noun phrase, I should be rendering it* a while. *Otherwise, it should be one word. Since this revelation, I have been compulsively tracking the use and spelling of* awhile *and* a while *in whatever I'm reading. I have discovered that breaches of the rule are rampant. In a number of publications, I have come across instances of* for awhile.

May we now consider it unnecessary to maintain a distinction between the two spellings? Please enlighten me.

This is just one of many little distinctions that a person with a subtle command of English is called upon to make. There's also—just for example—*anymore*, adverb (as in "I don't go there *anymore*"), and *any more*, pronoun phrase ("I don't have *any more*"); *any time*, noun phrase ("You may withdraw your money at *any time*"), and *anytime*, adverb ("You may withdraw it *anytime* you want"); *everyone*, pronoun ("*Everyone* has a checking account"), and *every one*, pronoun phrase ("*Every one* of us has a checking account"); *into*, preposition ("I put the check *into* my account"), and *in to*, adverb or particle plus the sign of an infinitive ("I went *in to* see the bank manager"). We can't simply gloss over all such distinctions, and none of them is especially harder than any of the others.

Not everyone does have a subtle command of English, though, and people do try to gloss over such distinctions. Just within the past week I've come across a form letter whose author assured me "I'll be happy to help *anyway* I can"; an advertisement boasting "*Everyday*, you can make a difference. We do"; and an advertisement promoting a watch with the slogan "Chronomat *For Ever*." No, no, no.

The choice between *a while* and *awhile* is easier than many of the others because the two-word version is never wrong. *Awhile* is possible except where the word follows a preposition, such as *after* or *for*. But even where it might be the usual form (say, in "Wait *awhile*"), we have the option of inserting an adjective between the *a* and the *while* ("Wait a *little* while.") Thus a case can always be made for considering the expression to be a noun phrase, and rendering it as two words.

A still easier distinction, incidentally, is between *a*

lot and *alot,* because there is no distinction to be made: *alot* is never right.

Back, Forward, Up

Help, help!!

I have noticed confusion regarding the use of the words back, forward, *and* up *as applied to events in time, timetables, and schedules. If one is referring to a planned future event, and if said event is going to be* moved back, *in my thinking the concept is that the event is being moved further into the future. However, I have encountered others who would interpret this expression to suggest that the event is being moved to an earlier date. This follows the logic that when a historical event or a transaction is* backdated, *the event is being moved closer to the beginning of time, the birth of Christ, the fall of Rome, or whatever.*

What are the rules regarding the use of these words in describing time-relevant events?

Back, forward, and *up* are the verbal equivalents of M. C. Escher drawings. One thing dictionaries will tell you is that *back* means "in, into, or toward the past"—an idea that when applied to the future suggests that *move back* should mean "make earlier." But dictionaries also define the word as meaning something like "farther away" ("Stand *back!*")—and obviously the later future is further from the here and now than the near future would be. In actual use, with respect to the future most people, most of the time, use *move back* to mean "make later" ("Let's *move* the dinner party *back* from Friday to Saturday"). What this usage has in common with the use of *back* with respect to the past is the movement in time away from the present.

As for *forward*: In future contexts (say, "What if we *move* the date of the party *forward*?"), on the one hand the word seems to mean "further into the future" and therefore to be a synonym for *back,* and on the other it seems of course to be the opposite of *back* ("I just can't decide whether to *move* it *forward* or *back*"). The picture is no clearer with respect to past contexts. *Forward* is used very inconsistently.

The easiest word of the three is *up*: in any context *move up* tends to mean "make earlier." That is, most people use it to mean the opposite of *back* with respect to the future and the same as *back* with respect to the past. Piece of cake, right?

If you ever find yourself wanting to discuss a change of time, now in the past, that was in the future when the change was made, God help you: "We forgot to tell him a month ago when we decided to move the party up a week." Unfortunately for this subject in general, at some point the future is certain to become the past, making *back* and *forward* in such contexts absolutely baffling.

My conclusion is that when you're referring to movement in time, if context doesn't spell out the direction of movement you mean, you'll do well to avoid saying "I need to *move* the dinner party *back*" or "I need to *move* the date *forward*." How about "I need to postpone the party" or "I need to move the party to an earlier date"? The alternative is to be prepared to be hospitable when, say, the dinner guests who are now expected two weeks from Saturday ring the doorbell this Saturday instead.

Beer

I have been in a continuous argument about this with every single person I know (except my mother) for about a month and a half now. What is the plural of beer? *I have always thought the plural was* beer, *not* beers. *Please respond, so that (hopefully) I can rub it in everyone's face that I am correct. Thank you* VERY *much.*

Do you mean the plural as in "He liked to have a couple of *beers* when he got home from work"? Or as in "Colorado is known for its *beer*"—which isn't actually a plural? Or as in "Colorado is known for its *deer*"—which, of course, is a different word? I'm sorry to have to break it to you, but the plural of *beer* is *beers*.

There are in fact nouns with a plural the same as the singular. These tend to name creatures that have been known to English since ancient times and have been hunted or fished or were used for food, such as *deer* and *bear* and *fowl*. In most cases, a form with an *s* on the end is also a proper plural, and this plural is likelier to refer to a limited number of individuals than to a multitude ("We feasted on two roast *fowls* in a room overlooking a pond full of *waterfowl* and *trout*"). But this distinction—which is not a rule, only a tendency, and one to which many exceptions exist—doesn't generally apply to liquids, since liquid en masse is a quantity of liquid, not a number of liquids, and is therefore singular ("Maybe we shouldn't have washed the meal down with so much *beer*"). Only when one is talking about individual glasses or bottles or brands ("So many *beers* to choose from!") does the word become plural.

"They have so many kinds of beer *I can't decide"—sounds plural to me. "They have so many kinds of* flowers *I can't decide."*

What you're taking to be evidence of a plural in fact points up the difference between "count nouns" and "mass nouns." A "count noun" names something that in quantity becomes plural and—surprise—can be counted. *Flower* is a good example: *one flower, two flowers.* Another is *bottle:* "ninety-nine *bottles* of beer on the wall." A "mass noun" lacks those qualities: think of the *water* in a vase or in several vases, or all the *beer* in those many bottles.

The distinction can be a perplexing one, I admit, because many mass nouns can also be used in a count-noun way: "The bar carries a range of sparkling *waters* and ninety-nine different *beers.*" I wish English were more straightforward, but I didn't invent it.

One of the many oddities I noticed when I moved to this country from Canada several years ago was that the word beer *was pluralized to* beers. *While surely Canada has its own peculiar slang, I would hazard that Canadians speak a truer form of the "Queen's English."*

Beg the question

In a recent music review in The Boston Globe, *I read,* "Begging the question *of whether simplicity is a virtue or a vice..." For centuries philosophers and logicians have used* beg the question *(and its Latin version,* petitio principii) *to refer to the fallacy of assuming that which is in dispute—as in the presumption behind the*

question "Have you stopped beating your wife?"
Lately, however, the phrase seems to have been turned
into a sorry attempt at an upscale version of either
evade *or* invite the question. *Is it too late to save this*
fine old phrase?

I can't find any evidence that the meaning "invite the question" is common, but reputable dictionaries have been accepting the meaning "evade the question" for decades. Still, things haven't reached the point where anyone is saying that the phrase in its traditional meaning is wrong. That meaning is in trouble because it is confusing. It has nothing to do with what most of us think of as begging; nor does it necessarily involve a question (an example of question-begging that appears in the second and third editions of *Modern English Usage* is that "capital punishment is necessary because without it murders would increase"). And *petitio principii,* from which the phrase was long ago translated, and which is generally given as a synonym, is an expression that doesn't come up much in conversation. So we have nothing to help us call to mind *beg the question* when it is wanted. Maybe we should all lodge the idea of "asserting or taking as a starting point what needs to be proved" in our minds. When that seems to be what's going on, it's the moment to say, "Excuse me—I do believe you're *begging the question.*"

This morning, in an obit for Princess Diana on CBC,
a member of the paparazzi tried to justify hounding
her. He said, "They were just doing their job."
   This may be an example of begging the question.
It is precisely their job that is being criticized. What
do you think?

I think you're right.

Although both my dictionaries give "evade the question" as a "loose" second choice, I confess to never having encountered beg the question *in its traditional, classical sense. I suspect that if you took a poll you would find that the loose version is the one now almost exclusively in use. The dictionaries are behind the times.*

You may well be right, too.

Behind your back

Doesn't behind your back *mean the exact opposite of what we're trying to say when we use that cliché? If someone is saying something* behind your back, *doesn't that really mean that he or she is saying something in front of you—in that area that is* behind your back? *I'd rather have people talk in front of my back than behind it.*

Please tell me you're just being whimsical.

Between

See Among, Between.

Bi-

How often would you expect a biannual *event to occur? I have always known this to mean every two years, but when I encountered a challenge to this interpretation as being only one quarter of the actual frequency (that is, twice a year, which to me would be* semiannual*), I incredulously consulted three different versions of* Webster's Dictionary *and also looked up* biweekly *and* bimonthly. Biweekly *was defined first as "every two weeks" and second as "twice a week."* Bi-monthly *was defined as "every two months, 'sometimes' twice a month," without further explanation.*

Confusion reigns. What are we to do, short of abandoning the prefix bi- *altogether?*

It's a good question, and my correspondent is right: *bi-* is useless for making clear a rate of recurrence. (Notwithstanding, *The American Heritage Dictionary* does distinguish between *biannual*, "happening twice each year," and *biennial*, "happening every second year.") When I received the letter, not having anything very interesting to say in response, I sent a form letter in reply:

Thank you for your letter. Because Word Court appears only six times a year, I am unable to respond to many questions—but I do hope to get to yours.

My correspondent wrote back:

I note that you avoided using the term bimonthly, *which proves my point!*

Bode

For years now I have noticed that commentators and columnists employ what seems to be a contradictory usage of bode. *They say that something* bodes ill, *as in "A poor showing in the Alps* bodes ill *for a Tour de France victory," using* bode *(correctly, I believe) as a transitive verb with the noun object* ill; *yet when things are looking up, these same pundits state that an event* bodes well, *as in "The many favorable reviews* bode well *for the film's Oscar chances." If something is said to* bode ill, *shouldn't a reversal of fortune lead us to say it* bodes good?

Although your logic and your knowledge of the way parts of speech function are impeccable, speakers and writers since Dryden, in 1700, have used *bodes well*. *Well,* an ancient word, can be grammatically slippery: for example, how would you parse "Leave *well enough* alone"? This, I admit, could just as well be used to explain why *bodes well* is considered a forgivable mistake. It is, however, considered correct. As scrupulous dictionaries indicate, an exception has been made for *well* to the otherwise reliable rule that *bode* (roughly speaking, a synonym for *foretell*) is transitive and therefore must lead into a noun.

Bring, Take

I am writing this in the desperate hope that you will save my marriage. My wife and I have nearly come to blows over the proper use of the words bring *and* take. *She keeps insisting that she will* bring *our daughter to the library, and I say that my daughter is going nowhere unless her mother* takes *her. I am unable to convince my wife that she is wrong about this and needs to turn from her grammatically evil ways. Please help this syntaxed family.*

The fundamental rule is that *bring,* in its relevant sense, refers to movement toward the speaker ("Will you *bring* me some new library books?"), and *take* to movement away from the speaker ("How nice of you to *take* back the ones I've read"). These verbs can also indicate movement toward or away from anyone from whose perspective the action is being viewed

("She *brought* the librarian a gift. The librarian *took* it home"). Curiously, with these words seemingly opposite meanings can overlap, particularly when people are *bringing* or *taking* someone or something with them ("Let's *bring* [or *take*] plenty of books with us"). But I gather that your daughter isn't just accompanying her mother; she's the reason for the trip. Your wife, diligent mother though she may be, then, is not *bringing* but *taking* her.

If the distinction between bring *and* take *is related to direction—toward or away—then whether the wife of the fellow who wrote that letter* brings *or* takes *their daughter to the library has more to do with her physical relationship to home and library than with whether the daughter is merely accompanying her or is the reason for the trip. So the man might ask his wife to* take *their daughter with her, whereas the librarian might call and say,* Why don't you *bring* your daughter with you? *Mom, on the other hand, might say things focused in either direction. She might say to herself, "I'm going to the library. I'd better* bring *Susan with me so that we can have a chat on the way." Or she might say to herself, "I'd better* take *Susan with me so that she can get away from her pedantic father for a while." It seems to me that Mom has a choice, each of which is perfectly legitimate.*

I don't disagree with any of your examples, and, in fact, my first response to that letter was the same as yours. But note that in the scenario you gave me Mom is bringing her daughter *with her,* implying that she'd be going anyway, and wants her daughter to *accompany* her. If, however, the object of the trip is to deliver the girl to the library, and if Mom is at home telling Dad that she plans to make that trip, then she's not supposed to say "I'll *bring* her to the library." That's all I meant.

But

See And, But, Or.

Chattel

This is a stupid mistake that I see all over the place in less carefully proofread media (newspapers and e-mail are major offenders). But I just came across it in an otherwise literate article in Harper's! *"Even as women were idealized, they were widely regarded as* chattel.*" Argh! They were regarded as* chattels. *It's a count noun! One* chattel, *two* chattels. *I wish people would stop confusing that word with* cattle *(a mass noun).*

There, I feel better now.

Right you are. The mistake isn't *so* stupid, though, because ultimately *chattel* and *cattle* derive from the same Latin source. Regardless, by now the "collective senses" of *chattel* given in the *Oxford English Dictionary* (including two that mean "cattle") are marked obsolete or rare.

Clear

See Transparent.

Closing, Closure

Ever since the federal government decided to reduce funding to support military bases all over the country by consolidating their functions, I have felt assaulted by newscasters, both local and national. Whenever a base was targeted for possible closing, *the newscaster would report that it was targeted for* closure. *While they may have had the need for* closure *in the social-emotional sense after they were shut down,* closure *seems to have been mistakenly used to mean* closing *(gerund). Even National Public Radio broadcasters perpetuated this incorrect usage throughout the process of identifying the cities to be affected and then implementing the* base-closing *(not* base-closure, *as some called it) plan. I could not have called in every time I heard it—it would have been a part-time job!! What does Word Court think of this apparent faux pas?*

I scoured dictionaries old and new for support for your position. They all support the idea that *closure* can be an act of *closing,* so there's nothing more to say except: Case closed.

Compare to, Compare with

I need to know when it is compared to *and when* compared with. *Here is the sentence: "... an imbalance of functions on one side of the brain as* compared with/to *the other side." The functions are the same but the facility with their use is different.*

When I first heard the Artist then known as Prince sing his "Nothing Compares 2 U," my heart went pitty-pat for an idiosyncratic reason that you can probably in this context guess. If the Artist can get *compare to* right, I don't see why we all can't.

Compare to indicates a likening: In "Shall I *compare* thee *to* a summer's day?" Shakespeare is likening thee to a summer's day. In "Nothing *compares to* you," the Artist's point is that nothing is like you.

Compare with indicates a contrasting, an exploration of differences as well as similarities: In "*Compare* great things *with* small," Virgil and, after him, Milton are contrasting the great and the small. They're not saying that great things and small are alike, any more than the Artist was saying that nothing contrasts with you. And in your sentence you don't mean to be saying that the two sides of the brain function alike; rather, you are contrasting the functioning of one side of the brain with that of the other. *Compare with,* therefore, is correct.

Comprise

In a recent press release from the White House about the Department of Veterans Affairs I read: "The Department is comprised of three organizations that administer programs to benefit veterans and their families." I think the correct use would be to say "The Department comprises three organizations."

You're right. The reason *comprise* is confusing to many people is the same reason that it's useful: it doesn't work the same way as similar words. "Three organizations *compose* the department" or "Three organizations *make up* the department" but "The department *comprises* three organizations": a whole *comprises* its parts. The word works, that is, like *consists of*—except that you mustn't use the *of* with *comprise,* for, as you suspect, that changes the picture.

Think again of *make up,* whose meaning is almost exactly the reverse of *comprise.* "Three organizations *make up* the department" and "The department *is made up of* three organizations," obviously, mean the same thing; *make up* is active, and *is made up of* is passive. *Is comprised of,* then, oughtn't to mean the same thing as *comprise.* And yet it's never used any other way; no one ever says "Three organizations *are comprised of* the department." For this reason, and because there's no sense using three words where one will do, it would be better if we all rooted *is comprised of* out of our vocabularies.

Convince, Persuade

It disturbs me to find convinced *followed by an infinitive in much current writing that seems to me otherwise literate. Shouldn't it be* persuaded? *My thought is: one should be* convinced that...

This punctilio is so commonly overlooked that it's hard to be stern about it. Nonetheless, why not get it right? The traditional distinction is that a person who *persuades* you induces you to act, whereas one who *convinces* you changes your opinion. Thus *convince to* is considered incongruous.

Of course, it's not easy to *persuade* people without at the same time *convincing* them. The senses of the words overlap, as perhaps this quotation from Joseph Conrad illustrates: "He who wants to *persuade* should put his trust not in the right argument, but in the right word. The power of sound has always been greater than the power of sense." Supposing Conrad had written *convince,* wouldn't his idea have been equally convincing?

Cull, Garner, Glean

What irritates me is that people use cull *to mean* gather, *when they should say* glean, *or even* garner.

It's like the imply-infer *thing—we seem to be halfway to accepting the switch between the two, because the error is made so often that we already know what is meant. I saw it again in an AP story today, about a book using old photographs "culled from antique shops to lend verisimilitude to the tale."*

The fact is that dictionaries have long allowed *cull* to be used in the senses of "select" and "gather": "They *culled* some raspberries from the bushes to make the dessert." You and I are not tempted to use the word that way, though, because we can't forget that a *cull,* noun, is something that has been separated out because it's no good. And so we prefer to restrict the verb *cull* to the process of removing the rejects: "I hope they *culled* the moldy raspberries before they mixed the fruit in." As for *glean,* think of indigents rummaging in the fields after the reapers have come and gone. To *glean* is to pick up whatever is of value that has been left behind: "See if you can *glean* any good raspberries from among the moldy ones." And to *garner* is to gather and store in a granary, or as if in one. It's not a word appropriate to raspberries, because, alas, they do get moldy if you store them for long.

Data

A demon that haunts me is the use of data *as a singular noun. I realize this is a losing battle, but I still would like to see a few more shots fired from my side. When I first encountered this usage, it was from people I thought of as illiterates, and I was inclined to write them off. Now I see it in daily newspapers as*

*well as in technical journals. It's wrong, wrong,
wrong, and I implore you to say so in public.*

Using *data* as a singular *is* wrong. It's also unnecessary, because the word works fine as a plural, and
because we have alternatives to it, such as the plural
statistics and the singular *information.* But people
keep getting *data* wrong because their English-
speakers' ears don't necessarily hear the Latin *-a* ending as plural. Even the plurals of some words ending
in *-um* that come to us from or via Latin are now typically formed in English with an *s*: *albums, condo-
miniums, gymnasiums, mausoleums, stadiums,* and
vacuums are examples that come to mind. And
agenda is a onetime plural that is now almost invariably regarded as singular, having the plural *agendas.*
Be that as it may, "The *datums are* in," of course,
sounds much worse than "The *data is* in."

"Very few *data are* in," I have to admit, sounds
hokey—less idiomatic, certainly, than "Very little *data
is* in." The word is trying to sneak into the singular
category by devious routes. I myself would not say
either one of those sentences, but I fear that the data
aren't all in yet on *data.*

Deceptively

*A friend and I cannot agree on the meaning of
phrases combining* deceptively *and a modifier—for
example,* deceptively easy. *I contend that something
that is* deceptively easy *is, in fact, easy and is decep-
tive because it appears difficult. My friend argues that
a* deceptively easy *task is one that appears easy but is
difficult. Please help.*

The sad truth is that at this moment in history *deceptively easy* means nothing in particular. *The American Heritage Dictionary* asked its usage panel, which is made up of mostly eminent "educated speakers," about *deceptively,* and, the dictionary reports, about a third of the panel thought that the word in effect contradicted the adjective (that is, *deceptively easy* would mean "hard"), half thought the opposite, and the remainder said they found the meaning ambiguous.

If you want to be understood, you need to phrase it some other way. In most cases, I suspect, doing that will be—hmm, easier than you might think.

Decimate, Devastate

Did I miss something? Has Norm Crosby become copy editor of The Atlantic Monthly? *Three times recently the word* decimated *has been used when it was clear from the context that* devastated *was meant. For example, an article about the decline in global whale populations stated that the populations had been* decimated. *I'm sure that those who are concerned about the welfare of whales would think that a loss of only 10 percent, while not desirable, is tolerable. The other instances were in the letters to the editor, which only indicates that the usage has become more and more prevalent. Let us hope that it does not become acceptable. If it does, I shall be* decimated.

You are, of course, referring to the fact that the origin of *decimate* is in a punishment anciently inflicted on mutinous Roman legions—the killing of every tenth man, chosen by lot. This origin is still apparent in that Latin *decim-*. But even in 1926 Fowler, who had taught classics, was declaring that when a large proportion of some population was being killed, *decimate* was acceptable so long as no number directly contradictory to the 10 percent idea was specified. And reputable dictionaries have long allowed the word in that sense. In your last sentence, though, you have zeroed in on the usage the dictionaries don't like: *decimate* applied to destruction other than killing.

When I start to feel fussy about an issue like this, I remind myself that, etymologically speaking, our language is heavily littered with bits and scraps of old meanings that no longer apply. *Litter,* for example, is a descendant of the Latin *lectus,* meaning "bed," and *heavily* has in its lineage the Goth word *hafjan,* meaning "lift." Should I not say "heavily littered" because it might call to mind, in someone with an etymological bent, a jumbled and irrelevant image of lifting a bed? In fact I try not to dwell on etymology more than is absolutely necessary for my job, because I fear that my sensitivity to the current meanings of words will be compromised if their history is too much with me.

True, even those of us who haven't studied etymology in depth are likely to think of "ten" or "a tenth" when we hear *decim-*; the *decimal* system has made sure of that. And words that bring irrelevant or inappropriate allusions to mind, unlooked-for, are best replaced. Otherwise, the results can be laughable—as in headlines like "Drunk Gets Nine Months in Violin Case," "Iraqi Head Seeks Arms," and "Prostitutes Appeal to Pope." If you don't want to, then, you needn't use *decimate* except to mean the killing of one in ten. In that case, you won't be using the word very often.

Degree, Diploma

I have assembled quite a stack of newspaper and mag-azine clippings that employ the phrase high-school de-gree. *It annoys me very much when I see this instead of* high-school diploma. *I didn't know that high schools were* degree-granting institutions.

Good point. I suspect this is one of the many things that aren't being taught in high school anymore. And while we're at it, another reader has written to object to "She *graduated* high school"—also a good point. *Graduate* may be transitive ("The school *graduated* her with honors"), but the graduating institution isn't allowed to be the object of the verb.

I'm sure you have heard by now from several other Central High School of Philadelphia graduates re-garding the squib (is this term still in use anywhere?) about degree *versus* diploma. *I have a diploma con-ferring a* degree *on me at my commencement in 1944. This by virtue of an Act of Assembly dated April 9, 1849, which provides that "The Controllers of the Public Schools of the First School District of Pennsyl-vania shall have and possess power to confer academ-ical* degrees *in the arts upon graduates of the Central High School…in the same and like power to confer* degrees…*which is now possessed by the University of Pennsylvania." The first* degrees *were conferred at the commencement of February, 1850. By my time this was not regarded as any more than an anachronism, and a conversation piece, and may by now have been discontinued.*

You are the exception that proves the rule. The last time I wrote that about anyone, by the way, I received in response the complaint that *proves* in this expression means "tests" or "verifies," not "demonstrates" or "illustrates." And so it does—and so you do.

Déjà vu

In the past few years, I have seen many reporters use the term déjà vu. *Not once, however, have I seen it used correctly. It is used to mean that one has been here before or done this before. (A recent example from* The Denver Post *reads, "Some voters may feel a sense of* deja vu *when they spot his name on the U.S. Senate ballot this fall.... The 90-year-old Heckman has unsuccessfully run for a slew of elected offices since retiring from the corporate world in the 1960s.") The reporters seem unaware of the second part of the definition: that one feels this way when one has* not *been here before or done this before. Don't these people own dictionaries?*

They probably do, but I suspect that their dictionaries are newer than yours. You are quite right about what *déjà vu* traditionally means, and what it means to psychologists. (Here's a citation from a 1941 article in the journal *Mind*: "However strong the feeling that this has all happened before, it may turn out that one is not remembering, but suffering from paramnesia, a feeling of *déjà vu*.") Regardless, dictionaries now also admit the broader sense you mention, even going as far as to let *déjà vu* mean "dull familiarity; monotony." Isn't it ironic that the expression itself has entered new territory in which it already seems all too familiar?

Denigrate

When Massachusetts Superior Court Judge Hiller Zobel released his ruling in the case of Louise Woodward [a British au pair who was tried for the killing of the baby in her charge], a fair number of eyebrows must have been raised on both sides of the Atlantic at the judge's totally incorrect use of the word denigrate. *"I do not* denigrate *Matthew Eappen's death nor his family's grief," said Judge Zobel.*

Webster defines denigrate *as "to defame, blacken someone's character." In his desire to use a fancier word than* minimize, *the judge really was in over his head.*

I think perhaps you are denigrating Judge Zobel when you call his use "totally incorrect," because recent editions of some dictionaries give the meaning "belittle" for *denigrate,* in addition to the traditional one that you cite. Nonetheless, it's surprising that there's been no hue and cry about this new use, for it parallels one that's been a staple of stern usage-guide commentary at least since Fowler's first edition. That is, we have long been cautioned not to confuse *deprecate,* which means "to express disapproval of," with *depreciate,* which means "to belittle." Lately, however, some commentators seem to have given up the fight, considering the "belittle" sense of *deprecate,* particularly with *self-* (as in "*self-deprecating* humor," for example), too firmly established to suppress. Now *denigrate,* which in its original sense is a near synonym for *deprecate* in *its* original sense, seems to be slithering down the path that *deprecate* has taken. From the *St. Louis Post-Dispatch*: "These comments are in no way intended to *denigrate* or minimize

Magic Johnson's terrible tragedy." Here, as in your example, *depreciate* or *belittle* would be better.

See also Minimal, for a discussion of *minimize.*

Deprecate, Depreciate

See Denigrate.

Devastate

See Decimate, Devastate.

Different from, Different than

A friendship of more than fifty years hinges on your expertise. One of us claims that something is different from *something else. The other claims that something is* different than *something else. We have found sources that support both views. Please solve this dilemma so that we can find something else, equally ridiculous, to argue about.*

Sticklers tend to insist that *than* is to be used with comparatives ("smart*er than* I," "*more* careful *than* she"). Nonetheless, they allow the exceptions of *else* and *other* ("what *else than* that?"; "what *other than* this?"). Tradition, which at least in language is not to be taken lightly (what else is there to teach us how to speak and write?), is the only reason why *different than* should be different from *other than*—that is, why *different than* should be frowned on.

All the same, it is frowned on by many. Sometimes observing the proprieties brings about a tortuous result, however, and then reputable writers have been known to overlook them. Consider "The word has a

meaning *different from* that which I thought it had."
Some people will have no objection to that sentence;
others will want to avoid the issue altogether with
something like "The word doesn't mean what I
thought"; and still others will cut straight to "The
word has a *different* meaning *than* I thought."

Diploma

See Degree, Diploma.

Disinterest

When Newt Gingrich declared himself determined to
restore assault weapons, Mary McGrory wrote,
"What is most fascinating is Gingrich's seeming and
total disinterest *in the effect reviving deadly weapons*
is having on his reputation.... His action says: 'You
bet I'm an extremist. Watch my dust.'" What do you
think of that?

You know and I know that *disinterest* means "a lack
of involvement," or the state that's the opposite of
being an interested party—a different kettle of fish
from being *uninterested,* or "failing to show interest
or concern." Because *uninterest,* per se, is an extremely rare word, I do sympathize with the impulse
to say or write *disinterest.* (I, too, came upon it not
long ago, in a book about the use of English abroad:
"Instead, he was met with silence. Not realizing this
was a normal Japanese custom, he interpreted it to
mean *disinterest,* even rejection.") But second—or are
we up to third?—thoughts will lead a careful user of
the language to *uninterest* or *lack of interest* or *indif-*
ference instead.

Done, Finished

During the holiday season, visiting relatives took issue with my family's use of the word done *instead of* finished *to indicate the completion of a task. For example, at dinnertime my children would announce "I'm* done*" and ask to be excused. My aunts insist that "I'm* finished*" is the appropriate phrase. Is this just a matter of taste? Is* finished *preferred only in the context of eating a meal? Aren't* done *and* finished *grammatically equivalent? Can I never be* done *with the dishes? Please help!*

Theodore M. Bernstein, in his *The Careful Writer,* published in 1965, asserted that the headline "Ecuador Rail Line *Done*" illustrated "an improper, casual use of *done,*" and at the time, his point of view was not unusual. But a slim majority of the usage panel for the first edition of *The American Heritage Dictionary,* which appeared four years later, did not object to the word even in an official-sounding context, and the current edition of the dictionary simply presents "finished" as one of the meanings of *done,* treating the matter as settled. The Boy Scouts, certainly, draw no distinction between *done* and *finished*: their lyrics for "Taps" begin, "Day is *done,* gone the sun"—and perhaps they are paraphrasing Shakespeare, who wrote, "The bright day is *done,* / And we are for the dark." Nowadays the distinction between the two words is observed more by aunts and grandmothers than by grammarians.

The inquiry about done *instead of* finished *is an interesting one, and your "Day is* done*" parallel seems to justify the virtual interchangeability of the two words.*

*But isn't there another grammatical point involved
here?*

*Seems to me that one can legitimately state that
day is* done *(or* finished*) when the message is "It's
over, gone, finito, dead." But when it comes to people,
rather than things, the correct English surely would
be not* I am done *(or* I am finished*) but, rather,* I have
finished *or, if you prefer,* I have done. *If I am done, I
am dead. Or is this just another of those forms that
are to be observed by aunts and grandmothers but not
grammarians?*

Good question. You're quite right that *done* and *finished* are not only adjectives but also verb forms, and
right, too, that the adjective *done* is being used in different senses in "Day is *done*" and "I am *done*." But
this doesn't prove that *I am done,* meaning that I have
finished something, is incorrect. *Webster's Second*
called the usage "colloquial"; *Webster's Third,* from
1961, had done with all such designations and simply
presented the usage together with a few citations, including "Will you never get *done* with that scraping."
Few commentators have objected to the like since.
Anywhere this adjective seems insufficiently elegant,
of course, you're free to say instead *I am finished* or *I
have finished* or *I am through.*

Double 0s

See Aughts.

Due to, Owing to

*When I learned my English, in England, we were
taught to use* due to *only after the verb* to be, *and*

otherwise the gerund construction owing to—*for example,* "*The delay is* due to *a cow on the line*" *and* "Owing to *the delay caused by that damned cow, I was late for dinner." I've seen the same principle enunciated in American grammar books, although few Americans seem to follow it, and some educated people here have even told me that they've never heard of* owing to. *Would you say that in America* owing to *has now capitulated to* due to?

At the restaurant where I had lunch yesterday, I read a sign: "Due to *the small size of our dining room, we are unable to provide a smoking section.*"

It's true that not even educated people necessarily hold to the rule about *due to*. Why, just the other day, in *The New York Times* I came across "Burberrys, famous for its classic trench coat..., developed coats for canines five years ago. *Due to* their popularity, the company has just introduced six new styles...." But many do observe the rule, the pure form of which is that *due* is an adjective, and must modify a noun, whereas *owing to* is a compound preposition, to be used where the sense of the entire clause is the effect or result in question. I can't argue that this rule makes any more sense than, say, the rule that one may wear white shoes only between Memorial Day and Labor Day, but it is traditional.

Your rule-of-thumb version seems like a good one, as long as people understand what's behind it and also recognize that *due* needs to follow the form of *to be* directly—that is, "I *was* late for dinner *due to* the delay caused by the cow" is no good. Correct forms would be "Our gratitude *is due to* his having gotten the cow off the line" and "We *are* grateful *owing to* his having gotten the cow off the line." You may also wish to try *because* or *because of* or other constructions anywhere that *owing to* sounds prissy: "We are grateful *because* he got the cow off the line" or "We are grateful *for* his help."

See also Thanks to.

Effect

See Affect, Effect, Impact.

Empathy, Sympathy

My flame and I are engaged in a spirited debate regarding what I claim are evolving contemporary definitions of the words empathy *and* sympathy. *Visits to my 1978 edition of* The American Heritage Dictionary *will not settle the debate; the words are defined with eerie similarity.*

I claim that empathy *is taking on a new meaning of a special class of* sympathy *that one can only offer if one is capable of experiencing the other's emotional or physical pain. For example, she cannot* empathize *with a person suffering from a migraine headache, since she has never had one. In contrast, anyone can be* sympathetic *towards anyone else; I can* sympathize *with her if her mother is ill or send a* sympathy *card if her uncle dies.*

My flame claims that I have the new meanings exactly reversed—that it is sympathy *that requires a common experience and* empathy *that does not. My only defense of my position is the notion that there are* sympathy *cards in common use (implying that anyone can be* sympathetic *with respect to or in response to anything), whereas there are no* empathy *cards—at least, not yet.*

The fact is that these two words aren't clearly distinguished. *Empathy* is a translation from German, *sympathy* a derivation from Latin, and they have settled into English on overlapping patches of conceptual territory.

Empathy tends to appear in psychological or aesthetic contexts ("the *empathy* artists have for their subjects," for example). And it is perhaps more likely than *sympathy* to be used where what is being felt for is nonhuman, or even nonliving ("*empathy* for the land," say).

Sympathy, "feeling with," is more likely to be a two-way street: think of *talking with*, as opposed to *talking to*, as an analogy, and also think of constructions like "They were in *sympathy*." But *sympathy* is broader in application than *empathy*, and may be used for almost any kind of entering into another's feelings, or understanding them.

Enamored

Which of the following uses is correct: enamored of, enamored by, *or* enamored with? *The examples given in most dictionaries use* of, *but I cannot remember ever having heard it used except as* enamored with. *C. S. Lewis used* enamored of, *but has modern usage changed?*

Nope. *Enamored of* remains standard usage. If you want to say *with*, say either *in love with* or *smitten with*. If you want to try *by*, say *smitten by*.

Enormity

In her Pulitzer Prize–winning novel The Stone Diaries, *Carol Shields writes, "Such a discovery, they had told her, would be enormous in its implications— it excited them just thinking about such* enormity— *but at the same time the proof of discovery could be held lightly in the palm of a hand, a small rock chip imprinted with the outline of a leaf."*

Has the time come to throw in the towel on William Strunk Jr.'s admonition in The Elements of Style *to use the word* enormity *only in the sense "monstrous wickedness"?*

Isn't it just like Americans to want to trade in one of very few words we have to denote real, unmitigated atrocity for yet another word that means large size? Granted, we might not have to think quite so hard about what we're saying if we could rely on the conversion processes by which *immense* became *immensity* to have done their work on *enormous* and *enormity.* But instead *enormousness* has become established, taking its place among *massiveness, spaciousness, vastness,* and so on. If we are moral people, we should strive to retain *enormity* as one of few words adequate to decry historic events on the scale of the Serbian slaughter of Albanians in Kosovo in 1999, the mid-1990s genocide in Rwanda, and Hitler's Holocaust.

Entitled, Titled

Are the words entitled *and* titled *interchangeable—as when a DJ says "This next song is* entitled *'Venus in Bluejeans'"? What do you think? Remember, we are all entitled to our opinions.*

Dictionaries will certainly tell you that the words can be used interchangeably in a sentence like your example. *Entitled* in that sense, though, strikes me as wasteful of syllables and ever so slightly pompous. I prefer to reserve the verb *title* for the titling of things and *entitle* for the more abstract idea that has to do with claims or rights.

Equivocate

See Prevaricate, Procrastinate.

Every day, Everyday

As part of my job teaching writing to first-year university students, I fight an ongoing battle against the everyday/every day *mix-up. I try to teach my students that there is a difference—but it seems that everywhere I go outside the classroom, this difference no longer exists, or is flouted shamelessly. I believe that even Toyota confuses the two in some of its television commercials. Are* everyday *and* every day *merging into one? (It's* everyday *that seems to be winning.) Can the process be stopped, or should I just surrender and concentrate on the difference between* its *and* it's?

I refuse to believe that most people can't tell an adverb or a noun from an adjective. After all, I tell them apart *every day,* and doing so is an *everyday* matter for you as well, is it not? *Every day* brings each of us new opportunities to distinguish the two forms. It's an *everyday* problem, and its difficulty will diminish if we practice solving it each and *every day.*
Whew. Your turn.

Fewer, Less

I'm sure we've all grimaced when standing in the express lane at the supermarket and reading a sign

like "Twelve items or less," *for we all know that*
"Twelve items or fewer*" is correct. But is the* less *vs.*
fewer *debate as clear-cut as that? How about the*
*phrase "*less *than 10 percent"? Wouldn't "*fewer *than*
10 percent" be as correct, or more correct?

This is a variation on the distinction between *amount*
and *number.* In the supermarket line, of course, the
point is the count, or the *number* of items in the cart.
For this purpose *fewer* is the right word. With percentages, though, what's at issue is very rarely the
number of percentage points, so ignore *percent*
and focus on whatever the percentage is of: "*less*
than 10 percent of the store's *stock*" but "*fewer* than
10 percent of all *items* in the store."

In most contexts it's not hard to decide whether
what's under consideration is an amount or a number
of things. But you're right to question whether the
distinction is always clear-cut. For example, we might
say "Employees who put in *fewer* than thirty-five
hours a week do not qualify for full benefits," reason-
ing that we really are counting hours. But "Employees
who put in *less* than thirty-five hours" can be justified, too, on the ground that the meaning is "less time
than that."

Finished

See Done, Finished.

For free

For free, for free, for free! *These words are used in-*
cessantly and don't even sound right. Is this usage
correct?

The phrase has been used often enough for it to qualify as accepted informal usage, but standard English it's not. *Free* means "for nothing," after all, not just "nothing." Once, *for free* was meant jocularly— rather the way some people use *irregardless* now. As your ear has told you, its grammar is peculiar. *Free* being an adjective or an adverb, it can't very well be the object of the preposition *for*. Dictionaries tend to call the phrase an idiom and treat it as a variant on *free* alone—which it is. Still, pity the person who has written "I wanted to get the car *free*." One can't tell whether the writer has entered a sweepstakes or called a tow truck. Here, if the sentence is about a sweepstakes, the temptation to write *for free* is great.

Fortuitous

On the Public Broadcasting System's program Washington Week in Review *not long ago, the author of a* Newsweek *cover article about Hillary Clinton said that the magazine happened to be planning to publish an excerpt from her book when the news story of Mrs. Clinton's discovered billing records broke. "It was* fortuitous *timing," the author said with a grin. There was another misuse of* fortuitous *in* The New York Times *about a week ago headlining a story, and in the story itself, about a major new scientific discovery.*

In fact *fortuitous* is not being misused in this anecdote about Hillary Clinton; the word means "happening by chance or accident," which is the idea here. It is true that over the past several decades the word has inched further from *accidental* in meaning, and closer to *lucky,* until something like "The billing records were found *fortuitously,* casting doubt on Hillary

Clinton's credibility" sounds very strange—except, no doubt, to Mrs. Clinton's detractors. What the word is still not allowed to mean is, simply, *fortunate,* this word being perfectly capable of doing its own job.

Forward

See Back, Forward, Up.

Free

The misuse of a word that bothers me most is the misuse of free *when the intended meaning is "included in the price of"—which does not mean* free.

You mean like "…*free* with purchase"? Or "Buy one, get one *free*"? I see your point, but I think your objection has more to do with sales psychology than with language per se. Advertising copywriters have had it drummed into them that *free!* sells things, whereas to my knowledge no one has ever demonstrated that *included* works nearly as well.

Could you please explain the history of using free *as a free-standing adjectival suffix? For example,* sugar free, lead free, *and* smoke free *seem to have entered our language within my lifetime, probably in the past two decades. When I was a child, I never heard these terms, and people said* sugarless *(as in gum) or* unleaded *(as in gasoline). The euphemistic* Smoke Free *seems to have replaced the simple imperative* No Smoking *(though chewing tobacco is still called* smokeless*). Likewise,* fat free *(which means there's absolutely no fat) is used in place of* lean *(meaning less fat than you're used to).*

The first coinage of this type I heard of (in a magazine article, years back, recounting a courageous public protest by German wives against government orders for the deportation of their Jewish husbands, which ultimately persuaded the regime to back down) was Goebbels's "Jew free," as in "Making Berlin Jew Free*" in time for Hitler's birthday in 1943. If this is indeed the etymological origin of the* free *suffix, shouldn't its unsavory genesis deter us from using it today in polite discourse?*

What do you say we blame the Nazis for the important things and leave them out of this? For one thing, *carefree, duty-free,* and *fancy-free* were, respectively, part of our language some one hundred, two hundred, and three hundred years before Hitler was born. For another, I don't think we need look any further than our own nation's advertising and marketing departments for an explanation of the explosion of *free*s. If you were writing an ad or deciding what words to put on new packaging, which word would you choose: *free* or *no*? The fact that *free* is often seen without the hyphen that you or I might prefer is evidence for this origin. Contrary to nature, which abhors a vacuum, advertisers and marketers abhor a hyphen and will write *sugar free* and *sodium free* and *caffeine free* without giving it a second thought. Are they *guilt free* or *guilt-free*? You decide.

See also For free.

-ful, Full

For some time a friend and I have been in disagreement over the use of joined words such as spoonfulls *and* cupfulls, *which supposedly describe a measurement (usually of recipe ingredients).*

I maintain that this usage is incorrect, since it attempts to join a legitimate word (spoon, cup) *with a nonexistent one,* fulls. *There is no such word! It must be* spoons full, cups full, *to describe the actual measurement or volume.*

Please, what is your judgment?

Full is a word and *ful* is not, but the latter is a legitimate suffix (so plurals may be added to it). A good thing, too, for any recipe calling for a "*teaspoon full of salt*" would be asking you to toss in the teaspoon along with the salt.

Fulsome

I read of "fulsome praise" *characterizing the positive reception that a fine new movie enjoyed.*

That *fulsome* means "offensively, excessively flattering; sycophantic; smarmy" appears now to be a closely held secret. Thus the word is perfect for, say, telling an unloved boss that he deserves *fulsome praise* for his latest initiative, or offering a dragon of a neighbor *fulsome apologies* for having held a noisy party.

Garner

See Cull, Garner, Glean.

Get

See Put.

Glean

See Cull, Garner, Glean.

Gravitas

Gravitas *is a word that pundits such as William Safire and William F. Buckley Jr. love to use. It's good to drive the reader to a dictionary from time to time— but shouldn't the word used be in the dictionary? What does the danged word mean?*

A direct borrowing from Latin, *gravitas* means "gravity" in the sense of solemnity or seriousness. By now it has appeared in a few English-language dictionaries, notably the *Oxford English* and *The Shorter Oxford*. You're quite right that it is unkind of authors to use unfamiliar words that leave their readers guessing. But aren't you glad that it's not only people with rings in their bellybuttons and skateboards under their toes who are giving us words for the dictionary makers to include in their next editions?

Grow

President Bill Clinton is fond of telling us he will "grow *the economy," and now other bureaucrats use the phrase. Corporate types are checking in with a "need to* grow *our business." What they mean, of course, is* expand *the economy or business. Although their usage may conform to a literal definition of* grow, *to my ear it sounds straight out of Dogpatch. What do you think?*

This isn't something that we can blame President Clinton for. *Grow* has been cropping up hither and yon for at least five hundred years. Nonetheless, having conducted a straw poll among young men who wear earrings as well as older ones in bow ties and women in stockings and pumps, I can say with confidence that your ear has plenty of company: the transitive verb in inanimate, metaphorical contexts is widely reviled. It's fine for people to *grow* roses or *grow* their hair, but they should *expand* or *strengthen* economies, businesses, and, if need be, their vocabularies.

Healthful, Healthy

Now that the Food and Drug Administration has imposed regulations concerning the use of the word healthy *in describing meat and poultry products, I suppose it spells the end of* healthful. *Apparently,* healthy *does not mean, as we might expect, that the animal was fit and disease-free prior to slaughter; it means that the food product does not exceed certain fat, sodium, or cholesterol limits per serving.* Healthful's *demise was inevitable after both Barney and Cookie Monster extolled the virtues of "healthy food" on public television. Barney, being a tyrannosaur, may have used the word in its true meaning, however, for I doubt that he would enjoy eating, say, a leprous elk.*

I myself like to observe the distinction you make, on the ground that where it is easy to denote a difference in meaning with different word forms—well, why not do it? All the same, *healthy* has been used in the sense of "conducive to good health" for some four centuries. In this it is no more protean than many other adjectives that no one complains about. Think of *happy child* and *happy hour,* or *harebrained person* and *harebrained scheme,* or *heavenly host* and *heavenly hash,* or *honest Abe* and *honest mistake.*

Home, Hone

The reporter on CNN this morning was the last straw. Standing in front of the White House discussing the recent mission to rescue a pilot in Bosnia, she said something like "They honed *in on the downed pilot's radio beacon."* Honed? *I have noticed this incorrect use of the word* hone *with increasing frequency recently. It is sort of like a squeaky hinge or having a kitten sharpen its claws on your head; at first it is only mildly annoying, but with repetition it becomes almost unbearable.*

Hone *refers to a stone used to sharpen some fine-edged object such as a razor or knife, or the act of sharpening such an object.* Home *is the word that would be correct when speaking about locating or directing something like a radio beacon.* Homed, hom-ing, homes, *verb, intransitive, "to be guided to a target..."; or* homing, *adjective, "assisting a craft home: a homing guidance system"*—The American Heritage Dictionary, 1978.

I think you've said it all.

Home, House

Whatever happened to the word house? *When I was a kid, a developer built* houses, *a realtor sold* houses, *and* home *was where you went after school. It was perfectly okay to say "I need to paint my* house *this weekend" and "That's a nice-looking* house." *I understand that realtors and developers believe that it is easier to sell a* home *than it is to sell a* house, *but why has the usage spread to ordinary folks? Somehow I find it jarring when the newspaper says that "this new construction will include 22 homes."*

Between such ideas loose in our culture as "A *house* is not a *home*" and "*Home* is where the heart is," and the need that advertisers, newspapers, and so-called shelter magazines have for a word that encompasses single-family dwellings, townhouses, co-ops, condos, apartments, and triple-deckers, it's remarkable that *house* hasn't been utterly demolished. This valuable word is under threat, though. In my newspaper not long ago appeared the information that in a small South Dakota town where a tornado had struck the day before, "only about two dozen *homes* survived, mostly along the two northernmost streets...." *Is* that trying to tell us that the count is of households, or did the writer mean *houses*? *Home* where *house* will do is imprecise. And it's a genteelism—like calling an office a *business establishment* or a man, apropos of nothing in particular, a *gentleman*.

Home town

Where I come from, home town *means where you came from, though others seem to use it to mean where you live. I live in San Diego, California; I was born in Canton, Ohio; but what I regard as my* home town *is Massillon, Ohio, where I grew up. Is* home town *a phrase whose usage varies regionally?*

Throughout America a person's *home town* (which some would write as one word) can be where he or she was born, grew up, or lives now. *Home* is indeed where the heart is.

Hone

See Home, Hone.

Honorable

See Reverend.

House

See Home, House.

-ic, -ical

Is there any rule that consistently determines the proper form of an adjective whose two possible forms end in -ic and -ical? For example, word pairs such as historic/historical, geographic/geographical, classic/classical, typic *(obsolete)*/typical, *and* exotic/exotical *(obsolete) seem less and less interchangeable. Not to mention the fact that although some people prefer* classical music *to* classic jazz, *they would never play* music chairs *in a* musical hall.

Without intending to sound whimsic *or* acerbical, *I'm certain that you can provide a* logic *rule to lessen my* tragical *ignorance. Given a choice, I'd prefer not to make this* grammar *error.*

R. W. Burchfield has researched this question exhaustively, setting forth his results in *The New Fowler's.* There is no logical rule. There are words, such as *alcoholic* and *patriotic,* for which only *-ic* will do; there are words, such as *practical* and *radical,* for which only *-ical* will do; there are words, such as *geographic* and *geographical, pedagogic* and *pedagogical,* for which either choice is possible and the difference be-

tween them is largely a matter of style; and there are
pairs of differentiated words, such as *classic* and
classical, economic and *economical,* and *historic* and
historical.

A question that you didn't quite ask but that is
raised by your examples is when to use a noun attributively, as in *music hall,* and when to use an adjective, as in *musical chairs* and *logical rule.* For this
there *is* a general rule, though the employment of it
can sometimes seem more like an art than like a science. If something possesses that quality, use the adjective; otherwise, use the noun. Thus *grammatical
error* but *grammar teacher, historical novel* but *history book, geographic knowledge* but *geography lesson, educational video* but *education degree.*

Where a choice is possible, people rarely misuse
the noun. An adjective where the noun belongs,
though, is a common mistake. For example, an advertisement I came across not long ago boasted that the
product in question "opens the whole *educational*
market to the art of sculpture." The meaning there
should be that the market is teaching someone something—it's *educational.* And a recent newspaper
article contained the sentence "There are about
50 types of businesses the city would allow, including
a bakery, bed and breakfast, brew pub, art gallery,
florist, jeweler, *musical* store..." That ought to mean
that the store would be *musical*—would be talented
or would play music or something like that.

Ice, Iced

We have a disagreement about whether to use ice *or*
iced *when describing chilled beverages such as water,*

coffee, or tea; is it iced tea *or* ice tea? *We've gone to the obvious sources, but they are ambiguous. For example, here are two dictionary entries.*

ice tea: *iced tea*

ice water: *chilled or iced water, esp. for drinking*

If they are variants, shouldn't they be labeled as such, or be cross-referenced? There is no entry for iced tea *or* iced water. *Please explain.*

As you can prove for yourself, if you like, in the wide world of World Wide Web pages, *ice* is by far the more common form when water is referred to, and *iced* is far more common when tea or coffee is referred to. Idiom for once makes a kind of sense, because ice *is* water and nothing else, whereas tea and coffee (and most other drinks served cold) will have had the different substance of ice added to them. *Ice beer* and *ice wine* are yet another case, being beverages in whose production ice has played a part.

If not

It would seem that I have a disagreement, if not a dispute, with almost everyone who writes English. For if if not *has not become writers' most cherished construction in the English language, I'm a monkey's uncle—if not a giraffe's aunt. Yet how is a reader supposed to know, confronted by that clichéd construction, whether I do or do not have a dispute with writers or consider myself a giraffe's aunt? Taken literally, I'm saying I'm* not *a giraffe's aunt; taken idiomatically, I am a giraffe's aunt—the very opposite of what the words say. And writers use it either way—even the same writer on the same page. The only possible clue to meaning in a particular instance is the context.*

A recent New York Times *"Week in Review" section illustrates the quandary.*

Example 1, where not almost surely *means "not":* "The Democrats, successfully if not *admirably, snatched the pillars of Republicanism, foreign policy, crime and cultural issues."*

Example 2, where not almost surely *means its opposite and* not *"not":* "This time a year ago, White-water seemed destined at the least to hang like a thunderhead over Mr. Clinton's 1996 campaign, if not tank his re-election altogether."

Example 3, where it's anyone's guess what not *means:* "A number of people seem to feel that pot, if not *acceptable, does not rank as a threat with co-caine, heroin or even, some argue, alcohol, and that users ought to be left alone."*

Why this infatuation with such an opaque construction?

Probably the explanation, as Theodore M. Bernstein notes in his *The Careful Writer,* is that in speech, tone readily distinguishes the *if not* that signals an intensification of meaning from the *if not* that turns meaning around. Hear it for yourself, reading "He's nice-looking, *if not* really handsome" both ways. When we write, we tend to hear our voices saying what we mean, and so it's natural enough to write *if not.* As you can attest, however, readers may not be sure what they're hearing, so a careful writer may wish to change the phrase to *even,* or *perhaps,* or *though not,* or some other unambiguous expression. It's never hard to find a substitute for either kind of *if not.*

Nonetheless, I must admit that when I suggest to authors that they change the phrase in their work, they often sputter "But it's perfectly obvious which way I mean it!" Sometimes I really can't tell which way they mean it, and still they say that. Then again, sometimes they have a point.

Impact

Today I received an e-mail message from a professor at an Ivy League university which included the following: "This impacts on *when it began to influence political ideas.... The question of when it began to* impact on *political thought can be studied through the three other texts that it clearly did influence...."*

I object to the use of impact *as a verb to mean "affect," and the redundant* on *strikes me as a sign that the writer recognizes, perhaps despite himself, that* impact *isn't the right word for the job here. I never use* impact *in this way, and I tell my students not to. But language changes, and this usage seems to have won acceptance among many college professors and journalists. I'm beginning to wonder whether we anti-impacters have already lost the battle and* impact *as a verb is here to stay.*

Do you think we should keep resisting the impact of impact*? Or is this verb now a legitimate choice even in contexts that haven't anything to do with physical objects crashing into each other?*

Resist, resist! Eighty-four percent of the usage panel of the current, third edition of *The American Heritage Dictionary* "disapproves of the construction *to impact on* ... and fully 95 percent disapproves of the use of *impact* as a transitive verb" meaning "affect," according to a note in the dictionary. It continues, "But even these figures do not reflect the degree of distaste with which critics view the usage...." In the oldest extant use of the verb, it means something like *pack* or *wedge*, but it may also properly appear, as you note, in contexts relating to physical collisions ("Meteorites often *impact* the moon").

I was struck by your final sentence in the impact *discussion. We astronomers tell our students to distinguish among three terms:* meteor, meteoroid, *and* meteorite. *A* meteor *is the luminous atmospheric phenomenon produced when a* meteoroid *enters the earth's atmosphere. A* meteoroid *is a small object in orbit about the sun; its entry into the atmosphere produces a* meteor. *A* meteorite *is what's left of the* meteoroid *after part of it has been ablated during passage through the atmosphere at high speed. As the petrographic* -ite *suffix indicates, it's the piece of rock (or other material) found on the earth. Thus I don't feel it's correct to say, as you did, that "meteorites* often *impact the moon." It seems to me that what strikes the moon is a* meteoroid, *not a* meteorite; *if anything is left of it* after *the impact, that would be the* meteorite. *Perhaps this discussion will have an impact on some future column of yours.*

I didn't know. Thanks!

Include

I have always understood the verb include *to refer to a number of items that make up a portion of a larger whole, as in "The alphabet contains twenty-six letters, including A, B, and Z." I constantly hear and read it used in a contrary sense, as designating a com-*

plete *listing of the items that make up a whole, as in "The alphabet contains twenty-six letters, including A through Z." This drives me crazy. Am I fighting a losing battle? Can I include you in my list of allies?*

You bet. And yet we mustn't carry this too far: "His friends *include* some absolute lunatics, and some perfectly nice people, too," for example, is not incorrect, nor does it necessarily imply that the fellow has still other friends, who don't fall into either category. The word can be legitimately used in a way that leaves what is or isn't *included* a bit vague.

Incredible

The word incredible *has become an all-purpose adjective that has been vacated of any substance. I guess it is used merely to add emphasis, but in the process the word has been damaged.* High *or* low, fast *or* slow, good *or* evil, tasty *or* awful, mean *or* generous—*all these and a thousand more adjectives are now simply collapsed into* incredible. *The nadir of this usage occurred recently when some babbling idiot on the radio stated that "This is the most* incredibly *believable movie I have ever seen!" Here is the utter demolition of rational discourse.*

Read on, please.

A recent Atlantic *contained a subscription appeal with this statement: "Subscribe to* The Atlantic Monthly *at* incredible *savings."*
   Does this mean what I think it says? My understanding of the word incredible, *as noted in* Webster's

International Dictionary, *is "surpassing belief: too extraordinary and improbable to admit of belief."*

Does this mean that I can't know in advance what the actual price will be and I'm to disregard the prices listed on the card?

On the one hand, I do take your point. On the other hand, you didn't believe the pitch for a minute, did you? So it *is* incredible—literally.

In line, On line

Mine is not a language dispute so much as it is a dilemma. In three score and nine years I have always stood in line. *This initially followed the order to "fall in" during World War II and continued during the Korean and Vietnam conflicts. Now I am confronted with a generation or two who stand* on line. *Are they doing the same thing in the checkout at the A&P/ Pathmark/Giant/Publix/Safeway/Vons as I am? If they are, please provide guidance on this matter and the benchmark event that moved me from* in *to* on—*and please don't tell me Bill Gates did it.*

No, Bill Gates didn't. He's from out west, and according to the *Dictionary of American Regional English, on line* in the sense of standing, um, *in* line is primarily a New York City–area regionalism. Maybe even New Yorkers will stop using it now that *online* means "hooked up by computer." Then again, there are *in-line* skates.

Intensive purposes, Intents and purposes

For years it has bothered me when someone says "for all intensive purposes." *I always thought it should be stated "for all* intents and purposes." *After a few conversations and some conflicting opinions, I need an authority's final word. Which is it?*

It's "for [or 'to'] all *intents and purposes.*"

Investigable, Investigatable

I work in a government office charged with the investigation of child-abuse allegations, which we receive mostly by telephone. Before we may begin our investigation, we must first determine if the allegations contain sufficient substance to be investigated.

Here's our problem. If these allegations meet certain criteria, are they considered investigable *or* investigatable? *I opt for the former, believing it follows grammatical practice:* educate, educable; *calculate,* calculable; *etc. Others, with no argument to support them, simply use* investigatable *(or is that* investigateable)?

Please investigate this situation and advise me.

Abominate, abominable; administrate, administrable; alienate, alienable; allocate, allocable; appreciate, appreciable—as Burchfield not only points out in *The New Fowler's* but demonstrates with a "reasonably full list of words in *-able*" (from which the examples above have been plucked), verbs of more than two syllables ending in *-ate* tend to lose this ending when *-able* is added to them. Neither *investigable* nor *investigatable* is on the list, but that's all right. Burchfield writes, "The suffix *-able* is a living one, and may be appended to any transitive verb to make an adjective...."

Irresponsible

I have been using, with my family, friends, and employees, the following sense of the word irresponsible:
When there is a problem or a mess, I ask, "Who is irresponsible *for this?" This sense of the word is not in* The Shorter Oxford Dictionary.
Did I invent this usage?

Yes, I think you can fairly claim...would it be *responsibility?*

Late

I have asked this question of friends both savvy and otherwise, and have received nothing but puzzled looks in reply: For how long after a person's death is he or she referred to in speech and print as the late ——— ? In the past several months I've heard Richard Nixon called "the late President Nixon" and John Fitzgerald Kennedy called "the late President Kennedy."

I can even show you references to "*the late* George Washington": "the sort of observance normally set aside to commemorate the birth dates of *the late* George Washington, Abraham Lincoln, and Martin Luther King, Jr." *(American Spectator)* and "belatedly paying Alaska's respects to *the late* George Washington" *(Washington Post)*.
Late serves two purposes. It can be a mark of respect. Thus "*the late* George Washington" and "*the late* Diana, Princess of Wales" are plausible, whereas "*the late* Genghis Khan" and "*the late* Eva Braun" sound ironic, do they not?
Late is also used where people are likely to need a

little nudge to recall that the person in question has died. Where context, or simply people's pre-existing mental furnishings, can be relied on to provide the information, there's no need for the word; that's why you'll rarely see it in an obituary. I can, though, imagine situations in which "*the late* George Washington" would be apropos from this point of view as well as from the other. Here's one: "In 1800 the reputation of *the late* George Washington was..." Even if we can all be expected to know that Washington is long gone, we might be grateful for a hint about how early he left.

Lead, Led

I see lead *used in place of* led *to indicate the past tense of that verb in an increasing number of references. I thought the first few instances were typos, but I've now seen it enough to be convinced it's intentional. Have I missed something lately or are these writers confusing the conjugation of* lead *with* read?

People bump into me on the sidewalk pretty often, but even so, I don't think it's intentional. The present-tense spelling *lead* for the past-tense *led* is nothing more than a very easy mistake to make, given that the metal is pronounced like the past-tense verb but spelled like the present-tense one, given the false analogy with the verb *read,* which you note, and given that the common words *bread, dead,* and *head* are miscues as well.

Lectern, Podium

You'll love this. I was working in my college's media center last night and there was an order for a podium microphone. So I went to set it up. When I got there,

what I found was not a podium *but a* lectern. Lecterns *don't have mike stands.* Podiums *do. There was
obviously some confusion when the order was placed.
The person in charge clearly doesn't know the difference between a* lectern *and a* podium. *Good thing
I do.*

If you were hoping that the person in charge would
go look up *podium* in a dictionary and straighten
himself or herself out about the word, too bad: most
contemporary American dictionaries will tell you that
one of the things a *lectern* might be is a *podium.* And
yet anyone who reflects on *podium* together with *po-
diatry* will understand immediately how much more
fitting it is that *podium* should refer to the platform
on which a speaker or conductor stands. This is certainly the traditional meaning. The *lectern,* of course,
is the stand on which the speaker rests *lecture* notes
or the like.

   Now just one source of confusion remains: What
do you mean "*Lecterns* don't have mike stands. *Podiums* do"? How can that be?

Led

See Lead, Led.

Less

See Fewer, Less.

Liaison

We just printed something with the word liaison *(our
own business cards, no less). Unfortunately, we
spelled* liaison *"liason." Now we are desperately*

looking for a source to justify our mistake. We looked
in dictionaries, and none of them has such an entry.
You are our last hope. I hope you can help us—other-
wise, we will have to reprint at great expense. By the
way, most people we asked spell it the way we do, so
if we are forced to write it correctly people may think
we made a mistake. Catch-22!

I can show you *Lias* in my unabridged dictionary, and
Liassic, but both words have to do with a division of
the Jurassic period—probably not the image you want
to convey. Alas, no *liason.* Hold your head high. It's
not every day that others can both learn from a person's mistake, as they can in reading this, and learn
from that person's newfound knowledge—as they'll
be able to on the new cards you need.

Like

See As, Like.

Likely

It may be that Funk, Wagnalls, and their cronies think
that likely *is an adverb, but isn't it true that it was*
originally sent to earth on the wings of the little word-
angels as an adjective?
    Exhibit A: "The President will likely *announce his*
plan later today." Isn't it true that that sentence—
well, maybe it doesn't stink, but it has a definite odor?
I'm convinced that likely *was pressed into service as*
an adverb by some harried editor who couldn't re-
member how to spell probably *or, worse, some tele-*
caster for whom probably *did not fall trippingly from*
the tongue.

The little idiosyncrasy of *likely* is that by tradition it may serve as an adverb if it is preceded by a modifier, such as *very* or *most* or *quite*. Or, as you know, it is always welcome as an adjective. Thus both "The President will *very likely* announce his plan later today" and "The President is *likely* to announce his plan later today" are unobjectionable. By now the stricture about the adverb may seem Anglophilic; rarely among educated speakers in England will one hear an unmodified adverbial *likely*, though it has become common in the United States. However, since we already have the two versions given above plus "The President will *probably* announce his plan later today" plus *is apt to, is expected to, perhaps, no doubt, may well*, and so on, to convey a number of other possible shades of meaning, I'm not sure we have any reason to stake our own claim to the unmodified adverbial *likely*.

Literally

I saw this sentence in a local newspaper today, in an article about a football player: "Against the Vols' four toughest opponents...Manning literally *performed surgery on some of the conference's best defenses." And in a piece by Daniel Patrick Moynihan in* The New York Review of Books: *"On the minority side an enormous fuss is now being made over adding a little extra child care, some odd bits of child nutrition aid, perhaps a little foster care:* literally *arranging flowers on the coffin of the provision for children in the Social Security Act." I have noticed such usages of the word* literally *many times in the past few years—that is, as a term of emphasis. What is your feeling about the correctness of this usage? What might serve as an alternative—one that preserves the original meaning of* literally *yet at the same time allows writers to convey the emphasis they evidently so desire?*

The figurative use of *literally* is like the common cold: widespread and evidently incurable. Certainly it's objectionable. For one thing, the whole idea is self-contradictory. For another, the results are often unintentionally so funny that the speaker or writer might as well have slipped on a banana peel—and few people think it's good form to do that.

Bless you, though, for recognizing that people who misuse the word have some goal in mind other than to make themselves ridiculous. The best alternative to misusing *literally* tends to be, simply, to leave it out and let one's figure of speech do its job. If one doesn't trust that figure of speech to make the point, then the figure is the problem, and weighing it down with *literally* isn't going to help.

The author of the letter about literally *expressed a desire for another word that might be used for emphasis. My suggestion would be to use* virtually *as a replacement.* Virtually *has a spoken and written feeling that is similar to that of* literally, *but it also has a semantic benefit—it is intentionally ambiguous and vague. Although this word, too, can be abused, it does satisfy the need for emphasis while removing the conflicting message. Since* virtually *carries the implication of "nearly" or "in effect," it can be used without fear of contradiction, yet it is strong enough to imply something very close to literality. It is not a perfect solution, but it's virtually perfect.*

I agree with you that *virtually* means roughly what abusers of *literally* want to say. But if you'll look back at the example sentences in the original letter, I suspect you'll agree with me that *virtually* would not serve any purpose but would only weaken the writing.

Masterful, Masterly

Confusion reigns whenever I have to decide whether to use masterful *or* masterly. *Can you help me master the difference?*

If you want everyone to approve of your word usage, you will use *masterful* only in a derogatory sense, to mean "domineering, overbearing." And you'll use *masterly* in the approving sense, to mean "showing the skill of a master."

Please note that you will see others using *masterful* as a synonym for *masterly.* The word is established in that sense, too. However, some punctilious people argue, reasonably enough, that if we could insist on a distinction between the two words, this would be useful, for then we'd be able to tell an insult from a compliment.

Mediate

The Word Court column, in its first appearance in The Atlantic Monthly, *contained a glaring misuse of language. You said, "Have you recently had a dispute about language which you would like this column to* mediate?*"—but you are not mediating! As a professional mediator and a graduate student in conflict resolution, I very nearly became apoplectic when I read that sentence.*

Mediators *help disputants reach their own mutually agreeable resolution without taking sides or making the decisions for them. Since you don't necessarily have anything to do with the other side in these language disputes, and since you have established yourself as a court and as the authoritative decision-maker, there is no way you can* mediate. *By the way, you are likewise not an* arbitrator. Arbitration *also requires the voluntary submission of both sides.*

I could show you dictionary definitions that leave me looking more punctilious than your letter does. Let me instead concede your point. It's your field, after all. And supposing I did disagree with you, whom could we possibly ask to settle the argument?

Meteor, Meteorite, Meteoroid

See Impact.

Minimal

I write concerning the use of minimal *to mean "small" rather than "as small as possible." I regret the loss of precision and the frequent introduction of ambiguity.*

Good point. We mustn't, though, let ourselves be pedantic about how small the smallest amount possible is. A diet, say, that contains "only a *minimal* amount of fat" needn't be fat-free; it may well call for as little fat as people will find tolerable.

While we're at it, the same goes for *minimize.* This verb means "make as small as possible," not simply "reduce." Therefore, modifying it with the likes of *considerably* and *substantially,* as is sometimes done, is illogical.

Mirror image

I have for some time noticed a double meaning for the expression mirror image. *At last, there is someone, somewhere, to clear up such an important matter.*

The most common usage appears to be declaring something to be an exact replica of some identified object or concept. Mirrors, after all, faithfully reproduce the content of whatever reflects in them. However, the expression is also used to indicate the opposite or reverse of the identified object or expression, probably on the basis that the image appearing in the mirror is reversed left-right.

A *mirror image* is supposed to be reversed left and right. The problem, I suspect, is that there is no equally emphatic but conversational way of saying "exact, unreversed image." *Just like* and similar phrases lack force, and *the very picture* and such phrases will tend to come across as prissy. What is perhaps the traditional expression—*spit and image* or *spitting image*—strikes many people as crude, and so they rifle their mental file cabinets until they come up with *mirror image* instead. Maybe that's the procedure that this writer for *Entertainment Weekly* followed: "The megalomaniacal producer characters in all those Depression-era musicals were *mirror images* of the thugs in gangster pictures, identical expressions of the same economic imperative to 'make it' or die...." An additional drawback to *spit and image* (it is the original, and *spitting image* the imitator) is that it's hopeless in the plural: *spit and images* or *spits and images*? Never mind which version is correct—both sound ridiculous. I think I would have wanted to write " ...were *identical* to the thugs in gangster pictures, expressions of the same..."

Moment, Moments

Is there any valid explanation for using the word moment *in the plural? The dictionary says a* moment *is "an indefinite short period of time." None of its eight other definitions recognizes the use of the word in the plural. When a person reads "Moments later shots were fired," he is justified in asking, How many moments later? and How long was each of these moments? A moment* can be fifteen seconds or a minute *and thirty-seven seconds or whatever you want to make it. Using* moments *this way seems plain, ordinary stupid. To me, it doesn't make any sense at all. I respectfully request a judicial opinion.*

Let's begin by considering anew whether your dictionary "recognizes the use of the word in the plural." If in the entry for *moment,* after the *"n,"* for noun, there isn't an *"-s,"* to show you the plural, then somewhere in the dictionary's front matter, I promise, appears the explanation that nouns are presumed to have plurals, and these are presumed to be formed by adding *s,* unless otherwise specified.

So *moments* exists. Is it utterly useless? Not according to whoever translated a sentence by the French littérateur Colette as follows: "There is no need to waste pity on young girls who are having their *moments* of disillusionment, for in another *moment* they will recover their illusion." That makes the point nicely, don't you think? *A few moments* is two or three moments longer than *a moment.*

Momentarily, Momently

I quite frequently get into arguments with friends over the use of the word momentarily, *which many use to mean both "for a moment" and "in a moment." The former is correct, but I was always taught (and still maintain) that* momently *should be used in the latter case. I know that Fowler agrees with me; what are your thoughts on the matter?*

It's quite true that *momentarily* is not supposed to be used to mean "in a moment," and the fact that a majority of the usage panel for the current edition of *The American Heritage Dictionary* objects when it is used that way suggests that this is no fussy, outmoded prohibition but contemporary higher English.

There is, unfortunately, no consensus that *momently* fills the gap. This word started out, more than three hundred years ago, meaning "from moment to moment," and since then has been used to mean that, and "for a moment," and, yes, "in a moment"— which is to say, practically everything that has to do with moments. It has never been used to mean any of these things very much, however, and will no doubt strike some as an affectation. Not long ago I was discussing this issue with a young woman who was brought up on British English and hears the "in a moment" kind of *momentarily* as a solecism—but when I explained that there were people who wanted to use *momently* instead, she burst out laughing.

For some reason, people tend to prefer expressing concepts with single words, but it's worth remembering that doing so is not always the most economical choice. At least, if we rule out *momently,* on grounds of artificiality and ambiguity, then *in a moment* is the briefest way to express the idea, it being one syllable shorter than *momentarily.*

Moot, Mute

I recently wrote a letter in which I used the phrase mute point. *My intention was to use it to describe something that was self-evident and did not require discussion. However, my wife corrected me, indicating that* moot point *was what I meant to say. Not taking correction from my wife lightly, I looked up* moot *in Webster's and found that the definition was "subject to argument or discussion: debatable." Mute, on the other hand, was defined as "not pronounced: silent." Thus it seemed to me that* mute *was more appropriate to my meaning than* moot.

I have checked this out with a couple of attorney friends, who were surprised by the definition of moot, *as they regularly use it for the meaning I intended. One of my former English teachers says that he explains the apparent contradiction by assuming that* moot *means "so debatable that there is nothing more to say on the question." I am now so perplexed that I am mute on the subject. Can you clear this up?*

The common expression is *moot point.* It seems to have derived from technical legal usage, in which the adjective *moot* has to do with a matter that is of no practical legal significance, such as the interpretation of an old law after a new law, superseding it, has been passed. In other contexts the idea has been extended, so that the word *moot* often means nothing more precise than "irrelevant." This usage isn't what I call higher English, and a word that in general contexts has long meant "debatable," as you note, certainly loses some force of precision when the additional meaning of "not worthy of debate" is heaped upon it. But that's where things stand.

More

What disturbs me greatly is the misuse of the comparative. Speakers, people on TV, and people who should know better say "He is more lucky *than I am" and "She is* more thin *now." It should be "He is* luckier *than I am" and "She is* thinner *now."*

The comparative of adjectives should usually include -ier *or* -er: lucky, luckier, luckiest; thin, thinner, thinnest.

Some, more, *and* most *generally are used with adverbs, as in "He is* more aware," "He is more fully aware," *and "She talked* more forcefully *this time."*

The distinction between adjectives and adverbs isn't the right one here, because a number of adjectives, including the great majority of those with three or more syllables, lack inflected comparative and superlative forms (I mean they lack *-er* and *-est* forms). Think of *more fortunate* and *more fortuitous* and *most macilent* (this last is a ten-dollar version of your example *thinnest*). A number of adverbs, however, particularly short ones, do have them. Here I won't improvise on the theme of your examples, because *aware* is actually another adjective. But think of "Run *faster!*" and "Work *smarter*, not *harder!*"

You're right, nonetheless, that comparatives are often cruelly abused. The abuse reflects poorly on those inflicting it—as abuse always does. Before we set a *more* or *most* in front of any adjective or adverb, it's worth asking ourselves whether an *-er* or an *-est* form of the word exists. Our ears know. If such a form does exist, we will seem both cleverer and more fully aware if we use it.

Move back, Move forward, Move up

See Back, Forward, Up.

Much

See Thanks much, Thank you much.

Mute

See Moot, Mute.

Myriad

When, if ever, is the preposition of *supposed to follow the word* myriad? *In the middle 1930s my high school English teacher criticized a composition of mine and gave it an A– instead of a straight A because I had left out that preposition in a sentence. I had written something like, "The civil war in Spain is giving me* myriad *troubled dreams."*

Since then, I have noticed myriad *being used both ways by equally grammatically correct writers. Is there one correct usage? As a septuagenarian, I think it is time to forget my concern. However, I could use your help, because I write for publication quite often, and using the word makes me nervous.*

I think you deserve an A retroactively—or maybe even an A+, considering all the grade inflation that has occurred in the decades since the 1930s. *Myriad* is both an adjective and a noun, and so the likes of "*myriad* dreams" (adjective) and "a *myriad* of dreams" (noun) are both correct.

Myself

I am befuddled by what seems to me to be a fairly recent and large increase in frequency of use of myself *in locutions in which* me *(or* my*) would do as well or better. For example, an airline employee at a gate said, "...and just hand your tickets to* myself.*" An airline pilot announced, "On behalf of* myself, *I want to thank you..." A TV newsperson recently said, "This is just between* myself *and him." I could go on. What advice do you have?*

Before any *myself,* or any other *-self* compound, comes out of our mouths, or our fingers write or type one, it's always worth asking ourselves whether a *-self*less form wouldn't be more natural. "Just hand your tickets to *me*" certainly passes that test. So does "This is just between *us*"; and even "This is just between *me* and him"—or, better, "...him and *me*"—should pass it, if our sense of such things hasn't been corrupted by hearing the incorrect "between you and I" once too often. (For more on this, see Chapter Three, No. 2, "Case of personal pronouns.")

"On behalf of *myself*" can't be corrected in the same way, for "on behalf of *me*" actually sounds worse. If the pilot had said "on *my own* behalf," he, or she, might have noticed that the whole phrase was a bit foolish and it would be better left off: people thanking others are presumed to be doing it on their own behalf, and it's only when they're doing the thanking on behalf of, say, their employers that any such thing needs to be specified. But we can't expect a

busy pilot to have the same consciousness of language
as a professional editor.

Well, a professional editor would tell you that a
-self compound may properly be added to an ordinary
pronoun for emphasis; *I myself,* for example, am an
editor and am telling you that. Or it may be reflexive—that is, used when the *thought* circles back on *itself.* In other circumstances, it is a genteelism—and
that's not a compliment.

See also the entry for "-self" in the "Double or
Nothing" section of Chapter Five.

Nauseated, Nauseous

*Am I justified in becoming annoyed at the frequent
use of the word* nauseous *when apparently* nauseated
*is intended? One sometimes hears on the radio news,
for instance, someone say, "The escaping gas made
me* nauseous." *I understand (and my dictionary seems
to agree) that* nauseous *means, roughly, "disgusting"
whereas* nauseated *means "sick to one's stomach." I
am surprised that anyone would admit publicly that
he or she considers himself or herself* nauseous.

It's satisfying to know the little distinction between
nauseous and *nauseated* (which is almost exactly like
the one between *sickening* and *sickened*), but bad
form to point it out to anyone who doesn't know it—
say, a person who has just misused *nauseous.* So the
misuse has become widespread, some dictionaries
now accept the new sense of the word, and I don't
know what there is to do about it. Feeling superior to
others isn't, ultimately, very pleasurable, but I admit I
do enjoy a cruel little frisson when I hear people

unwittingly describe themselves as disgusting and politeness forbids me to contradict them.

Near miss

Would you please discuss near miss *to describe the non-collision of planes or other objects?* Near hit *or* close call *would be accurate, because there was, after all, a miss.*

Dictionaries now tend to give *near miss* an entry of its own, because the meaning of the expression is indeed not apparent from the meanings of its component words. It's in there all the same: *near* means not only "almost a," as in *near replica,* but also "a particularly intimate kind of," as in *near relative.* The latter, less common sense of the word is the one that pertains in *near miss.*

Need

It seems to me that people commonly use the verb need *in peculiar ways. One often hears statements such as "A program* needs *to be started for that," instead of "We* need *to start a program for that."*

Such a construction essentially transfers the condition of needing, in this case from us to the program. The program needs nothing—rather, it is we who need the program. For that matter, is it even possible for something not yet existing to need anything, including its own creation?

Similarly bizarre are statements such as "Teenage pregnancy needs *to be stopped now." Here one is faced with the irony of an entity necessitating its own demise.*

Strange to say, the subject of the verb *need* need not be who or what is actually feeling a need for something; the relationship between the word and the concept of necessity is looser than that. This is not a peculiarity of *need* alone: think of "These projections *assume* that the program will be started," "Teenage pregnancy *suggests* that a larger cultural problem exists," and even "One good turn *deserves* another."

It so happens that *need,* an ancient word, does have a special property. Not only can it be a main verb, as it is in your examples, but in negative and interrogative constructions, like my phrase "*need* not be," above, it can also be an auxiliary—like *should* or *must.* Now, with the sentence "The program *should* be funded immediately," the question Who says it should? never arises. Similarly, in "The program *need* not be started," the question of whose need it is needn't come up. Equivalent to that sentence, and probably a commoner way to put it these days, is "The program doesn't *need* to be started"—and there you are.

New Year's Eve

My wife and I were married on December 31, 1986. Were we married on New Year's Eve 1986 or 1987? Having endured yet another of "Dick Clark's New Year's Rockin' Eve" extravaganzas, I think I ought at least to know the truth.

In *New Year's Eve, New Year's* is just a modifier; *Eve* is the operative word. You were married on *New Year's Eve* of 1986.

Here's another question for you, which I bring up because I often see this phrase misused: When you celebrated your anniversary at the *turn of the century,* was that the *turn of the twentieth century* or the *turn of the twenty-first*?

Actually, neither. The phrase, which is comparable to *turn of the tide,* has to do with one century rolling over into the next. Thus the event was simply the *latest turn of the century,* and the one that occurred when the nineteenth century rolled over into the twentieth was the *previous turn of the century* or some such.

Well might you also wonder whether the new century, and the new millennium, began in 2000, the day after your thirteenth anniversary, or—on the eminently logical theory that the Year One of any millennium or century should be a year ending in *1*—will begin in 2001, after your fourteenth. The popular answer is the former; the precisian's answer is the latter; and I would bet that the general question will never be resolved but will blossom as regularly as a century plant does in myth—every hundred years.

Next

I am puzzled by the different ways that people use the word next. *For example, I am writing this note on Wednesday. In my mind,* next Tuesday *is six days away and* next Thursday *is eight days away. To my wife,* next Thursday *is tomorrow, which, she forces me to concede, is indeed the* next Thursday. *This has caused us several mishaps in planning for social events: most inviters use* next *in the same manner that I do. Are we alone in this confusion?*

No, you're not. In *next* I think I detect the handiwork of the same folks who decided that Sunday should be not only the *first* day of the week but also half of the week*end*. Your understanding of *next Thursday* is the usual one, the *next* in the phrase typically referring to next week. Never, not even on Wednesday, is *next Thursday* tomorrow. Ordinarily a week does begin on Sunday, or thereabouts, so on Friday *next Thursday* is six days away, not thirteen (as you know). And on Sunday or Monday—well, maybe we shouldn't speak of *next Thursday* on either of those days, except with heavy emphasis on *next*. Otherwise, we'll get ourselves into something like this: "See you *next Thursday*!" "Oh, I thought we were getting together a week from Thursday." "That's what I mean." "But you said..."

Not...but

I keep bumping into constructions like "He treats not the sick but the well" in which the writers have inserted commas before the not *or before the* but, *or both. My intuition tells me that they are attempting to make a parenthetical remark out of a construction that will not accept it. But aren't they really just separating the grammatical object from the verb?*

Yes, indeed. A pair of commas around a phrase often amounts to a detour sign, indicating that the main line of the sentence will resume on the other side of the phrase. But if one sets off "*not* the sick" with commas, then the main line of the sentence reads "He treats *but* the well"—a bit of a garble. Worse still is the lone comma either before or after a *not* phrase. This causes not just an ill-conceived detour but a derailment, for the reader is pushed off the track and never shown where to pick it up again.

Not and *but* sometimes turn up together in constructions different from the one in your example, and then a comma may be wanted. For example, "His bedside manner was *not* all it could have been, *but* at least he rarely lost his patients."

Number

See Amount, Number.

Officious

For a number of years I used the word officious *incorrectly. For example, I might have described a waiter as* officious *who was haughty, uncooperative, a martinet, inflexibly sticking to established policies, lacking in eros, and flaunting his power, instead of meaning that he was hoveringly oversolicitous and too much "in your face," which is the correct usage.*

I forget when it was that I learned the correct usage, but since that time I've heard many people use it the way I formerly used it. In fact, I've seen it in print several times, most recently in James Michener's Mexico, *where it was clearly meant to describe behavior in which someone relied on the power of his office to justify an obnoxiously uncooperative manner.*

Have you been monitoring this adjective?

It seems I don't need to. You've been doing the job wonderfully well.

Ohs

See Aughts.

One

I am writing to find out the correct connection between the word one *used as a neutral pronoun and their, he/she, or he and she. In other words, is it proper to say "One can enjoy the sound, rhythm, and beat of a band, but they can completely miss what the band is saying in their lyrics"?*

No, it's not. As a reference to an unspecified person, the pronoun *one* doesn't connect to other pronouns; it may not be an antecedent at all. Thus one must keep in mind one's possible lack of patience with one's need to keep repeating *one* in some constructions, and plan accordingly.

On line

See In line, On line.

Only

I have a question about only. *I feel that it should modify only the phrase (or clause or word) of the sentence which is intended to be limited or intensified. But increasingly* only *is being extended to include the verb that precedes that phrase.*

A simple example: "He only plays to win." This implies that all he does is play. But the intended meaning of the sentence is that when he does play, he has the intention of winning.

I say that such placement modifies the verb, thereby distorting the meaning of the sentence. Am I right, or am I simply an antique gentleman out of touch with the world of today?

Compared with the debate on this question, you're a young fellow—it has been going on for some two hundred years. Certainly, we can employ an easy, almost automatic process (asking ourselves, Is the idea "*only* plays" or "*only* to win"?) to determine what we intend to qualify and then place *only* just before that element. And yet it's on exactly this point that we find Fowler railing against "pedants" who for no good reason "are turning English into an exact science or an automatic machine."

Fowler recognizes that a misplaced *only* can sow confusion, and demonstrates the problem with the citation "Mackenzie *only* seems to go wrong when he lets in yellow; and yellow seems to be still the standing difficulty of the colour printer." But he also points out that "heterodox" early placement of the word can sometimes steer the reader right both more artfully and sooner than "orthodox" placement would do. Consider this example he gives of a pedantically correct sentence: "It would be safe to prophesy success to this heroic enterprise *only* if reward and merit always corresponded." The way most people would naturally say this is "It would *only* be safe to prophesy..." What's more, the more natural version serves timely notice, as the original fails to, that the writer really has in mind that under certain conditions it would *not* be safe to prophesy success. Note, too, that *only* can sometimes follow the word it modifies, as in Fowler's citation "The address to be written on this side *only*"—so it's not as if there were always and only one proper placement.

What there is to argue about has hardly changed since Fowler's day. Good writers continue to place

their *only*s variously, and there can be little objection
if they do it thoughtfully, avoiding sentences like the
one about Mackenzie, above, in which the word is
truly misleading. I don't believe "He *only* plays to
win" is in that league.

Or

See And, But, Or.

Oral, Verbal

News reports sometimes refer to verbal *agreements in
contexts suggesting that the reporters mean* oral *agreements rather than written ones. It would seem that the
word* verbal *could refer to either a written or an oral
agreement, and my old (1958* Webster's Collegiate*)
dictionary seems to say that this was once the accepted
distinction, but it gives the following as meaning No.
2: "Expressed in words, whether written or spoken,
but commonly in spoken words; hence, by confusion,
spoken; oral; not written, as a* verbal *contract." It
seems a shame to lose the distinction between* verbal
and oral. *Has this battle been lost? (Do attorneys really refer to* verbal *contracts when they mean* oral?*)
Do you have any hypotheses about why people turned
to* verbal *when* oral *made more sense? Are people perhaps squeamish about using the word* oral?

Let me introduce you to another of my correspondents, who as he listened to unfolding news reports
not long ago got an idea about how people's understanding of these two words might be modified. I
think you'll find it, um, suggestive.

With all the talk and print there has been about President Clinton and Monica Lewinsky, perhaps verbal *now has an opportunity to be clearly distinguished in at least one particular context. Ms. Lewinsky testified that President Clinton engaged in oral sex with her as well as dirty talk over the telephone. I don't think I need to go into an explanation of what* oral sex *is, but talking dirty over the telephone might be termed* verbal sex *to avoid possible confusion with it.*

Thanks, you two, for making it clear what the issues are. In a few set phrases, such as *verbal agreement* and, yes, *verbal contract, verbal* is generally understood to refer to the spoken word. But anyone using an original turn of phrase who wants to be precise on that point will do well to stick with *oral*.

Ouster

A strange spat I had with my wife occurred while reading a newspaper headline that contained the word ouster. *Would you please explain the correct usage of this word.*

The verb *oust*, of course, refers to ejecting or forcing out—not, generally, in senses like getting the toothpaste out of the tube but as in getting rid of a dictator. The tricky part is that *-er* ending, which isn't the ordinary suffix, meaning "one who" or "the agent of"; rather, it's the tag end of an Anglo-French infinitive. The word means either the act of ousting or the state of being ousted. Because that *-er* is tricky, though, some dictionaries allow the word to mean "one who ousts" as well.

Owing to

See Due to, Owing to.

Parlay, Parley

Quoting from The Atlantic Monthly: *"——— has
passed up every opportunity to* parley *his award…"
Should not the word be* parlay?

My Webster's Dictionary *defines* parley *as "to
have a conference or discussion, esp. with an enemy,"
etc.* Parlay, *on the other hand, is defined as "to exploit
an asset successfully."*

How about that?

I've checked into this for you. The real story, the author of the article tells me, is that the man he was
writing about refused to garnish his award with sprigs
of a fluffy green herb; the correct word would have
been *parsley.*

Just kidding. You're so right. The relevant color is
not herb green but face red. Thanks!

People, Persons

I had written you about the use of persons *instead of*
people *as the plural of* person. *You kindly wrote back,
requesting a specific example. I enclose two encountered at random last week.*

*(1) "Summary Notice of Pendency of Class Ac-
tion—To: All* persons *throughout the United States
and its territories who suffered damages as a result of
the inhalation of albuterol sulfate…*

Class Definition: The persons *included within the
class in this action are all* persons *throughout the*

United States and its territories who suffered damages
as a result of...”

(2) “This membership gain is important because it
results from a net gain in increases over decreases—
that is, there are more persons *being baptized, re-*
ceived, confirmed, and restored from inactive status
than there are losses by death, transfer out or re-
moved for other reasons.”

The plural *persons* is one of the distinguishing characteristics of legalese, pseudo-legalese, and Englishese—
jargons, as in your examples. I wouldn't have been
surprised, either, if you'd turned up examples like
“Wait*persons* wanted” and “The chair*persons* of all
departments are requested...,” for recent coinages
that self-consciously employ -*person* so as not to be
sexist are frequently even more creative in their plurals
than in their singulars. (More on this topic appears in
Chapter Two, under “Sex and the Single Pronoun.”)

People who hope to sound at all elegant should
not, however, use *persons* except in the set phrase
missing persons or when referring to a specific number of individuals: “Six *persons* said they would come
to the dinner but failed to attend.” Authorities on language sometimes try to turn this use of *persons,* or a
similar one, into an out-and-out rule, but there's no
evidence that any such rule is widely followed anymore or that the few people who do follow it are better speakers and writers than the many who don't:
“Six *people* said they would come to the dinner”
strikes me, at any rate, as more natural. In contemporary American English, then, there's little reason to
use *persons* except in—well, jargon and cant. Read
on, please, for further thoughts.

*Did I miss the memo announcing that the new plural
form of the word* person *is* persons? *I am sure that
the people who taught me the nuances of our great
language would like a copy as well. Whether it's the
announcer on the PA system at the Philadelphia
Flower Show requesting* "persons *separated from
their parties to report to the information booth" or a
writer for* Newsweek *who recently referred to "some
category of* persons," *it seems that the use of* people *is
being abandoned.* Persons, *however, is nowhere to be
found in my trusty dictionary. So I ask, Why the pro-
liferation of* persons? *And is this proper?*

As the fellow who wrote me about *moments* can attest, some dictionaries presume that there's no need to
specify it when a noun has a regular, -*s* plural, because
the great majority of nouns do have them; the plural
form of *person* has always been *persons*. But in fact
persons is being used less and less (maybe that's why it
sounds strange to you), and *people* is taking over most
of what was once considered *persons'* territory—
namely, references to specific numbers of individuals.

People, not *persons,* is the anomaly. It can be singular, as it is in "We are a *people* fond of gardening,"
and it can take a regular, -*s* plural, as in "The *peoples*
of Australia and New Zealand vie with the British in
their love of horticulture." But when it's unmistakably
plural, as in, say, "Ten thousand *people* attended the
flower show," it doesn't have a singular form of its
own. This may be why newspaper copy desks, in particular, long crossed out *people* wherever it came after
a number, and substituted *persons*. It's hardly a good
reason, though, for idiomatic English is abloom with
anomalies.

Where did you get the notion that newspaper copy desks have long crossed out people *and substituted* persons? *I've worked on major newspaper copy desks (seven of them) for almost thirty years.* The Associated Press Stylebook, *which is the guide for most newspapers, has been telling us just the opposite for as long as I can remember.*

You'll notice that I used the past tense; my source was Theodore M. Bernstein, late of *The New York Times.* I'm delighted that today's newspaper copy desks are peopled with editors of a mind with me.

Perspective, Prospective

Ever since the O. J. Simpson trial, when discussing jury impanelments in Denver, Little Rock, and so forth, radio and TV news broadcasters have referred to those likely to become jurors as perspective *jurors.*
Perhaps perspective *is a little easier to say than* prospective, *but I think the latter adjective is the correct one. Have the broadcasters gotten tongue-tied in the midst of all this judicial excitement or can* perspective *be stretched to include those waiting to be called to perform this civic duty?*

I was hoping to be able to report, after I looked into whether *perspective jurors* was showing up in writing, that no doubt you were mishearing *prospective* (which, of course, means "likely to become or to be or to happen") as *perspective* (which has to do with vision, literal or metaphorical). They do, after all, sound a lot alike. But the mistake *is* showing up in writing, in various places on the World Wide Web, including law-related sites, and even in professionally edited material like newspapers. Where it's not just a careless error, it's an awfully foolish one: "With approximately 1,000 *perspective jurors* called for the March 24th selection process, Judge John Ryan ruled that the pool is large enough and enough time has passed since the incident, the pretrial publicity should not be a factor in finding a fair jury pool." Egad!

Persuade

See Convince, Persuade.

Podium

See Lectern, Podium.

Presently

I always read my two children a story before they go to bed. These tales are usually straightforward and have never before piqued my curiosity in matters of grammar. However, upon reading a rendition of "Goldilocks and the Three Bears," I came across a passage where Goldilocks was approaching the bears' home. The text of the story reads: "Presently she came to the clearing where the bears' cottage stood." The word presently *seems redundant—or is it? I have a feeling that this version originated in an older version where this verbiage was acceptable. Please advise.*

In higher English, as in somewhat older English, *presently* means "soon," and it's *at present* that means "now." Thus the *presently* in your "Goldilocks" seems apt enough to me. In modern everyday usage, though, as in very early citations (those from the fifteenth to the seventeenth century), *presently* often means "at present." If someone who is careful about language is going to renounce one use or the other, this is the one to renounce.

You might think a word that could be indicating either the near future or the present deserves to be renounced entirely, on the ground that it is inherently ambiguous. Nearly always, though, context manages to make clear which meaning is intended: "*Presently* I'm having some porridge. I'm eating as fast as I can, because I know the bears will be returning *presently.*"

Prevaricate, Procrastinate

This year, in three books by different authors, I have found prevaricate *where the context calls for* procrastinate. *Grant sends a note to Lee at Appomattox asking for a meeting but Lee* prevaricates. *Henry the Eighth wants the Pope to annul his marriage to Anne Boleyn but the Pope* prevaricates. *Charles the First, trying to hold his throne, endlessly* prevaricates. *What is going on? I am exasperated. Or should I say* exacerbated?

I certainly don't need to tell *you* that *prevaricate* means "lie or evade the truth," and that *procrastinate* means "postpone or delay"—but maybe others will be glad of the reminder. For my own part, I wonder whether the word each of your writers was groping after may have been *equivocate,* which means "be evasive; avoid or postpone saying anything definite." The meaning of this word, it seems to me, is about halfway between the meanings of the ones you give.

Prospective

See Perspective, Prospective.

Prove

See Degree, Diploma.

Proved, Proven

Last night on the news on TV I heard again a word usage I particularly hate: "Seeger Ford has proven that it offers the best deals." Whatever happened to good old proved as the past tense of the verb prove? I have always considered proven to be an adjective. Am I being too fussy, or even wrong?

I happen to observe the distinction you make ("I *proved* it was the shortest route" but "I followed a *proven* route"). The authorities are far from being united about it, though, so when others fail to observe the distinction, let's not get on our high horses. That's the wrong mode of transportation.

Put

Why is the verb put so carefully avoided? "Place stamp here" sounds okay, but not "Place into," which I often see. And in The Washington Post, I recently came upon the sentence "She was jailed briefly after tossing 15 cents into two expired parking meters as a police officer, who told her to stop, was writing a ticket for one of the vehicles." This seems to me a particularly ludicrous result of avoiding put. My guess is that the word has a smutty meaning I don't know.

You'll see the same thing happening where *get* would be the natural word, if you monitor uses of *acquire* and *obtain* and *receive* and *retrieve* and so forth. Sure, you *can* do smutty things with either of these verbs. And no wonder: my three current unabridged dictionaries give eighteen, twenty-two, and thirty meanings for the verb *put,* and twenty-one, twenty-eight, and thirty-four meanings for *get,* and that's without counting phrasal verbs like *put up* and *get down* and *get up* and *put down.*

These are tremendously versatile words. In words as in tools and electronic devices and kitchen implements, however, people love special-purpose gadgets—and this, I suspect, is the real reason they're found straining after a special-purpose synonym rather than making use of the handy, all-purpose *put* or *get.*

Quarter, Quarterly

A major corporation I own stock in sends its financial statements out titled "First [or 'Second,' etc.] Quarterly Report." The -ly sounds wrong. Am I right?

I do agree that "First *Quarterly* Report" sounds peculiar—but note that the company is indeed sending out *quarterly report.* The first one it ever issued was its *first quarterly report.* Logically, though, the first one in its second year was its *fifth quarterly report.*

Then again, the report that pertains to the first three months of any year covers the *first quarter*; it's the *first-quarter quarterly report.* So much for precision. "*First-Quarter* Report" is probably better than "First *Quarterly* Report," but not by much.

Reluctant, Reticent

I have noticed the increasing use of reticent *in situations where I believe* reluctant *is intended. The gardening section of our local paper recently featured this headline: "Fig trees produce bumper crops; rhododendrons* reticent *to bloom." I understand* reticence *as a reluctance to speak. One is* reticent *on a subject or one is* reluctant *to discuss it. Please help.*

I'm with you. The time-honored meaning of *reticent* is indeed "quiet" or "reserved"; someone can be *reticent,* period, and really oughtn't to be reticent *to do* anything at all. But the assertion that a person is *reluctant* cries out for more information—reluctant to do what? I must admit that the current edition of *The American Heritage Dictionary* gives "reluctant" as one of the meanings of *reticent.* However, previous editions did not. It's hard to see what's gained if the two words come to have the same meaning, and easy to see what's lost. Thus I am reluctant to accept the shift in meaning—and not reticent about saying so.

In your response to a reader who questioned the common tendency to equate reticent *with* reluctant, *you quite correctly agreed with the reader that* reticent *refers specifically to a reluctance to speak. Hence it cannot be a synonym for* reluctant. *However, after all this, you commit a redundancy yourself in your use of* reticent *in your last sentence. Surely if* reticent *means "reluctant to say," then "reticent about saying" is redundant. No meaning would have been lost if you*

*had said "Thus I am reluctant to accept the shift in
meaning—and not reticent about it." In "reticent
about saying," reticent is simply being used as a synonym for reluctant, which, we've already agreed, it
cannot be!*

Dear reader, I will leave it to you to read the section
on redundancies ("Double or Nothing") in Chapter
Five, and judge whether I should leap to my own defense
or allow this objection to stand.

Reverend

*My minister and I seem to disagree as to the common
usage—or misusage—of the title Reverend in the
modern world. We agree that the word alone as a
form of address is misused. I have always thought
(and taught) that the adjectival title Reverend is correctly used as part of a fuller religious title, as in "The
Right Reverend Will B. Dunn." To refer to a minister
as Reverend (as in, "Hiya, Reverend") is both incorrect and gauche (just as you would not introduce a
judge as "Honorable Jones"). I notice, however, that
an increasing number of clergy of some congregations
seem not only to allow such usage but to encourage it.
If a clergyman should actually identify himself as
"Reverend Dunn," or be commonly (I use the word
advisedly) called so by his parishioners, it would seem
to be good manners to accept the usage. However, it
also seems to be a bit patronizing to mimic such misusage. Usually, though, this misuse of Reverend seems
to me innocent and free of any taint of sarcasm. My
friend and minister (Episcopalian) disagrees. He says
that in his experience "the word Reverend used as a
title is almost invariably spoken with a sneer" by*

people who dislike religion and the ministry and are uncomfortable with religious titles of any sort.

Who am I to tell a minister I've never met that he's inappropriately suspicious of others? Nonetheless, in my experience people who write "*Reverend* Dunn" and "*Rev.* Dunn"—or "*Honorable* [or *Hon.*] Galese"—don't know that there's anything wrong with those forms, and are eager to change them when the problem is pointed out. The problem is that *Reverend* and *Honorable* are not courtesy titles, like *Judge* and *Professor* and *Dr.* and *Mrs.*, but honorifics. As such, they are not to be used except before a courtesy title *(the Reverend Dr. Dunn)* or with a full name *(the Honorable Lee Galese)*.

People who aren't sure of their ability to use honorifics properly—and it's not something that most of us get a lot of practice in—may find it helpful to mentally substitute *the late*: we wouldn't say "*the late* Dunn," but we would say "*the late* Dr. Dunn," for example, or "*the late* Lee Galese." Do not, however, be tempted into "*the Honorable Judge* Lee Galese"— that's redundant, like "*Dr.* L. Ness, *M.D.*"

In writing, by the way, when *Reverend* or *Honorable* is spelled out, the *the* belongs with it; when one of these words is abbreviated, that article should be left off *(Rev. Will B. Dunn; Hon. Lee Galese)*.

Savings

For the past several years I have noticed the word savings *used where there is clearly only one saving, as if it were a singular form such as* politics, *for example. You see such things as "A savings of $10.00 can be made on this item."*

It seems this annoying usage started in advertising and other commercial writing, but now is seen in political statements, essays, newspaper reporting, and so on.

Sometimes a word change fills a real need and is welcomed into the language. But in the case of savings *being used as a singular, I can see no fulfillment of a need. On the contrary, it even clouds the issue when the plural is intended.*

I sincerely hope that I and the editors of my dictionary are not the only ones who are bugged by this creeping and useless neologism.

Savings began creeping over the line from plural to singular years and years ago, when people began referring to *savings accounts* and *savings bonds*: nouns used as adjectives are generally (though not invariably) singular. We don't say *stocks market* or *investments counselor* or *dollars equivalent,* for example.

But you're right that *savings* hasn't crept as far as *politics* in the singular direction, and *a savings,* particularly, is considered poor form. This can make it hard to know what to do with the likes of "a penny of additional *savings,*" "the government would have reduced its *saving* (increased its borrowing)," and "one way to increase national *savings*"—all phrases that appeared recently in *The Atlantic Monthly,* just as they are given here. What's under discussion may be either the process of *saving* or a pool of (plural) *savings,* but the distinction is worth keeping in mind and trying to denote in a consistent way.

Seasonable, Seasonal

My Webster's *and* American Heritage *dictionaries claim distinctions between the adjectives* seasonal *and* seasonable, *yet most weathercasters (local and national) use the terms interchangeably. Are they undereducated or are my dictionaries dated? Or am I, to be bothered by their usage?*

I'm with you, and your dictionaries. What is *seasonable* is more of a judgment call than what is *seasonal,* for the former word means "appropriate to the season" or "timely," whereas the latter means just "of the season" or "dependent on the season." The example that *The American Heritage Dictionary* gives distinguishes the two words very neatly: "Rains are *seasonal* if they occur at a certain time of the year. They are *seasonable* at any time if they save the crops."

Shall, Will

My grandmother used to illustrate the difference between will *and* shall *with the following two sentences: "I* shall *drown; no one* will *save me" and "I* will *drown; no one* shall *save me." One sentence denotes intention; the other denotes desperation. But which is which?*

You're not the only one who's confused by *shall* and *will.* Not long ago, attempting to hammer out a budget bill, the two political parties' leaders in the Senate were at a loss for the proper wording. "Holding a dictionary between them and pouring [sic] through its pages," *The New York Times* reported, "the two leaders agreed that the words were synonymous. They agreed on *shall.*"

I wish they'd called me. The traditional distinction made in England is that in the first person *will* has to do with willpower—that is, it denotes intentionality—and *shall* with simple futurity, whereas the second and third persons reverse the pattern. Thus your two sentences mean, respectively, "I am going to drown, and no one is going to save me" and "I mean to drown, and no one had better save me." (In fact, the latter of your sentences is the punch line of an antique joke about a Scotsman whom well-brought-up English folk mistakenly allowed to drown, because—well, you get the idea.)

There are, however, many traditional exceptions to the traditional rule, and even the Fowlers, H.W. and his brother, F.G.—admirable watchdogs of traditional English English—were forced to admit, in their 1906 book *The King's English,* that the idiomatic use of the two words, "while it comes by nature to southern Englishmen,...is so complicated that those who are not to the manner born can hardly acquire it."

In the United States today, most authorities agree, *will* does the better part of the jobs that it once took the two words to do, and what *will* doesn't do is generally taken care of in other ways, such as by *is going to* or the cleverly vague *'ll.* Except in set phrases like "*Shall* we dance?" and "We *shall* overcome," *shall* now strikes most Americans as an affectation. When you're in doubt, therefore, use *will.* Politicians notwithstanding, it's the all-American choice.

Allow me to point out that shall *persists in one very special usage, familiar to all architects and engineers who write or interpret specifications: "The contractor* shall *provide access to the work area at all times to inspectors, other trades, and lienholders."*

Here shall *means "must" and in general is legally enforceable.*

You quote "...is so complicated that those who are not to the manner born can hardly acquire it."
I am very familiar with this phrase, but have always thought it to read "those to the manor born," indicating those born in the manor house to prestige and position, as opposed to the uneducated, common masses.
Have I been deluded all these years? Please enlighten me. If it is indeed manner, *that doesn't make much sense to me.*

Your idea about *to the manner born* is certainly logical, but the phrase is a quotation from *Hamlet*:

> *But to my mind, though I am native here*
> *And* to the manner born,—*it is a custom*
> *More honoured in the breach than the observance.*

Shelled

For a recipe, my wife requested that I get her some shelled almonds. *I knew that she meant "whole almonds sans shells"; however, Generation X employees at three stores showed me whole almonds with their shells intact. At one of the three I overheard a young employee joking with another regarding my (to her) confused request. What does Ms. Grammar think of my recent forays into the world of retail customer service?*

It is curious that a person is said to be *undressed* and a package *unwrapped,* whereas an almond and a

potato in comparable states are properly called
shelled and *peeled*. In cases like these, the two forms
reflect a thought pattern in which *un-* designates tasks
that remain to be done or have been reversed *(un-
washed, unpacked, untied),* and the lack of *un-* designates tasks already done that have involved some kind
of removal *(skinned, gutted, cored).* Ignorance of such
niceties of our language, it seems to me, is its own
punishment.

Sneaked, Snuck

*When I was in school, many years ago, we were
taught that usage changes according to what is acceptable among people whose taste and training qualify them to make judgments. While acknowledging
that language is dynamic, and necessarily adds new
words and alters the meanings of others, I wonder
whether such a group of judges still exists. A grating
example of usage that troubles me is* snuck, *rather
than* sneaked, *for the past tense of the verb* sneak.
*The way things are going, I think one could write
"When the burglar* snuck *into the room, a floorboard*
cruck, *and the mouse* squuck *in alarm."*

Seriously, for many years I understood the word
snuck *to be a rustic illiteracy of the sort used for dialogue in old Western films. Now I find it as part of the
standard vocabulary in books and even on radio. Perhaps I should just admit that I'm getting old and
stodgy—that I* puck *years ago and have been going
downhill ever since.*

As I was transcribing another correspondent's letter
recently, my computer's spell-checker picked up a
snuck. I was delighted. But then I clicked the mouse

button to see what correction the computer would suggest and was offered this list to choose from: *snack, snick, suck, shuck,* and *stuck.* People are still better than computers—but we all need to keep working at it if we want to stay a step ahead.

The American Heritage Dictionary has, in fact, assembled a usage panel of the kind of people you have in mind as judges of our language. And almost exactly two thirds of them, according to the current edition of the dictionary, disapprove of *snuck.* Although the word is quite common in informal use, *sneaked* remains the standard past tense of *sneak.*

Spit and image, Spitting image

See Mirror image.

Substitute

Is it my imagination or has the verb substitute *changed its meaning in the past few years? I have always thought it meant "take the place of" and usually required the preposition* for, *as in "Would you substitute a salad* for *the hushpuppies, please?" Similarly in the noun form, a* substitution *would require a preposition—preferably* of, *as in "Sorry, the cook doesn't permit the* substitution of *fresh foods for fried."*

But more and more frequently I am seeing constructions that imply that substitute *now means "replace." For example, when a landscape planner notes that "we should* substitute *willow oaks by red maples here," I wonder which species will end up being planted.*

Recently I found the following column headings in a piece of the online help for a leading

word-processing software application: "Font ... sub-
stituted to." In the table that followed, I avoided utter
confusion only by recognizing the names of the fonts
in column B that were being substituted for those in
column A. (The substitution of font *for* typeface *is yet*
another matter.)

Is it really correct to use substitute *where* replace
(or change*) is meant? Why would anyone want to do*
that?

You're right about the way substitute, verb, is supposed to work, though the problem of its working the
way it shouldn't isn't only a recent one: *The New
Fowler's* traces the switch back to the seventeenth century. What generally seems to happen is that someone
begins to say, or write, something like "I'd like to *substitute* ..."; then blurts out the thing that's to be replaced, "hushpuppies," before the substitute, "a
salad"; and then blunders about looking for a preposition, like *to* or *by,* that might sort of turn the verb
around. If we think about this any further, we're just
going to get ourselves confused. Suffice it to say that
the mistake is easy to make, but a mistake it is.

Suspect

I am bothered by the increasing misuse among
Chicago newscasters of the noun suspect. *The word is*
an important protection for a person suspected but
not yet convicted of a crime. No doubt the statement
"A man has been stabbed and the police are searching
for suspects*" (when they have no idea who the culprit*
might be) is meant as bending over backwards to be
fair. But doesn't it tend to undermine the very prin-

ciple of "innocent until proven guilty" by making suspect *a synonym for* perpetrator?

A spokesperson for the National Association of Chiefs of Police and also several representatives of the legal profession agree with you that *suspect* can be insidious. The paradox is that although the police are indeed searching for *perpetrators* and *killers* and so on, anyone they arrest will necessarily be merely a *suspect* until he or she is found guilty of the crime.

Sympathy

See Empathy, Sympathy.

Systematic, Systemic

An article in The Wall Street Journal *the other day said, "Top officials of Columbia/HCA Healthcare Corp. engaged in a* 'systemic' *effort to defraud government health-care programs, federal investigators state in an affidavit unsealed yesterday in Florida." Has my medical-school training led me astray? Can* systemic *possibly be the right word here?* Systematic?

You can find meanings like "of or relating to a system" for both words in most dictionaries—a technicality in those federal investigators' favor. Nonetheless, as you know, *systemic* tends to mean "within or throughout a biological system" (such as the nervous or circulatory system or an entire organism), whereas for the most part *systematic* means "according to a method or plan." Unless something very peculiar is going on in this legal case, *systemic* does seem out of kilter here.

Take

See Bring, Take.

Temperature

A very common usage emanating from radio and television has me baffled. I hear the following from the weather reporter: "Get out a warm jacket, because tomorrow we will have cold temperatures *in our area."*

I have always thought of temperature *as a dimension, with the word modifiable only by* high *or* low. *I believe that* cold *and* hot *are adjectives defining the reactions that animals or plants manifest to* low *or* high *temperatures. How can a* temperature *be cold? Am I all wet here, or are we seeing a mass misuse of the language?*

You're quite right that *hot* or *cold*—or *warm* or *cool*—*temperatures* may not always be the best way to put it. Recently, for example, I came across "He employed humor as a way of reducing tension often caused by the *hot temperature* and humidity." How about *heat*?

And yet if the problem were just as you say, how could the recommended jacket be *warm*? The conceptual relationships of English adjectives to their nouns are multifarious, and it will be a *sad day,* a *sorry state of affairs,* an *unhappy turn of events,* and so forth if our language ever loses this characteristic. *Hot* and the rest of them as modifiers for *temperature* fall well within the acceptable bounds. Indeed, these examples convey something subtler than what could be conveyed with *high* or *low*: "Gardenia augusta...demands a sunny south window, *warm temperatures* (above 65 degrees day and night), high humidity and an acid soil underfoot"; "Cheesemaking in the Cheddar Valley, where the famous caves were used to store cheese at a constant *cool temperature,* can be traced back more than 800 years."

Thanks much, Thank you much

Perhaps I should reread my old (very old) college English books before I write, but somehow I don't believe I would find my answer there. I'm sure that you can help.

My problem is the word much. *Is it correct to use it unqualified, as in* Thanks much *or* Thank you much? *I hear it more and more from TV announcers, the last time from a well-known and respected CNN reporter.*

This use of the word, to me, if not wrong is certainly awkward. Is it correct or is it wrong?

Thank you so much for your help.

The short answer is that *Thanks much* and *Thank you much* are jocular formations—not quite in the same ballpark as *Who'd of thunk?* but perhaps lurking outside the gates, at a nearby souvenir stand.

Note how *much* does not work alone with verbs: "I hate you *much*" and "It surprises me *much* to hear you say so" are not idiomatic, although "I like you *very much*" and "That does *not* surprise me *much*" are. The expression *Thank you much* is a shortening of "I [or 'We'] *thank you much*"—which is on the first, unidiomatic pattern, whereas *Thank you very much* or *Thank you so much* is on the second, permissible one. So much for *thank you.*

With *Thanks much,* you have a choice about how

to think of *thanks,* though the phrase is substandard according to both viewpoints. *Thanks* here might be either a plural noun (as it is in *Many thanks,* which is a pared-down version of something like "I offer you *many thanks"*) or a further shortened version of *Thank you* (compare *Thanks very much!*). In fact, there's a *"Much thanks"* in Shakespeare somewhere, but if there weren't, there'd be no excuse for this phrase today.

Thanks to

Of late I have been meeting up with the use of thanks to *in contexts like these: "A three-stall car wash was missing one wall* thanks to *the rushing waters of the Delaware" and "We will continue to have...escalating crime* thanks to *children who grow up in combat zones." These may not be grammatical errors, but they strike me as illogical uses of the phrase. Whatever happened to* due to?

Where blame is more to the point than gratitude, *thanks to* is indeed out of place. However, there are traditional limits on the use of *due to* that keep it from being an all-purpose solution to the problem. A noun is allowed to be *due* to something ("The *need* to repair the car wash is *due to* the storm"), but a clause may not be ("*The car wash needs repairs due to* the storm," for example, is wrong). It's usually possible to revise one's sentence to conform to the rule. But changing *due to*—or *thanks to*—to *owing to* or *because of* is almost always the simplest solution.

Why is *owing to* allowed where *due to* is not? It has been in use much longer in such prepositional contexts, *due* having been nothing more than an ordinary adjective ("Repairs are certainly *due*") a century ago. Those precisians who fifty or thirty years ago denounced the preposition *due to* as an arriviste have tainted its reputation.

See also Due to, Owing to.

Thank you, You're welcome

Have you noticed that the expression You're welcome, *which used to follow someone's saying* Thank you, *has all but disappeared from television and radio interviews?* "Thank you *for being here,*" *says the interviewer.* "Thank you," *replies the guest. Occasionally I'll hear someone respond,* "With pleasure." *And this morning on National Public Radio's* Weekend Edition, *someone simply answered,* "Okay." *But most of the time the program's closing features mutual expressions of gratitude. Is* Thank you *on its way to becoming like* Shalom—*employed for both greetings & farewells? Is saying* You're welcome *in some sense elitist?*

Our mothers all made sure long ago that we'd have the little call-and-response pattern *Thank you, You're welcome* etched into our brains. Nonetheless, a person who, for example, has been given a chance to talk to a national audience about his life's work or a person who is promoting her new book hardly deserves censure for feeling that gratitude for the interview ought to run in both directions. The impulse is much like that in "It's a pleasure to meet you," "The pleasure is mine." All the same, the "With pleasure" you report having heard as a response to *Thank you* strikes me as a non sequitur.

For my own part, I like to keep three shades of

meaning at the ready: my mom's good old-fashioned
Thank you, You're welcome for situations in which
the gratitude is unidirectional; *Thank you, Thank
you,* with the emphasis in the response on the *you,* for
those the-feeling-is-mutual cases; and *Thank you, Not
at all* for the range of meaning in between.

That, adverb

I am always puzzled about how bad that *bad is, or is
not, or how cold, or how late, or whatever else.
Sometimes it also seems as if* not that *is one word.*

To illustrate: "What is the temperature?" "It's
notthat *cold." Or: "What time is it?" "It's* notthat
late." (Could it be this *late?)*

*It always sounds as if the person feels the need to
say something but has not taken the time to find out
what he really means, and hopes that the listener will
understand anyway. He does not know* that *much—
sometimes not even* tha-a-a-at *much, or* notallthat
much.

*I hope you will not mind commenting on this all
that much, or this much, or any other much.*

Half a century ago the adverbial *that* was regarded as
merely a colloquial or dialect form, and even today
"It's not *that* cold" doesn't pass muster as standard
English, let alone higher English. But the word is only
substituting for the perfectly acceptable *so,* and has as
much meaning as many English words do. The idea
that *that* or *so* conveys is "to a certain degree or extent" or, often, "to the expected degree or extent."
Moreover, "Is it really *that* bad?" will strike many as
plainspoken and idiomatic rather than bumpkin-like

these days, and it's hard to see why "Is it really *so* bad?" must be preferred.

All that is a shade more colloquial than *that* alone: "Is it really *all that* bad?" is indeed a little bit bad.

That, conjunction

Have you noticed that announcers on the radio often screen the word that *out of their reports? Initial ambiguities force the listener to decide upon the meaning, rather than perceive it clearly as the sentences proceed. Two of a number of examples I have collected: The Saudi group "demanded U.S. troops be removed" (the group wants U.S. troops—oh, no, it doesn't). "He doubts many members would like it" (first he doubts the members, then their preference).*

And another letter:

I've noticed an increased use of the word that, *encountering it so often, in fact, that it has begun to irritate me. Would not the sentence "Mr. Smith advised me* that *he would be departing next weekend and* that *he would return the following weekend" be better stated in this manner: "Mr. Smith advised me he would depart next weekend and return the following weekend"? Is there a rule of grammar or syntax covering this point?*

I have received other letters, too, about *that* in its role as a conjunction, in which it typically connects a subordinate clause to a main one. The two of you will surely want to know that by a margin of four to one my correspondents wish they saw or heard more of these *that*s, not fewer.

The magic of *that* is that at the same time it connects, it puts a bit of distance between two elements of a sentence—a neat trick that often comes in handy. As the examples in the first of your two letters illustrate, sometimes one wants to make clear that the object of the verb is the whole clause and not the noun at the start of the clause, and *that* does this job with a minimum of fuss. Or one may want to put the distance between two (or more) subordinate clauses that express very different ideas. In the "Mr. Smith" sentences, one *that* (after "Mr. Smith advised me") is surely enough, and I don't mind the version in which there are no *that*s at all. But I would add two to "Mr. Smith advised me he would depart next weekend and the roses need pruning," to make manifest that Mr. Smith advised me of two things, and disparate things at—well, that.

Where to prune *that* is either where ideas are closely related, as they are in the first "Mr. Smith" example, or where multiple *that*s begin to sound like a drumbeat: "He said *that* he had advised me *that* the departure *that* he planned..."

These ones

Maybe I am oversensitive, but there is something I hear used all the time, by all age groups, that I find grating. Last week I heard Charles Gibson on Good Morning America *repeat the phrase after a guest had said it, and I thought, "Enough! Now they are doing it on national television, as if it is correct." Please tell me whether* these ones *has now become accepted as correct use. I believe* these *means more than one, while* one *is one, unless you have a pile of actual*

numbers on the floor or desk—or perhaps it could be
used when referring to times tables. If you could clear
this up, I would be grateful.

Self-evident though it may seem, the idea that "*one* is
one" isn't quite right. Think of the sentence "I don't
watch many television programs, but the *ones* I like, I
watch faithfully." Then again, what we might expect
a well-spoken person to say next is "*These* tend to be
nature shows"—as opposed to "*These ones* tend
to be..."

Not only, however, can *these* function as a stand-
alone demonstrative pronoun, referring to a prior
noun, as it is doing in "*These* tend to be..."; it can
also be an adjective, modifying, say, *programs*
("*These programs* tend to be..."), and there's no
grammatical reason why it shouldn't be allowed to
modify the pronoun *ones*. The singular of this construction is quite common, and no one objects to it:
"*This one* is my favorite show." We might choose to
be slightly more frugal and say, "*This* is my favorite
show." But must we really fret over every tiny extrav-
agance—assuming no word is utterly wasted? In fact
this one is a bit more emphatic than *this*.

Now, why we should deny the advantages of emphasis to a plural when we grant them to the singular,
I don't know. And yet I have to agree with you that
these ones is often grating. My conclusion is that we
should try not to use the phrase habitually but should
also not object to its use where the special emphasis it
imparts is wanted. ("Which programs did you say you
liked?" "*These*—the ones this review is discussing."
"What did you say? I wasn't paying attention."
"*These ones. These ones* here!")

Times

I have been bothered lately by writers, especially those of scientific articles, comparing objects in terms of negative qualities. For example, a certain star will be described as ten times fainter *than another. Unless this is a convention agreed upon lately, I just can't think what it could mean. How much faintness does a star have, and if another has ten times as much, how bright does that make it? Or if one star is* one time fainter *than another, wouldn't that make it have zero brightness?*

Even when the quality in question isn't negative, the construction you're referring to is a bad idea. Think of *ten times brighter,* for example. We all know what that's supposed to mean, but then what's *one time brighter?* You'd think it would mean *twice as bright*— so *ten times brighter* must be *eleven times as bright?* This way madness lies. *Ten times as bright as* is how it ought to be said, and making such a revision is usually painless. As you note, when the quality is negative, it only makes matters worse. *A tenth as bright* is much, much clearer than *ten times fainter.*

While I also hate ten times fainter, *and I agree with your conclusion, you have a misconception about the word* times. *The word* times *is never written without the final* s. *(See* The American Heritage Dictionary, *third edition.) It is proper to say* one times one *or* seven times one *or* one times twelve. *The* times *refers to the multiplication operation, not the number of occurrences of something, and the multiplication operation always has that pesky final* s.

How obnoxious I am to argue with someone who says he agrees with me. But *one times twelve* isn't quite the same construction as *ten times brighter*. Furthermore, I can't accustom myself to the idea that *brighter* should ever be synonymous with *as bright,* as it is if *ten times brighter* is regarded as synonymous with *ten times as bright.* Nor do I see why we need this way of putting it, since we have not only *ten times as bright* but also phrases like *tenfold increase* and *ten times the brightness.* You'll notice that I didn't call *ten times brighter* wrong—but I hope you'll keep that to yourself.

Titled

See Entitled, Titled.

To the manner born, To the manor born

See Shall, Will.

Transparent

Could you discuss the term transparent? *My impression is that it is used with two opposite meanings. Among engineers and other technical types, it seems to mean that the inner workings of something are invisible to the user, while among the politically inclined (bureaucrats and newsmagazines), it seems to mean that inner workings are fully visible to the public. For example, in his book* Envisioning Information, *Edward R. Tufte used the word to mean "undetectable" when he wrote, "By giving the focus over to data rather than data-containers, these design strategies are* transparent *and self-effacing in character. Designs so good that they are invisible." But in* The Economist *the word meant "fully visible": "The best solution [to campaign finance scandals] is not to restrict political donations or spending, but to make them transparent. Every penny a party receives should be made public and its source named."*

Come to think of it, *clear* has the same peculiarity: "Those sliding glass doors are so *clear* that I walked right into one—it was invisible!" and "What you mean is perfectly *clear* to everyone—it's obvious!" The possible ambiguity is worth keeping in mind when using either word in a context where it won't be—well, clear.

Troops

When I was growing up, I was a member of a Boy Scout troop. We went on camping trips with five or ten different troops from other parts of the state. Each troop had about fifty members. Through grammar school and then on to high school, I always assumed a troop *was a group of people.*

During my college years I developed a keen interest in military history. For some inexplicable reason, my professors referred to individual soldiers as troops. *Being somewhat naïve, I first assumed that "50,000* troops *killed in Vietnam" meant probably a million or more dead soldiers. I soon learned otherwise, but the grammatical miscue has never made sense. Never a week goes by when a major daily does not refer to* troops *as individual people. Yet one would never call a single infantryman a* troop.

The difference between Boy Scouts and the military that's most relevant here is that each *troop* of the former is made up of Scouts, whereas *troops* in the latter can consist of soldiers, sailors, Marines, Seals, airmen, airwomen, and so on. In a context like the number of casualties in a war or battle, using any one of those words would often be inaccurate, using *all* of them would often be inaccurate as well, and using most of them would only make clutter. Hence the need for a single word that means "a member of the Armed Forces."

There isn't one, and that's why *troops* has been sent into the breach. The convention that has arisen about this word reminds me a bit of the military's "Don't ask, don't tell" policy: We are to ignore the special qualities of *troops* when the word appears in a context like "5,000 *troops* were sent overseas," in which it means a body of soldiers and the number is indicating the size of that body. But when these qualities call attention to themselves, as when only a few soldiers and Marines are under discussion ("Five *troops* have gone AWOL," say, would be wrong) or when members of the Armed Forces are doing something as individuals ("A thousand of the *troops* married Vietnamese women" would also be wrong), then regulations call for us to discharge the word and replace it with a fresh recruit.

Trustee, Trusty

Here's an esoteric one for you. I am a managerial-level deputy sheriff of several years' experience. In my line of work I am continually afflicted by the misuse of the word trustee. *As you may know, some of our guests in the county jail are allowed to work at certain unpaid jobs in the jail system by virtue of their trustworthiness. It has always been thus, so in early jails in English-speaking areas such individuals were referred to as* trusty *prisoners. Over time this adjective became a noun, so that the prisoner was known as a* trusty. *Several such inmates would be* trusties. *Most newspaper editors seem to know this.*

Nowadays, however, much to my aggravation and in spite of the good work of the newspaper editors, there are more and more lazy minds who do not seem to hesitate to apply the word trustee *to these inmate workers. They do this without regard to any knowledge of the inmate's possible free-world status as a member of a school board or in another position properly carrying the title.*

My position in our organization has allowed me to pull rank on our own folks and clarify for them why I am right and they are not on this point, but, quite frankly, I'm getting tired of it. Besides, there are names for people like me. To top it all off, there is now at least one popular dictionary that makes the same mistake as some of these benighted blighted souls. I think I am about to lose the battle. Are you with me or against me here?

I wrote the fellow back to assure him that I was with him, and to ask which dictionary presents *trustee* as a synonym for *trusty*. This is how he responded:

Here are two that are good and two that aren't.

Good: The American Heritage Dictionary *and* Webster's Ninth New Collegiate Dictionary.

Bad: The American Century Dictionary *and the* Random House Webster's Dictionary, Unabridged.

I note that the name Laurence Urdang appears on both the suspect volumes, as the editor of the first and

a contributor to the second. I am currently research-
ing our local ordinances for... I'm sorry. I can't
go on. Ongoing investigations must be handled
discreetly.

Tuck, Tux

My father and my aunt, both wise, well-informed,
and mature adults, are engaged in an intense discus-
sion about the shortened form of tuxedo. *One says*
the correct word is tuck, *and the other vehemently*
disagrees. Please help us resolve this minor but linger-
ing point.

English isn't like arithmetic, where if one answer is
right, the others have to be wrong. Unabridged dictionaries give both *tuck* and *tux*.

With regard to whether tuck *or* tux *is the suitable ab-*
breviation for tuxedo: tuxedo *is itself a vulgar slang*
term for an informal dinner jacket, used generally by
people who rent that particular garment. It comes
from the fact that the short-tailed dinner jacket, worn
with a black bow tie, was introduced at a party at
Tuxedo Park, New York, about a hundred years ago,
as an informal alternative to a tailcoat and white tie.
Persons of breeding thus refer to a dinner party at
which white tie and tails are worn as formal *and a*
dinner jacket / black tie affair as informal. *The word*
tuxedo *is little used in polite circles.*

Another letter made much the same point.

My father, who died over sixty years ago, said
this: "Tuxes are for gents; dinner jackets are for
gentlemen."

Turn of the century

See New Year's Eve.

12:00 A.M., 12:00 P.M.

One of my language pet peeves is the use of
12:00 A.M. *and* 12:00 P.M. *There are no such things,*
since A.M. *stands for* ante meridiem, *and* P.M. post
meridiem. *Since* 12:00 *is* meridiem, *it cannot be* ante
or post. *I suggest that those who have trouble with*
this, and won't say noon *or* midnight, *change their*
schedules to read 12:01 A.M. *or* 12:01 P.M.*!*

Well, now, there's an idea. But perhaps you'll agree
that *12:00 noon* and *12:00 midnight* are better, for
they serve as discreet little signs of connoisseurship of
the language.

2000s

See Aughts.

Un-

See Shelled.

Under way, Underway

It seems that nearly every day I read, either in print or
in correspondence, an example of someone using the
word underway. *I think that should be two words—*
under way. *The word* underway *suggests to me some*
sort of subterranean passageway, perhaps the opposite
of overpass. Is it a word at all? Is there a change in
usage that has been under way in the twenty years
since my last grammar and usage course?

Under way remains the dictionaries' form of choice, though *underway* is on the march, to judge by comparing older and newer dictionaries' entries. Maybe by the time you are really old, *underway* will have overtaken its predecessor—but by that time it will be charming of you to insist on using the outmoded form.

Up

See Back, Forward, Up.

Verbal

See Oral, Verbal.

Vicious circle, Vicious cycle

I often encounter the phrase vicious cycle *in speech or in print in my native country, the Philippines, but I have always used* vicious circle, *thinking it the only correct form. Recently, though, I came across the former phrase in* U.S. News & World Report, *to describe an aspect of the economic plight of women. I think the author should have said* circle *instead of* cycle. *Am I mistaken?*

No, not really. But I suppose that once policymakers began trying to break the *cycle of welfare dependency,* it became inevitable that some linguistic confusion would result. Indeed, *vicious cycle* does turn up fairly often these days. Here's a typical example, found on the World Wide Web: "One fate awaits homeless animals. If they're not picked up and gassed, they linger on the street—sick, starved and maimed. How many are yours? This *vicious cycle,* unfortunately, is not make-believe." Quite a few of the other references I found on the Web, though, were just making some punning allusion to motorcycles or mountain biking.

Most dictionaries give *vicious circle,* and do not give *vicious cycle* even as a variant, so perhaps the swing toward *vicious cycle* has yet to become a vicious circle.

Virtually

See Literally.

Where

I work for an attorney and proofread his documents. I always cross out phrases in which he uses where, *an adverb, to modify a noun—for example, "a case* where*" or "a situation* where.*" He always ignores my notes and leaves the script as is. I say it should be "a case* in which,*" and so forth. What do you say?*

The court finds for you. You cannot, however, object to your boss's constructions on strictly grammatical grounds. *Where* isn't only an adverb; it can also be a subordinating conjunction, one of whose jobs is to attach certain other parts of a sentence to a noun.

What you *can* say, though, is that it is considered a stylistic flaw to use *where* where the meaning has little or nothing to do with places or space: "The restaurant *where* we met for dinner"—fine. "A case *where* I was at a loss"—no, better not.

Various language experts use words like "immature style" and "amateurish" when they describe this flaw. Needless to say, I'm not recommending that you tell your boss that. That one is right is unpleasant enough for others when one is tactful about it.

While

Would you wish to turn your attention to the slovenly use of the all-purpose while? *Although, though, whereas, and sometimes even* while *I would not be such a purist as to insist that it be used only in the literal sense of "at the same time as," I resent having to reread a sentence to know which meaning is to be taken. And it is distracting when used frequently and indefinitely.*

As long as it is conceivable that *at the same time as* could be substituted for *while,* we who are reading or listening are supposed to disregard any suspicions we may have that such a substitution would result in a lie, and ignore the word's temporal aspect. For instance, "*While* I'm very fond of cookies, I like potato chips more" is a passable sentence, though it requires a bit of willful ignoring: it doesn't necessarily mean that I crave cookies and potato chips simultaneously. And yet it happens surprisingly often that *at the same time as* couldn't possibly replace *while.* Here is a typical paradox created by the misuse of *while*: "*While* the company had long avoided debt, it was happy to borrow the capital it needed to expand."

Curiously, if a sentence's main clause contains a negative, *while* can create a problem even when the things it joins are going on simultaneously. (In these sentences think of *at the same time as* in the sense of "as long as.") For example, "*While* I was hungry, I didn't want to eat a big meal." Do I eat big meals only when I'm *not* hungry? Or what about "*While* the management team believes that a new sales strategy is necessary, it will not sabotage the old strategy"? Potentially, this stops just short of declaring that if the management team ever decides against developing a new strategy, it will get busy sabotaging the one it has.

Mentally substituting *at the same time as* or *as long as* would have smoked out all these problems, by making evident how different that meaning was from the intended one. Where there's no risk of any significant misunderstanding (as in the "cookies and potato chips" sentence), a person can be forgiven for deciding to stick with *while*. In all the other examples, one of the other choices from your nice little list of near synonyms would have been greatly preferable.

Will

See Shall, Will.

-wise

I shudder when I hear someone attach the vogue suffix -wise *to nouns when such usage is simply a shortcut. Our language has such beautiful (albeit stuffy, I suppose) substitutes. I would certainly prefer* in terms of today's weather *to* weatherwise, *or* with regard to one's finances *to* financewise. *The other day I heard* musically speaking *and found myself greatly relieved, for I had anticipated* musicwise.

Let's hope a word to the wise will be sufficient.

Wreaked, Wrought

I am constantly coming across the word wreaked *as the past tense and participle of* wreak. *I find this usage awkward and grating on both eye and ear. I insist the proper word is* wrought. *I have written to several editors concerning this solecism, including the editor of* Maclean's *(Canada's national magazine!), but have elicited no response. Am I old before my time?*

Wreaked doesn't reek so badly as you think. *Wrought* is a past tense of *work,* believe it or not (as in "finely *wrought* gold jewelry"), and *wreaked* is good contemporary English.

Your call will be answered...

When I make a telephone call and am put on hold, in many cases a recorded message says, "Your call will be answered in the order in which it was received." Shouldn't it say something like "Calls are answered in the order in which they are received"? I get this message very frequently. Can you tell me what rule is being violated?

When the sentence is in the singular, it's like the Zen koan that asks, What is the sound of one hand clapping? What is the order in which one call is received? Logic, not grammar, is being toyed with here.

You're welcome

See Thank you, You're welcome.

Zeds, Zeros

See Aughts.

Shelf Life
(Useful Reference Books)

Sometimes with language-reference books as with ingredients for a recipe, nothing but the newest and freshest will do. At other times—for instance, when one is trying to determine if a usage is well established or when the recipe calls for cheddar cheese—a bit of age is a good thing. And when, say, one is researching the rationale behind some standard proscription or reaching for a can of tomato paste, age isn't much of an issue one way or the other, so long as what's on the shelf is of good quality.

A distinctive feature (or is it?) of dipping into language reference is that if the results are going to impress anyone, others have to have heard of one's source. At least, someone editing a friend's prose, or conferring with a colleague about the wording of a pamphlet, or engaged in any other kind of give and take about language, can cite Fowler, or Strunk and White, or *The American Heritage Dictionary,* or *The Chicago Manual of Style,* and say, with feeling, "What do you mean you're not familiar with it? It's widely recognized as authoritative." Citing less well-known sources is less likely to win arguments hands down.

There are many books, of course, that suit uncontentious purposes. Like a cook with her pots and pans—a flat omelet pan, a bulbous double boiler, a butter

warmer, a lobster kettle—I delight in and use quite a
few. The oldest reference book on my shelves is an 1836
Dictionary for Primary Schools, by Noah Webster,
LL.D. And I have a cheap 1994 facsimile of Rev. H. J.
Todd's 1818 edition of Dr. Samuel Johnson's *Dictionary
of the English Language,* whose contents are, obviously,
even older than my little *Webster's.* The newest heavy
tome to have taken its place alongside the others is *The
New Fowler's Modern English Usage,* edited by R. W.
Burchfield. Newer and heavier still, but occupying a virtual shelf, is an online *Oxford English Dictionary, Second Edition*—a multicolored, high-tech incarnation of
the awe-inspiring scholarly project that has been under
way since 1858. My virtual shelf teeters under its
weight, together with the weight of the Nexis database
of newspaper and magazine articles (which when I last
checked was said to be growing by some 120,000 articles a day) and the World Wide Web in general. These
last two are invaluable primary sources for researching
up-to-the-minute usage.

I am, though, chiefly concerned with durable usage—which we might define as language that doesn't
make older people wince and that we can hope will still
be easy to understand fifty or a hundred years hence—
and so I don't insist on having the latest edition of everything. In fact I'm quite fond of certain books of mine
from the 1940s, 1950s, and 1960s. Some of these I came
to know because they belonged to my father, a college
professor. Others I've picked up for a few dollars at
used-book stores. Named in what follows are all the reference books I have cited in the present volume, and a
few more, which I've had no occasion to cite here but to

which I often refer. The dates given are those of the first printing of the edition I use.

Dictionaries

The first language-reference book anyone needs is a good dictionary. Because this will contain features of other kinds of reference books, such as comparisons of synonyms and usage notes about controversial words, few people need to invest in anything else until they've gotten to know their dictionary well and seen whether it leaves any of their questions unanswered. I'm not complaining, but it is amazing to me how many questions people bother to write down, put in an envelope, spend a stamp on, and mail off to me though they could have answered those questions for themselves if they'd just cracked open a dictionary.

I think *The American Heritage Dictionary* (third edition, 1992) is the best dictionary in existence for Americans. It's complete enough that one might think twice about using (outside a specialized context, such as an academic paper) any word that doesn't appear in it. It's reasonably up-to-date, and its many usage notes knowledgeably discuss disputed words and meanings, often reporting the results of polls of the dictionary's distinguished usage panel. I have the *American Heritage* both on paper and on a CD-ROM. I've grown to love this and other electronic reference books, in part for the very unintellectual reason that I don't even have to take the two steps over to the bookcase to use them.

Besides the current *AHD,* I use nine other dictionaries, or editions of dictionaries. The most notable of them is that whiz-bang virtual *Oxford English Dictionary.* I'd also hate to be without *Webster's New International Dictionary of the English Language, Second Edition, Unabridged* (this was first published in 1934; my copy dates from 1954). This is a classic of erudite American usage, which even now some favor over its younger, more liberated sister, *Webster's Third* (1961).

Usage Guides

As if you hadn't already noticed, I think *the* invaluable usage book is *Modern English Usage,* by H. W. Fowler, in either its first edition (1926) or its second (revised by Sir Ernest Gowers, 1965). Although the third edition, called *The New Fowler's Modern English Usage* (1996), by R. W. Burchfield, is the product of new, impressive scholarship and covers many more topics and strives to be more objective than its forebears, it fails to wield the same authority. With the passage of time, Fowler himself has been canonized, even deified, whereas Burchfield still gives the impression of being an ordinary mortal.

Fowler's Anglocentrism is, from the point of view of an American, certainly a shortcoming, and I wish I could report that Burchfield had rectified it. In his preface Burchfield assures the reader that he has tried to reflect American usage equally with British (and usage in other English-speaking countries to a lesser extent), but it's clear throughout the book that his mind really isn't on his American readership. The entry for the noun *office,* for example, begins, "In AmE the ordinary word for a doctor's surgery," and the one for *pacifier* explains that this "is the customary word in AmE for a baby's dummy." If, however, being an American, you want to look up *surgery* or *dummy,* to have the corresponding mystery explained, you won't find any entry to translate British usage for you. The book is good but not perfect, and, alas, not lovable like the real Fowler.

The Reader Over Your Shoulder (1947), by Robert Graves and Alan Hodge, is worth seeking out. It's unlike any other usage guide. Rather than being arranged in dictionary form, it's filled with rules like "There should never be any doubt left as to where something happened or is expected to happen" and "No unnecessary strain should be put on the reader's memory." (Don't worry— these rather cryptic pronouncements are thoroughly explained.) Eleanor Gould, of *The New Yorker,* told me not long ago that she's so fond of this book that at one point she arranged for all of *The New Yorker*'s writers to be issued their own copies. The book was reprinted in 1990 under the title *The Use and Abuse of the English Language.* I've been told that the first edition, published in 1943, is better still, but I've never run across it.

Other usage books I like to consult include *The Careful Writer* (1965), by Theodore M. Bernstein; *American Usage and Style: The Consensus* (1980), by Roy H. Copperud; *Modern American Usage* (1966), by Wilson Follett (an idiosyncratic book whose 1998 revision, by Erik Wensberg, I haven't had the chance to get to know); *The King's English,* by H. W. and F. G. Fowler (third edition, 1985); *A Dictionary of Modern American Usage* (1998), by Bryan A. Garner; *The Complete Plain Words* (first U.S. edition, 1988), by Sir Ernest Gowers; *Merriam-Webster's Dictionary of English Usage* (1994); the *Harper Dictionary of Contemporary Usage* (second edition, 1985), by William and Mary Morris; and *The Elements of Style* (third edition, 1979), by William Strunk Jr. and E. B. White.

Style Manuals

As I explained in the aside at the end of Chapter Two, style manuals make suggestions about what to capitalize, when to spell out numbers, how to use punctuation, and so on. Like dictionaries, they tend to incorporate other kinds of material as well, such as notes about usage and grammar. *The Atlantic* has long employed *Words Into Type* (third edition, 1974) as its primary source of this kind. *The Chicago Manual of Style* (fourteenth edition, 1993) is certainly more up-to-date, and it's better known and therefore can be considered more authoritative. It was, though, designed with the needs of academic, rather than commercial, publishing in mind. Many other style manuals exist, intended for various audiences. Here the main point is to have *some* wide-ranging reference, because you will get terribly weary trying to remember, say, whether you decided to capitalize *army* always, in some situations, or never.

When you're ready to spring for a style manual, presumably you'll have some questions in mind that you'd like to have the manual's help in answering. If other things are equal and you don't know which book to choose, carry notes on a few such questions with you to the largest bookstore in town, and look up your questions in as many books as the store sells. See which book gives rules that you can find readily and that make sense to you. I'll admit that this advice is too practical for most people to follow, but if you do follow it, it will serve you well. It works for other reference books, too—thesauri, for example.

Thesauri

As a bit of wisdom shared with the young freelance writer that I then was, John McPhee told me years ago that he considers using a thesaurus tacky, and that writers do better to rely on the words they know. His procedure indeed helps a writer remain honest and direct. Editors, though, find thesauri invaluable, because we're often searching for a word that will express an idea not our own, in a style not our own. I happen to like best a 1940 *Roget's* that I inherited from my father. Many of the words in it are classics; they've worn well and can be expected to continue to do so. Nevertheless, the version of *Roget's* that's part of Microsoft Bookshelf is winning me over, because it's so handy. I have reservations about it, however, for, unlike my father's volume, it doesn't offer me many words I've never seen before. John McPhee, should he ever find himself at a loss for words, might prefer it for that very reason.

Most thesauri call themselves *Roget's,* and derive from a classification of words or the ideas underlying them that Peter Mark Roget developed in England in the nineteenth century; most thesauri are, therefore, a lot alike. The comprehensive ones—among which the most comprehensive is probably *Roget's International Thesaurus* (fifth edition, 1992)—tend to expect you to start with their indexes and then go rifling through various categories. J. I. Rodale's *The Synonym Finder* (revision, 1979) is different. It is conveniently in dictionary form, and its editors seem to have done much more than simply reorganize a *Roget's*. My impression is that *The Synonym Finder* contains at least as many useful words as *Roget's International*.

If, by the way, you unearth in a thesaurus a word treasure not thoroughly familiar to you, imagine the expression on John McPhee's face and, before you put your new word to use, look it up in a dictionary. Words are grouped together in a thesaurus because the ideas they express are related, not because they're identical. The connotations of or limitations on a given word may surprise you. My father's *Roget's* gives *enormity* under the heading "size"; my online *Roget's* has the word under "greatness"; and yet, as we discussed in Chapter Four proper under "Enormity" (or as *The American Heritage Dictionary,* among other sources, will tell you), using *enormity* in this way is considered a solecism.

Miscellaneous

Thesauri and the lists of synonyms often given in dictionaries might seem to have synonyms covered, so who needs a dictionary of synonyms? I do! Here again I like an old book that belonged to my father—a 1942 *Webster's*. It is wonderful for the loving detail in which it explores the similarities and differences among words.

George O. Curme's two-volume *A Grammar of the English Language* (1931 and 1935) is a tremendous descriptive source for odd little points about how our language is used, though it is not for the faint of heart. A sample sentence: "In all the above Middle English groups only the synthetic genitive—the genitive formed by an ending—is given, but alongside of it was in wide use the newer *of*-genitive, which arose in Old English, at first employed in only a few categories, but gradually spreading to others."

We are edging toward the point of view of linguistics now, and to understand that conceptual framework Steven Pinker's *The Language Instinct* (1994) is useful— and it is enjoyable as well. Two classics in this field are Otto Jespersen's *Growth and Structure of the English Language* (1905) and his monumental *Modern English Grammar on Historical Principles* (1946).

Fascinating books about the history of English, its development, and its spread around the globe include *The Mother Tongue* (1990), by Bill Bryson; *The Cambridge Encyclopedia of the English Language* (1995), by David Crystal; *The Story of English* (1986), by Robert McCrum, William Cran, and Robert MacNeil; and *The New Englishes* (1984), by John Platt, Heidi Weber, and Ho Mian Lian. *They Have a Word for It* (1988), by Howard Rheingold, is actually about words we *don't* have in English, and it's fascinating as well.

The classic on the history and distinctive characteristics of American English is H. L. Mencken's *The American Language* (fourth edition, 1936). Good books both newer and lighter on this subject are *Made in America* (1994), by Bill Bryson; *I Hear America Talking* (1976) and *Listening to America* (1982), both by Stuart Berg Flexner; and *Speaking Freely* (1997), by Stuart Berg Flexner and Anne Soukhanov. Scholars or connoisseurs of regionalisms will also want to know about the *Dictionary of American Regional English,* though they'll wish its authors would hurry up. Its first fascicle, *A–C,* appeared in 1985, and to date just two more have been published, bringing what's in print only as far as the letter O.

Dictionaries of quotations are worth keeping on hand, too; I have an older *Bartlett's Familiar Quotations,* and also the latest edition of *The Columbia Dictionary of Quotations* online. These help me ensure that I have the right wording for any borrowed bit, and that I haven't ignorantly attributed, for example, "I disapprove of what you say, but I will defend to the death your right to say it" to Thomas Paine when it was, rather, Voltaire who said it. Actually, Voltaire only said something like it (in French, of course), and this well-known rendering of his remark is a 1907 paraphrase. And if I hadn't just told you how I know that, wouldn't you be impressed that I do?

Anyone drawn to aspects of English other than those discussed here should get his or her hands on Bryan A. Garner's *A Dictionary of Modern American Usage* and have a look in the appendixes "A Timeline of Books on Usage" and "Select Bibliography." These can steer a person toward quite a few more of the many existing books on aspects of language.

CHAPTER FIVE

Immaterial Questions

E pluribus unum. ("Out of many, one.")
—Motto for the Seal of the United States

This chapter, let's be frank, is a grab bag of topics I wanted to bring up that haven't fitted in elsewhere. As it happens, they are all in some way ethereal—things immaterial in *that* sense. Here we will be answering questions that no one has asked; defining words that don't exist; poking around among pronunciations, which, of course, are invisible on the page; and exploring redundancies and wastes of words—single expressions that somehow manage to express their ideas more than once, and words that express nothing at all.

Unquestioned Answers

Maybe by now it seems as if the readers of the Word Court column had asked me every language-related question that anyone could possibly be interested in—at any rate, it sometimes seems that way to me. But from time to time, as I'm reading, I'll come upon a mistake that makes me think, Why doesn't someone ask me about *that*?

As

As may well be the most abused word in the English language. Not only is it often ignored in favor of *like* (about which, see the entry for "As" in Chapter Four), but also there is a widespread tendency to precede a construction like "Dull as that was, I found equally boring..." with another *as*—as in "*As* dull as that was..." This is a mistake. Wherever the one *as* could be replaced with a *though*—"Dull *though* that was"—that one *as* is all that's needed or wanted.

Some books that discuss this point explain that the double *as* is comparative, whereas the single one is wanted when nothing is being compared. But as you can see from the example I've given, that's misleading, for "dull as that was" makes a comparison of some sort. But contrast "dull *as* that was" with "*as* sharp *as* a tack." "Sharp *though* a tack..."? Certainly not. Note also that the distinction between the two forms will be neatly preserved, and you'll never be wrong, if you refrain from using one *as* (that is, if you never say "sharp *as* a tack") where two would do and a *though* would not.

Another nicety relating to *as*: The choice between "Shakespeare said, 'The ripest fruit first falls' " and "*As* Shakespeare said, 'The ripest fruit first falls' " is not a matter of indifference. In the first case, the main clause points out that Shakespeare said something; that he did so is the point. In the second case, that clause has become a subordinate element, and the quotation is the main clause—and the point. The former is the version you'd probably want to choose if you were writing about Shakespeare, whereas the latter is more appropriate when you are, essentially, borrowing his words to make a point of your own. Thus, "Virtually all our greatest authors have used agricultural imagery. Shakespeare said, 'The ripest fruit...'" Or else "The problem of achieving ripeness without bruising and spoilage has always been with us. *As* Shakespeare said, 'The ripest fruit...'"

Based, Basis

What is it about these words that anyone likes? I can see the sense in noting that, say, a consulting group is *based* in Chicago, but it makes me wince when people say the same thing about themselves, or about other individuals, as they often seem to want to. Since when is a person *based* somewhere, rather than *living* somewhere?

And *basis* often just takes up space. Wouldn't "providing both fresh and frozen seafood from around the world on a daily *basis*" be better said, "daily providing fresh and frozen seafood from around the world"? Wouldn't "Each of our core service lines can be provided on a stand alone *basis* or networked together" be much better said, "Our core service lines can be provided individually or networked together"?

Cannot help but

From *The New York Times*: "We *cannot help but* keep journeying, witnessing, connecting"; " 'You *can't help but* think he's not the same leader that he was four or five weeks ago,' said Mr. Mueller." Here and wherever you see it or hear it, *help but* might as well be a stutter. The right forms are "*cannot help* continuing to journey" or "*cannot but* keep journeying" and "*can't help* thinking" or "*can't but* think." Elvis Presley comes to my aid when I need to remember this punctilio, for in my mind's ear I hear him singing, "Wise men say…*can't help falling* in love with you."

Commas

People do ask me about comma placement in various situations, but no one has shown any interest in two tricky ones about which the advice readily available elsewhere is incomplete.

An example of the advice I mean is one of the eleven "Elementary Rules of Usage" in Strunk and White's *Elements of Style*: "Place a comma before a conjunction introducing an independent clause." Some version of this rule can be found in virtually any explanation of how to use commas. Only rarely is it mentioned that every now and then two grammatically independent clauses will be conceptually interdependent, and then the comma should be left out. Consider this comment to a stargazer: "Look for the comet and you'll see Venus." Surely it means that *if* one finds the comet, one will have no trouble spotting Venus; the two clauses are not truly independent, as are the two in, say, "Look for the comet, and see if you can't find Venus, too." Other examples that may help illuminate the difference are "Come outside and I'll show you the comet" and "Come outside, and don't forget to shut the screen door"; and "We gazed at the stars and our problems looked small" and "We gazed at the stars, and our friends watched TV." Few will ever tell you're wrong to put a comma in a sentence consisting of two grammatically independent clauses. Even so, the only way I know to signal the unusual conceptual relationship between the clauses in the first sentence in each of the foregoing pairs is to leave the comma out.

The second tricky situation, as it happens, conflicts with another of Strunk and White's elementary rules: "Do not join independent clauses by a comma." Strunk and White—and I—would like either a period or a semicolon to replace the comma in "It's not a comet, I can see through the telescope it's a meteor." But exceptions ought to be made to this rule as well—notably, when the whole point of two clauses is to contrast negative and affirmative assertions: "It's not a comet, it's a meteor." Punctuating this sentence with a semicolon would be like using a C-clamp to hold a sandwich together.

Many language critics inveigh, rightly, against the "comma splice." Few so much as hint that there might ever be a use for it. Wilson Follett, in a fine section on the point (under "sentence, the") in his *Modern American Usage,* writes:

> *The distinction between desirable and deplorable commas of this class is often subtle and paper-thin.* He composed this symphony in 1885, it was never performed until after his death *is illiterate.* This was not only his first concerto, it was his best *is neither illiterate nor colloquial: it is swift and emphatic. The difference is definable, yet difficult to define for those writers who most need the definition. Whoever finds it hard to perceive the difference between the comma fault and the legitimate splicing by commas will do well to avoid the second form and seek safety through semicolons, conjunctions, or separate sentences.*

Danglers

Everyone knows that participles aren't to be left dangling, or hanging, or unattached. That is, we've all been warned not to begin a sentence with a participle, or a phrase containing a participle, and then give it a subject different from what the participle modifies. "*Eating,* the serving platter served as my plate" and "When *carving* the duck, the cats were fascinated" are typical examples of the fault. (Note that there are two common kinds of exceptions to the rule. "When *serving* duck, it is imprudent to leave cats unsupervised in the dining room" is acceptable, because it would never cross anyone's mind that the *it* could be serving. "*Speaking* of imprudent, did you notice that they used a beautiful antique tablecloth and served red wine?" is acceptable, too, for no clear reason beyond that tradition sanctions *speaking of*—along with *considering, allowing for,* and various additional participles—in such constructions.)

But other parts of speech can be danglers, too. One day, I found this in a mail-order catalogue selling French kitchen towels: "*Handsome enough to frame,* we could not resist the grape and vine motif so evocative of the Burgundian countryside." What's more, danglers—dependent elements that seem to attach to the wrong word or phrase—can dangle from elsewhere in the sentence. Lists of hilarious headlines, funny signs, and funny lines from things like medical records often illustrate this: "Two Sisters Reunited After 18 Years in Checkout Counter"; "You are welcome to visit the cemetery where famous Russian and Soviet composers, artists, and writers are buried daily except Thursday"; and "The patient lives at home with his mother, father, and pet turtle, who is presently enrolled in day care three times a week."

It might appear self-evident that modifiers shouldn't be placed where they can seem to modify the wrong thing. If we pursue this idea beyond the funny lists and take it seriously, though, the implications are many. Doesn't "Tomorrow I'll bet you that the dinner will be lavish" have me doing my *betting* tomorrow? In the abstract it may seem easy to correct this impression in either of two ways, and in many contexts one or the other of them will do just fine. We can move *tomorrow* closer to what it modifies—can make the sentence read *tomorrow's dinner* or *the dinner tomorrow*. But we may not want to, if, for example, the previous sentence reads "Today our meals are frugal" and we like the parallelism in the placement of *today* and *tomorrow*. The other possibility is to turn *I'll bet you* into an interpolation: "Tomorrow, I'll bet you, the dinner will be lavish." (The key thing about an interpolation is that it is not to be followed by a conjunction like the *that* in the original sentence. The conjunction makes what comes after it subordinate to what comes before, binding those two parts together instead of allowing the main line of the sentence to begin at the beginning, leap over the interpolated middle, and coast along to the end. An interpolation doesn't always need to be set off by commas, though if this particular one weren't set off, the *tomorrow* would still be trying to attach to *I'll bet you*.)

Suppose, however, the original sentence had read "Tomorrow I'll give you any odds you like that the dinner will be lavish" and we were adamant about keeping *tomorrow* at the beginning of the sentence. A really complicated sentence may need so much reworking that we'll wish we had failed to notice the problem in the first place.

Some will say that all of this is pedantry—that there's no possibility of misunderstanding "Tomorrow I'll bet you..." For me, the trouble with this argument is that, having trained myself to scour text for dangling modifiers, it's hard (just kidding—read, "I find it hard, very hard") to know where to stop. If you perceive "Tomorrow I plan to enjoy myself" to be utterly innocent, you will probably be untroubled by "Tomorrow I expect the long-awaited celebration to take place." (Indeed, because tomorrow is in the future and the verbs are present-tense ones, there's a strong case to be made that these sentences aren't truly ambiguous.) But how do you feel about "Yesterday I would have expected the long-awaited celebration to take place"? Is the idea that the expectation or the celebration was to have taken place yesterday or that both were? Here it seems obvious to me that *yesterday* is when I would have expected ... but is not when the celebration was to have occurred. And so I do not find it natural for *tomorrow* in the parallel "I expect" sentence to be the date of the celebration. Certainly, clarity would not suffer if we were all suspicious of such constructions.

People who do take this idea seriously find reminders everywhere that they're in the minority. Consider this staple of airplane washrooms: "As a courtesy to the next passenger may we suggest you use your towel to wipe off the wash basin." Here, surely, the airline hopes to encourage you to do the next passenger a courtesy, but isn't it in fact boasting that *it* is doing the next passenger a courtesy simply by making the suggestion?

This sentence is ungratifying to recast. "May we suggest you use your towel to wipe off the wash basin as a courtesy to the next passenger" is no improvement; it's confusing, and now the courtesy seems like an afterthought. "May we suggest that as a courtesy to the next passenger you use your towel to wipe off the wash basin" is workmanlike, but not inspired. Of course, there's no rule stipulating that all we can do is reshuffle the words we are dealt. We can say, "As a courtesy to the next passenger, kindly use your towel to wipe off the wash basin" or "Be so good as to ..." or "The next passenger will thank you for using..."

I like to think, at any rate, that we will do our readers a courtesy if we keep a sharp eye out for danglers of all kinds.

Diagnose

It's so common and so convenient a formula that railing against it is probably demented. All the same, *diagnose with*—as in "I was *diagnosed with* obsessive-compulsive disorder"—is poor form. The verb is a back-formation from *diagnosis* ("The doctor made a *diagnosis* of obsessive-compulsive disorder"), and it supposedly means something like "identify by diagnosis": "The doctor *diagnosed* my problem as obsessive-compulsive disorder" or "She *diagnosed* obsessive-compulsive disorder." Less good form are the likes of "I was *diagnosed* as having obsessive-compulsive disorder" and "She *diagnosed* me as suffering from obsessive-compulsive disorder." Worse still—and relative to the other sentences doesn't this one sound crude?—is "I was *diagnosed with* obsessive-compulsive disorder." I won't go on and on about this. I won't go on and on about this.

Grill, Grille

A *grill* is a device for cooking food over an open flame or a restaurant that wishes to advertise that its kitchen contains such a device. A *grille* is the ornamental open-work covering on your radiator or the front of your car, for heaven's sake. Restaurants that call themselves *grilles* are guilty both of manhandling the language and of pretentiousness.

How

Respectable dictionaries and some of the more permissive usage books will tell you that the conjunction *how* can mean "that," at least in informal contexts. An example of this usage would be a sentence by Martha Gellhorn, originally published in *The Atlantic* in the month and year I was born, and more recently cited in *Merriam-Webster's Dictionary of English Usage*: "It was odd *how* writers never seemed to have anything to do except write or live." This sentence in itself is pretty harmless. Just a short distance further down the slippery slope, though, comes "It was odd *how* he wrote me"—intended to mean that it was odd *that* he did write. Using *how* as a synonym for *that* risks ambiguity.

In behalf of, On behalf of

According to a little-known fine point of English, these two compound prepositions mean different things. *In behalf of* means "in [someone's or something's] interest"; *on behalf of* means "as [someone's or something's] agent" or "in [someone's or something's] stead." And so, for example, "He appeared *on behalf of* Elizabeth Taylor at the benefit *in behalf of* victims of AIDS."

Italics

Throughout this book I have used italics to set off what others have written and also to designate words under consideration *as* words, as opposed to words being used in the ordinary way, symbolizing other things. And there are various additional legitimate technical uses of italics, such as for book titles, for the names of newspapers and ships, for foreign words, for legal citations.

And then there are the *annoying* uses of italics. Sometimes when writers want to be *emphatic,* they *italicize* the words to which they wish to give emphasis. But there is *no point* in doing this when readers, in their own minds, would *naturally* emphasize those very words. In fact, it's *intrusive* and *irritating—don't you think so?* To the argument that *sometimes* an idea just needs a *little* more *oomph!* I would respond that when one does, this is the fault of the words used to express it, and the words should be revised, not tricked out in *silly, giddy* italics.

Yikes! The use of italics for emphasis is legitimate, all the same, where you want to emphasize a word that it wouldn't naturally occur to people to emphasize on their own. Note the *as* in the first paragraph of this entry.

Like

Like sometimes means "resembling": "I've always wanted a cat *like* a tiger but smaller." A common super-stition notwithstanding, *like* may also mean "such as": "Cats *like* tigers and ocelots can make good pets, but not if you're house-proud." Yes, this state of affairs can give rise to ambiguity—but it does so less often than you might think. Only if real confusion seems probable is there any point in changing *like* to something else. For instance, out of context, "What would you think if I got a cat *like* that one?" is ambiguous: is our ailurophile in-terested in that particular cat or just a similar animal?

R. W. Burchfield, in *The New Fowler's,* illustrates the ambiguous use with the title of a Kingsley Amis novel: *Take a Girl* Like *You.* (The book was published in 1960, so don't start about that *"girl."*) Burchfield com-ments, "Had the title been 'Take a Girl Such as You', there would have been no such ambiguity." He's right, of course: without reading the novel, we can't tell whether Amis had in mind a girl who resembled some-one or he had in mind the very girl. But Burchfield can't seriously believe (let's give him the benefit of the doubt) that *Take a Girl* Such as *You* would have been a better title. "A girl *like* you" is idiomatic, and "a girl *such as* you" is pedantic. Not only that but a bit of ambiguity in the title of a work of fiction is often a good thing—as in, if you're so curious, read the book.

See also "Plurals with single examples," later in this section.

One word or more?

People who want to use language well spend a good deal of time hunting for just the right way to say something. A lesson we all learned early about words is that the fewer the better: not *very difficult* but *formidable,* not *mingled in together* but *conflated,* not *employing no more words than necessary* but *succinct.* We've all been taught, too, I hope, to choose the plain word over the fancy one: not *plebeian* but *common,* not *uncomplicated* but *simple,* not *perspicuous* but *clear.*

Sometimes these two principles conflict; we may seek out the exact word only to realize that it's a little too special. Two or three short, common words are often preferable to a single longer one. Doesn't "She *took part*" sound more conversational than "She *participated*"? Doesn't "I was confused *for a moment*" seem more human than "I was *momentarily* confused"? Doesn't "I hope you don't think this idea is worthless" say it better than "I hope this idea won't engender *floccinaucinihilipilification*"?

Partially, Partly

Partially is supposed to be reserved for when something happened to some extent, or partway. *Partly* is the only indisputably correct choice when talking about what happened to a portion, or part, of something. "The western sky is clear but there are clouds to the east; the sky is *partly* overcast. The clouds are light and hazy, so the rising sun is only *partially* obscured." *Partly* is not wrong in this latter sense, either, so it's the one to use whenever you're in doubt.

Percentages

Percentages are a handy tool, enabling us to describe proportions, large or small, in an exact way: for example, "Same-store sales increased by *12 percent* over the period." But when we're actually sizing things up very approximately, the scientific precision of percentages threatens to turn into fatuous pseudoscience. "*Nearly 50 percent* of the U.S. population, or 135 million people, will communicate via e-mail by 2001" is a bit silly; the writer had nothing more precise than *almost half* in mind. "Since a majority *(over 50 percent)* was required by German law for the election of a president..." is very silly; the parenthetical phrase serves no purpose at all.

In this citation the problem is the opposite: "While 82 percent of companies are currently involved in quality programs, only one-third (33 percent) calculate the cost of quality and 40 percent believe that knowing the cost of their quality programs may be a good idea." The silly part, that is, is *"one-third,"* since what's under discussion throughout is exact percentages—the number of parts per hundred.

Plurals with single examples

From a newspaper article: "Free money....It is a phenomenon that *fabled economists like John Maynard Keynes* hinted at in their writings, conjuring up *colorful terms like 'pushing on a string'* to describe one potential effect." Hmmm. How many "fabled economists like John Maynard Keynes" do you suppose there have been—like him, that is, in having hinted at the free-money phenomenon in their writings? And just how many "colorful terms like 'pushing on a string'" did those fabled economists come up with?

Those are sneaky phrases. Their author is implying that he has in mind a whole coterie of relevant economists and a range of relevant terms, and that certainly he, and probably we, know who and what they are. But do you think any of that is true? And isn't it strange that a writer who knows his economists and his terminology so well can't be bothered to cite an extra example or two? More honest, it seems to me, would have been for the writer to say "a fabled economist like John Maynard Keynes" or, even better, "the fabled economist John Maynard Keynes." Or if he was indeed thinking of a group, he should have named some additional members of it. In that case, though, he'd be stuck with the chore of making clear which one of his economists came up with the expression "pushing on a string" and, to be really scrupulous, finding comparable phrases by the others he cited.

Writers of suspect plurals with single examples aren't necessarily putting on airs. Some of them seem to be having trouble deciding what they want to talk about—the group or the example. Take, for instance, this (run-on) sentence that I found on the World Wide Web: "*Men like Hitler* knew the power of books, that's why so many books were burned by the Nazis." Might not the thought be better expressed as "The Nazis knew the power of books; that's why they burned so many"? Or maybe Der Führer specifically is being blamed, and the idea is: "Hitler knew the power of books; that's why he had the Nazis burn so many of them."

Illustrating a plural noun with a single example can

sometimes be legitimate. In our present context, for instance, I wouldn't mind a phrase like *phrases like this one.* Here there really *is* a group of things to be discussed, not just a lone case that the writer or speaker is hoping to turn into a trend. And the example is enough to make clear what group that is—we would have no trouble coming up with other examples if we wanted to. When these criteria are met, no purpose is served by changing the plural to a singular or giving additional examples.

Question marks

Most written questions make no problems for anyone, because it is obvious that they are questions. A small minority of sentences that are or might be questions causes the preponderance of trouble. This minority comprises several types. One is sentences that are nominally questions but are in fact meant as politely expressed commands—for example, "Will you please button your raincoat." These are not supposed to end with question marks.

There are, as well, sentences that are nominally commands or declarative sentences but are meant as questions, as would be apparent if they were spoken aloud—for example, "He went out like that in public?" and "Call his therapist? Or call the police?" These *are* supposed to end with question marks.

In considering the example sentences just given, we might decide that what determines whether to use a question mark is whether a voice speaking the sentence would end with a rising inflection. Some people have been taught that this is a good test. (Listen, in your mind, to "Call his therapist" and "Call his therapist?") Nonetheless, it is not the case that every true question would end in a rising inflection if the question were said aloud. Think of "What's he done now?" or "What sort of pleasure do you suppose he gets out of embarrassing people?" The real point of distinction is whether or not the idea is interrogative.

And here we have wended our way back to a question raised at the outset of Chapter One: Should it be "Who cares" or "Who cares?" The answer is, It depends. The former is not a question. It might be the presentation of a topic; that is, perhaps it could be restated as "Which people care"—the way it was intended in Chapter One. Or it might be a flat, jaded assertion that amounts to "I don't care and I don't think you should, either"—as might be appropriate in our recent context.

The "Who cares?" version *is* a question, meaning something like "Does anyone care?" The difference between this and the assertion can be subtle, perhaps amounting to whether or not it seems that the writer or speaker is hoping for an answer. ("Who cares?" "Not I!")

As for the other part of the question asked many pages ago, question marks differ from quotation marks in that there's rarely any point in doubling them up. Thus the right way to render *that* was "Should that be 'Who Cares?'" and not "Should *that* be '"Who Cares?"'?"

So, So that

The point of *so* is that something is the cause of or reason for something else. The point of *so that* is that something was *intended* for such a purpose: "I left home early *so that* I could be there to help you clean the house, give the twins their bath, and wash all the pots and pans for you before your party. But there was a traffic jam, *so* I was late after all. What? What do you mean I was wearing my party dress when I arrived *so* you know I can't be telling the truth? Silly! I was wearing the dress *so that* ummm…hmmm…*so that* when I arrived early, you could be the first to see it!"

Then

Then is not a conjunction, so unless you would say "He ate, slept," you shouldn't say "He ate, *then* slept." It's "He ate *and then* slept." Here I'm caviling at sources ranging from the *Encyclopedia of Biological Sciences* ("Abiotic synthesis of organic compounds, first simple *then* complex, preceded the origin of life on earth") to *The New York Times* ("He opened with a tribute to 'freedom fighters,' *then* turned to his main subjects: ribald jokes…, run-ins with the police and the ups and downs of his career") and on to recent fiction ("I put on some music and abluted, *then* made two Nescafés"— *Absolute Beginners,* Colin MacInnes). This construction is fairly common and you'll be in pretty good company if you use it. But I happen to think you'll be in better company if you don't.

Word Fugitives

I often receive letters from people wanting to know whether there's a word for something or other. Even while they haven't a clue about what their word might be, they feel that it must exist, or it should.

They have a point. Strange to say after I have been working with words for so many years, but I marvel at the abundance of things we do have words for. Consider the body. Every part of it has a name: *hair, scalp, forehead, face, ears, eyes, pupils, irises, eyelids, eyelashes, nose, bridge of the nose, nostrils, cheeks, mouth, lips, teeth, tongue* . . . And that's just the very top of the list of our familiar external parts. All our internal parts have names, too, and everything around us has a name, and the parts of most of these things have their own names, and so do the parts of the parts—right on down to molecules that have their own names, and the elements of which they are composed.

And then there are the words that specify the characteristics of things: *my* hair, *messy* hair, *mouse-brown* hair. And words for actions: *muss* my hair, *mousse* my hair, *miss* my hair after it's been cut. And words that specify the characteristics of actions: *merrily* muss, *miserably* muss.

Besides the words for physical things and what happens to them, of course, words exist to describe all sorts of ideas. For example, there are words about words. Consider *macaronic,* "characterized by a mixture of languages"; *metalinguistics,* "the study of the interrelationship between language and other culture-determined behavior"; *metonymy,* "a figure of speech in which one word or phrase is substituted for a related one, as in the use of *Washington* to mean *the United States*"; *misnomer,* "a wrong or unsuitable name"; *mnemonic,* "a device, such as a formula or rhyme, to assist memory"; *monosyllabic,* "employing words of one syllable"; *mood,* "a set of verb forms or inflections indicating whether the speaker considers the action or state referred to as fact or in some other manner"; *moot,* "subject to debate" or "of no practical significance"; *morpheme,* "a meaningful linguistic unit that cannot be divided into smaller meaningful parts"; *mumbo jumbo,* "gibberish"; and *mytacism,* "excessive or wrong use of the letter *m,* or of the sound it represents."

Altogether, at least a million English "lexemes"—words, abbreviations, plant and animal names, and so forth—are in current use, according to David Crystal's *The Cambridge Encyclopedia of the English Language.* Paradoxically, if we started counting those lexemes and recording as new lexemes all the numbers we used that weren't already on the list ("...six hundred fifty-four thousand and one, six hundred fifty-four thousand and two..."), we would end up adding almost another million words. Counting those would add nearly another million, and counting those would—etc. The explanation of the paradox is that numbers made up of other numbers, along with plurals, inflected forms of verbs, and those kinds of things, aren't considered to be lexemes in their own right.

Some thousands of new terms, besides, are coined each year. My colleague Anne Soukhanov presents resonant examples of these in her Word Watch column for *The Atlantic:* among the ones she has recently brought to readers' attention are *Beltropolis, explornography, muscle candy, para-parenting,* and *push polling.*

Nonetheless, our language can exhibit startling gaps. For instance, as Bill Bryson explains in his droll book *Made in America,* "Walking was such an unquestioned feature of everyday life that until 1791, when William Wordsworth coined the term *pedestrian,* there was no special word to describe someone on foot. (Interestingly, *pedestrian* as an adjective meaning dull or unimaginative is significantly older, having been coined in 1716.)"

Even today we lack a concise way to say "because of, or perhaps in spite of." (If there were a single word that could replace what is in effect a seven-word-long preposition, these citations, for example, might be rejiggered to be much more readable: "*Because of, or perhaps in spite of,* the speed and scope of change, other fundamental continuities exist. These are the barriers to world progress" and "*Although—or maybe because*—it looks to the past, it is one of the show's most beautiful objects.") We have no word for the French *voilà*—except *voilà*. Among my reference books is one, *They Have a Word for It,* by Howard Rheingold, devoted entirely to foreign words for which we have no equivalent. In truth, English has directly imported some of these, like *Zeitgeist,* from German, and *mantra,* from Sanskrit. Others are perhaps more culture- or climate-specific—too bad! For instance, in Bantu *mbuki-mvuki* means "to shuck off clothes in order to dance."

All this is by way of saying who knows whether an established word exists for any of the ideas in the letters that follow—ideas that I have taken to calling "word fugitives." (The comedian Rich Hall dubbed such things *sniglets* in the mid-1980s, a period that will no doubt go down in history as the Golden Age of recreational word-coining, owing to the appearance of Hall's book *Sniglets* [1984] on the heels of *The Meaning of Liff* [1983], by Douglas Adams and John Lloyd, which had a similar theme.) Unfortunately, no reference book can readily settle whether such words do exist. "Reverse dictionaries" try their best, but they don't work very well.

Like neologisms, the words that people wish were

available to them tell us something about life today—as you'll see. Most of the letters here came to me by way of a Word Fugitives feature that I created for *The Atlantic*'s Web site. Visitors to the site tried to meet the letter writers' needs with, usually, inventions of their own. I've also included some of these responses here, along with a few of my contributions. You'll notice a widespread cheerful obliviousness of the sensibility that led H. W. Fowler, in *Modern English Usage,* to fulminate against "hybrid derivatives." "Word-making," he wrote, "like other manufactures, should be done by those who know how to do it; others should neither attempt it for themselves, nor assist the deplorable activities of amateurs by giving currency to fresh coinages before there has been time to test them."

> *I'm looking for a word (I'd settle for a phrase!) to describe the children of one's parent's live-in lover.* Significant-siblings? Quasi-step-siblings? *I have a pair of boys in my class, and I find myself saying "your b—— Joe." What is the relationship here?*

> *I have heard of* ovolactovegetarians, vegans, *and* vegetarians. *What are people called who eat fish and poultry (and vegetables and fruit) but not red meat or "the other white meat"? These people will not eat any mammals.*

Would semicarnivore *be specific enough?*

And someone who eats fish but not chicken—or the other way around—would be a *semidemicarnivore.*

> *A friend of mine recently told me about a date he had with a young Russian woman. He wasn't*

extraordinarily fond of her, but he said she had a cer-
tain je ne sais quoi *about her. When I dug deeper into*
this, we made the discovery that he associated qualities
of adorability with her because, in part, she was foreign.

Smithing a word for "cute because foreign" has
been my assignment for some weeks now, and I've not
been able to come up with much other than xenador-
ability *and* xenocute, *both of which I find unpalatable*
and lacking.

Three suggestions: xenerotic, outlandelicious, *and*
geographoxy.

If we shortened the xeno *part to simply* x, *that would*
yield . . . x appeal.

Often I will see the checkout person at the local su-
permarket do it when he or she reaches for a plastic
bag or picks up and counts out my change in paper
currency. I've even seen politicians doing it on TV be-
fore flipping a page in their prepared text.

I'm referring to that nasty, disgusting act of licking
one's thumb and index finger before attempting to
turn a page in a book or handle paper in general. Is
there a name or phrase to describe this very wide-
spread habit? If so, none of my local library re-
searchers has come up with it.

I used this letter to lead off the inaugural group of
Word Fugitives appearing on the Web site. When the
little word NEW appeared on my screen to tell me that
the first suggestion in response to it had come in, I
clicked on the item eagerly. The intellectual dialogue
among *The Atlantic*'s sophisticated, highly literate

readership had begun! Someone had written to suggest
digilingus. I put my head in my hands and groaned.

*My wife and I, in our newlywedded bliss, could not
wait a whole year to celebrate our anniversary. So
we've been marking the day of the month in which we
were married. After five months we decided that we
couldn't call this an anniversary, since the word an-*
niversary *comes from the Latin* annus, *"year."*

*About twenty-five years ago I interviewed a newlywed
couple. She was in her eighties and he was close to
ninety, as I recall. They, because of their advanced
age, had been celebrating what they called* monthiver-
saries, *and that word has been in my vocabulary ever
since.*

Lunaversary, *from the name of the Roman goddess of
the moon, might work, although it may be too close
to lunacy to be sufficiently romantic. Another possibility is* seleniversary, *for the Greek goddess of the
moon, Selene.*

*We need a word for people whose bodies or minds
have some slight flaw or impairment and thus do not
conform to our ideas of "normal," and whose lives
are made difficult by invidious comparisons with this
norm.*
 *The word would need to be less strong than the
dramatic word* disabled, *which draws all attention to
the few things that these mildly impaired people can't
do, instead of the multitude of things they* can *do. It
would be stronger than* different, *since everyone is*

*different. It would need to express "deviating from
the norm," but not with all the negative connotations
of perversion that the word* deviant *has. And it would
be less mawkish and awkward than the oft-lampooned*
differently abled.

*This whole problem could be solved by deleting
the word* normal *from the lexicon. It came into the
English language in its current usage only in the mid
nineteenth century. Previously, it referred to a carpen-
ters' tool. Hard to believe, but for most of recorded
history no one found it necessary to go around saying
things like "You're just not* normal*" and "Try acting*
normal *for once in your life!"*

The main reason the word normal *is dangerous is that
there are two meanings that are not commonly distinguished: 1) "commonplace or average, conforming to
a norm," and 2) "healthy." If we find ourselves being
or doing like most people, we may erroneously conclude that we are healthy—and that if we are different, we must be impaired. Huck Finn, for example,
thought he was a very bad kid for helping Jim escape.
In some places it is still normal to smoke—but
nowhere is it healthy. This goes beyond the word,
doesn't it?*

I am curious about the origin of the word palindrome, *since it seems odd that anyone would feel the
need to devise such a word. But as long as we have it,
how about a word to describe words that read the
same right side up or upside down, such as* dollop?
    And as long as we have onomatopoeia *to describe
words whose sound suggests their meaning, how*

*about a word to describe those whose appearance
suggests their meaning—such as* level, *which is not
only perfectly level in its appearance but even has a
fulcrum in the form of a* v *at its center point?*

dollop = flipnym
level = optonomatopy

I like flipnym. *Can you think of any besides* dollop?

There can't be very many. How about mow?

solos
pod

And don't forget *I.*

If I like English things, I'm an Anglophile. *If I dislike
them, what am I? Not an* Anglophobe—*I'm not
afraid of them. Perhaps a* misanglist, *a coinage similar
to* misanthrope, *but that's pretty awkward.*

In fact *-phobe* can indicate dislike as well as fear—but
if the two emotions were all of a piece, Hunter S.
Thompson's title *Fear and Loathing in Las Vegas*
would be redundant. I heartily agree that our language would benefit from having a new suffix that allowed us to disentangle fear from loathing.

How about Anglodisser? *I know* dis *is short for "disrespect," but we could use it to signify dislike, too. A
cat-hater, who may or may not also be an* ailuro-
phobe, *would thus be called an* ailurodisser. *Poor
soul.*

How about misanglope? *May not be etymologically
correct, but it's cute, and the meaning is obvious.*

What about -o-, or -i-, thope? I don't see it in the dictionary and it has a pseudoscientific ring to it.

From the Toronto Serial Diners Collective: We must say up front that we like -thope a lot. We endorse it heartily, and dismiss all thope-ithopes.

But that didn't stop us from coming up with our own answers. Our two favourites are -defile, which makes for a nice converse to -phile (e.g., Anglodefile); and -bile, which also pairs nicely with -phile (e.g., Anglobile). The latter one suggests hatred strongly, and this can't be confused with fear as the emotion under discussion.

I wish we had more words to describe the different kinds of love. You know: parental love, godly love, sexual love, spousal love, food love, pet love, and so on. Apparently, though I haven't verified this, there are fifty different words in Arabic for different kinds of love. That's what we need!

This idea about Arabic is evidently just a myth, right up there with the myth that Eskimo languages have dozens of words for snow. (Responsible anthropologists and linguists have been trying for some years to lay to rest the one about Eskimos.) A man I know who himself speaks Arabic fluently writes, "I've had a friend do some sleuthing, and even in classical Arabic he can only come up with about ten words for *love* in Arabic, the best of which is *huyaam*: 'a state of wandering about at random in consequence of overpowering love.' But in Arabic as it's spoken today, there really is only one commonly used term, *hubb*, which includes the sense of both *love* and *like*."

Don't you think there should be a word for when a pet and its owner start to look alike? Maybe the word could also apply when a husband and wife start to resemble each other after years of living together.

How about sympatimorphosis?

Symp*eti*morphosis!

Is there a word one may use to express the opposite of emulate? *I find none, but consider using* contraemulate *or* disemulate *when advising, suggesting, or directing that someone's example not be followed.*

I am not quite satisfied with these terms, so in practice I fall back on something like "Don't emulate," and usually get my point across. But I sense a need for a term somewhere between a negative command and a euphemism.

Contradict *in the sense "be contrary to; be inconsistent with" is closely opposite. So, for that matter, is* oppose.

I gather, though, that the letter writer wants a verb that could begin a sentence like "*??* President Clinton in how you conduct your personal life."

"Conduct your personal life to contradict President Clinton's behavioral standards." Not exactly a familiar usage, perhaps.

Shun *is another possibility: "Shun President Clinton's behavior when conducting your personal life."*

Shun is good, because it's an old, simple word falling into desuetude. There's a lot to be said for extending the meanings of, say, the four-letter combinations that already mean something, rather than inventing new combinations, which tend to be longer and more complicated. All the same, *shun* doesn't quite do what the letter writer is asking his word to. Evidently, there's room for a new coinage, too.

Antiemulate. *It seems to work well enough in our sample sentence ("Antiemulate President Clinton's behaviour…"), is instinctively clear, and, as a bonus, affords the possibility for vast amusement by allowing you to construct such sentences as "Antiemulate! Antiemulate! Don't treat Toto as badly as everyone else does!"*

I'm looking for a word to describe the feeling that I'm about to drop my car keys down a sewer drain. I only have this feeling when I take my keys out of my pocket as I'm walking across the parking lot to my car, and I respond by clutching my keys even tighter. Suggestions?

I know of no male counterpart to slut.

What word might describe the female equivalent of cuckold?

I am looking for a word to describe what happens when two people try to pass each other on the street, or in a corridor, and they each rotate to the same side (right-left) three or four times while attempting to establish passing lanes.

❧

Is there a word to describe the last few strands of hair on some balding men that are grown out and combed over to cover a bald spot?

❧

What do you call the stuff left on a car window by a dog?

❧

Here's my question, which my mother and I have been wondering about for years: When you dig a hole in the ground with a shovel, and pile the excavated earth next to the hole, you stand on the ground between the hole and the pile. Is there a name for the area or piece of ground that you are standing on between the nascent hole and the growing pile?

What good sports Word Fugitives readers are! Just look at these responses to that last one:

In math we call the little flat area between a dip and a hill an inflection point. *That is, the curvature changes sign there but the slope does not.*

Or in waves it is called a node—*the point between a hill and a trough.*

Most remarkable of all, no one but me demanded to know exactly why that man was asking.

No Blunders Aloud

More consequential, surely, than our language's lack of any of those specific words is the lack of a direct connection between pronunciation and spelling. For some reason. I have long been on the mailing list of "Dhe Kånådån Nuzletter," apparently a one-man effort, dedicated to phoneticizing Canadian English. Whenever I skim the latest copy, I reflect that if phonetic language would impart to me the phonemes of, say, Emma Thompson or Diana Rigg, I would enlist in the cause today. But what I hear in my mind when I read a "nuz" item like

> *Britan: For sevverål senturies dhe neim ûv dhe british nåsion-ståt hav bied misspeled åz 'Britain' ! No li-idor, nor skolor, håv propozed å korreksion ! It iz taim for dhe Bleir-Labor Government tu korrekt dhis ling-gwistik kriim*

leaves me convinced that we're all better off as we are. In *The Reader Over Your Shoulder,* Robert Graves and Alan Hodge made clear that they thought so, too, explaining:

> *There is to the English eye something distasteful in phonetic spelling. . . . One would have less objection to phonetic or 'simplified' spelling if it could be introduced retrospectively in one's grandfather's days; but nobody likes to make such sacrifices for the sake of his grandchildren.*

Writers, faced with the nuisance of needing to know how to spell, can now get help from spell-checkers as well as from dictionaries. (Although spell-checkers are notoriously unable to distinguish between or among words, like *faced* and *phased,* or *to* and *too* and *two,* they clean up true spelling errors such as *"nusance"* and *"dictonaries"* very effectively.) The most nearly comparable pronunciation tool is the loudspeaker-like icons that appear as part of my CD-ROM dictionary's entries: I can click on one of them if I can't be bothered to make sense of the pronunciation symbols and want to hear the word said properly. Many of us, though, can easily let the computer look our writing over before human beings do, but we tend to do our important speaking directly to people. Thus poor pronunciation is liable to make someone seem more conspicuously ignorant than an inability to spell.

In other ways, too, spelling and pronouncing are not fully comparable—a point worth elaborating on, in case I have elsewhere given the impression that I think spoken and written English are simply two forms of the same thing. They're not, quite. People as a group have been speaking English far longer than they have been writing it. And, of course, each of us learned first to speak and only later to write. Writing, though based on speech, is a somewhat artificial and stripped-down version of it. For example, the tools of writing are quite limited in their ability to convey tone of voice, or inflection, which in spoken English can affect the message dramatically.

Consider, for example, the commonplace sentence "I would never think of that." As written, it is heard in the mind's ear with a light emphasis on both the words *never* and *think*—the sentence's natural inflection. As we discussed above, in the "Unquestioned Answer" about italics, if we think it's important for the written sentence to have a different inflection, we can convey that with italics (some use underlining instead): "*I* would never think of that" suggests by contrast that someone else would do so or has done so; "I *would* never think of that" is objecting to having been contradicted; "I would *never* think of that" is emphatic; "I would never *think* of that" is amazed; and "I would never think of *that*" declares that one has been thinking of something else. But if we were saying this sentence aloud, imagine all the indignant or sly or contemptuous or shamefaced or admiring additional tones that we could communicate. A writer must arrange the context so that readers themselves generate those tones of voice—all the better if it's to their surprise.

Here, though, we are concerned with pronouncing words—pronouncing them one at a time. There are reasons to care about the pronunciations even of words we will never say aloud. Again and again I've had the experience of reading a word—maybe *automaton* or *boustrophedon* or *chaise longue* or *desultory*—and wondering what it's supposed to sound like in my head ("AUtamaton" or "auTOMaton"? "booSTROFedon" or "boostraFEEdon"? and so on). Any word that I can't confidently sound distracts and annoys me, like an itchy mosquito bite. I'm leery of just guessing at the pronunciation and making myself hear the word that way, for someday I may want to say it aloud, and at that point I'll do well to remember that I don't know how to.

Even if none of this is striking a chord in you, please note that, as we'll see, others will judge you on the basis of pronunciation, much the way they will on the basis of spelling and grammar.

Acronyms

I am on a statewide committee working on the development of a computer system. The committee is titled

Statewide Computer Users Group, known as SCUG, *and pronounced "skug," presumably (I thought) because the word computer has a hard* c *or* k *sound. The new system is called the Court Information Processing System, or* CIPS, *which from its inception was pronounced "sips" by the techies. I want to pronounce it "kips," because it seems logical that the sound of the letters in the acronym would follow the sound of the original words. But then, we always think that logic is on our side, don't we?*

Perhaps logic is, but that's not quite the point. You may find history instructive: during World War II the Navy designated a "Commander in Chief of the U.S. Fleet" in the Pacific, but soon discovered that everyone was pronouncing *CinCUS*, the pertinent acronym, "sink us"—and so they changed the name. Today *CERN* (for the Conseil Européen Pour la Recherche Nucléaire) is not pronounced "kern," nor is *UNICEF* (for the United Nations International Children's Emergency Fund) pronounced "unichef." Acronyms, once coined, go off and lead lives separate from those of the words that gave rise to them. They are almost invariably pronounced as they would be if they were wholly independent words.

Conch

A close friend and I have had a bitter dispute over how to pronounce the word conch. *Is the* ch *pronounced as in* cherry, *or does it have a hard* k *sound, or are both pronunciations considered correct?*

Dictionaries give both pronunciations for *conch*, but all of mine give the "conk" pronunciation first.

Certainly, this is the pronunciation that tends to be heard in the Caribbean (first pronunciation "CaribBEun," second "CaRIBbeun"), where much conch meat and many conch shells come from.

Coup de grâce

Nearly three decades ago I heard one of my young colleagues (an assistant professor of English) pronounce coup de grâce *rhyming with* Mardi gras. *I gently suggested (as I blushed) that he should consult an* American *dictionary. He did, and he blushed.*

Since then, for the last three decades, I have heard all the major anchorpersons (except for those from Canada?) and just about everybody (not yet any U.S. President?) pronounce the phrase the non-American-dictionary way. A sudden panic drove this paranoiac to look it up in an American dictionary—Webster's New Collegiate—while writing this line, and to my great relief, nothing has changed.

That's right. In fact, this one is pronounced with a final *s* sound even in French. It's "mardee grah" but "coo de gras." "Zheh neh pahl pah frhonsay" comes in handy, too, at times.

Filet, Fillet

I wish that grocery stores would stop trying to sell "fill-its" of fish and that framing shops would stop trying to put "fee-lays" of decorative molding around the inside of their mats and frames.

My old two-dollar Webster's *(which I got at a gro-*

cery store) makes the distinction, but The American Heritage Dictionary, *in my opinion, is in error.*

My own preference is to buy *fish fillets* and *filets of beef,* both to be pronounced "feLAY," and to ask for *fillets* on frames, to be pronounced "FILLits." But I can't pretend that this opinion is definitive; well-regarded up-to-date dictionaries don't unanimously agree—or out-and-out disagree—with either you or me.

Forte

Describing my attributes to a prospective client in Princeton, New Jersey (I am a freelance writer), I stated that writing long pieces—brochures and such—is my forte, *pronouncing it "fort." During the ensuing discussion, the man interviewing me referred to my* forte, *pronouncing it "FORtay," not so subtly letting me know that he felt I had used the incorrect pronunciation. I couldn't help hearing a hint of condescension in his tone. However, I do believe my pronunciation was correct:* forte *pronounced "fort" is a thing a person does particularly well, as opposed to* forte *pronounced "FORtay," a musical term meaning "loud." I believe this man's mistake is a very common one. Then again, do the wordsmiths in Princeton know something those in less academic communities do not?*

Your interviewer does seem to have had exceptional knowledge of how to sow self-doubt in others. You're quite right about the preferred pronunciations for *forte* in its different meanings—and right, too, not to have tried to correct a sales prospect's pronunciation.

Gantlet, Gauntlet

We should not confuse a gauntlet *with a* gantlet, *though* gantlet *may be spelled "gauntlet" and* gauntlet *may be spelled "gantlet." If* gantlet *is spelled "gaunt- let," therefore, should it be pronounced "gauntlet" or "gantlet," and if* gauntlet *is spelled "gantlet," should it be pronounced "gantlet" or "gauntlet"?*

These days both the glove one throws down and the line some have been forced to run as punishment tend to be spelled *"gauntlet,"* and pronounced that way, too. The only indisputable *gantlet* remaining is, ac- cording to *The American Heritage Dictionary,* "a section of double railroad tracks formed by the tem- porary convergence of two parallel tracks in such a way that each set remains independent."

Pachelbel

How to pronounce foreign words is sometimes of concern, and within this broad area composers' names are a small but significant field. Knowledgeable people know that Chopin *doesn't sound the way it looks and* Tchaikovsky *has a silent* T *(which begs us to ask, Why is it there, since it isn't in the original Cyrillic spelling?). But my question involves yet an- other composer, whose name, I believe, is mispro- nounced even by music scholars more often than it is pronounced correctly. At least, according to some of my German friends it is. This composer (who was German) is noted for only one composition, popular at weddings and occasionally other venues: Canon in D. The composer:* Pachelbel. *This one composition of*

*his is enough to give rise to a need to say his name,
but he's too obscure to be found in the standard home
references that give pronunciations. (For the record,
we Americans tend to pronounce* Pachelbel *with the
accent on the first syllable, but the Germans accent
the second.) Can you tell me—not on the basis of how
the local classical DJ says it but on that of international authority—the correct pronunciation?*

There *is* no international standard pronunciation for
names—either personal or geographic ones. (Think of
Paris, whose denizens call it "ParhEE"; think of
Mexico, whose citizens call it "MAYheeco.") The way
German people pronounce *Pachelbel* isn't quite
relevant to the way you'll want to pronounce it,
therefore. I'd go with the standard American
pronunciation you describe: "PACKelbel."

The author of the original letter wrote me back:

Thanks. Paris *is a good example of our inconsistency.
The classical-music genre has, however, been an exception to the colloquialization (is that a word?) of
foreign words. I know of no intentional exception in
the pronunciation of composers' names from their
original. Even names as common as* Charles *get the
"Sharl" pronunciation if the composer was French.*
Bach *is pronounced with the guttural sound that is
characteristic of German and rare or absent in
English. I still think we in the classical-music area
would seek international authority.*

There's certainly nothing to stop you from pronouncing any name as nearly as you can to the way the person holding it would, or would have. And it's true

that the great majority of names are pronounced so as to imitate the original pronunciation. (The only exceptions I can think of are translations of names bestowed according to their meaning, such as that of the English royal Crusader *Richard the Lion-Hearted,* also known as *Richard Cœur de Lion.*)

Not everyone, though, will be impressed if you strew the stream of your English discourse with foreign phonemes. The effect is much like the one achieved by someone who habitually drops little French *je ne sais quois* into conversation. *C'est-à-dire,* it can seem affected, *n'est-ce pas?* Besides, switching back and forth from the phonemes of one language to those of another is even more awkward to do than it is to hear. In pronouncing foreign names, as in playing music, artfulness demands that we avoid seeming to try too hard.

I'm saying all this so that you won't think everyone's just being slipshod if I am now able to convince you that classical-music mavens don't in fact attempt to say every composer's name just as it would be said in the composer's native language. At least, I have it on the authority of a film-score composer who has worked in France that French musicians pronounce *Mozart* so that it rhymes with *beaux-arts.* And Chinese ones, so I am told by a native speaker of Mandarin, tackle *Tchaikovsky* (one of several possible romanizations of that name, effected according to a common and consistent, if unintuitive, system of transliteration) by rendering it with characters that appear as *"Cai Ke Fu Si Ji"* when spelled according to the Pinyin system (itself an unintuitive romanization) and are pronounced something like "Tsy-kuh-foo-suh-jee."

Palette

Is it good form to pronounce palette *in the French way if one is American? The alternative not only sounds inelegant but already has two other meanings ("upper part of the mouth" and "skid for loading heavy objects").*

American dictionaries do seem to think that the only proper pronunciation is "PALit," and yet I understand your objections to saying it this way. As for "paLET," not only is it the proper French pronunciation but also no oral contortions are required to get it out in the midst of an English sentence. The choice is yours—but see the entry for "Valet," later in this chapter, before making up your mind.

Primer

My boss and I disagree with just about everyone (not an unusual circumstance) on the pronunciation of the word primer. *Most people, it seems, pronounce it as if it were spelled "primmer," as in the phrase* prim *and* proper. *We think it should be pronounced "prime-r" as in* the prime rate *or to* prime a pump. *Please advise.*

What meaning of *primer* did you have in mind? *The American Heritage Dictionary* and *Webster's Third* both think that a "prime-r" is a blasting cap or an undercoat of paint, and that a "primmer" is a basic book.

T

Many years ago I was a speech teacher in Wichita, Kansas. We tried to get our students to pronounce the h *in* what, why, wheel, *etc. We lost the* h *battle. Are we about to lose the battle for* t *in words such as* painter, center, *and* county? *I've heard these words on TV and radio pronounced as if there were no* t *in them at all. They are pronounced "painer," "cener," "couny." I have even heard "Alana" for* Atlanta.

Just a moment, please—I'm not ready to concede that the *h* battle *is* lost. As for those *t*s, I have not yet begun to fight!

The

I am disturbed by the disappearance of the distinction between the long-e pronunciation and the schwa pronunciation of our definite article the. *It has gotten to the point where entire segments of our population see no use for the long-e version before a word that has an initial vowel sound. Many educated speakers seem to be ignoring this (to me) very important difference. From President Clinton tonight, in an interview with Jim Lehrer: "What's 'thuh' issue, what's 'thuh' answer?" In the case of actors in their roles on TV, I wonder, Are they directed by their directors to deliberately use the wrong* the, *or do they just not know the difference?*

As a teacher of fifth-grade youngsters here in the Bronx, New York, I have been noticing for many years that my students rarely make this distinction.

Just to make your point more concrete: you are referring to the difference in pronunciation between *the* in front of a vowel and *the* before a consonant—between " 'thuh' definite article" and " 'thee' article," or " 'thuh' question" and " 'thee' answer." This distinction is still considered to be basic to standard English. Many native speakers, however, are not even aware that they are observing this distinction, so let's hope it never needs to be widely and vigorously defended, or it's likely to be in trouble. Perhaps it already is in trouble. The psycholinguist Jean Fox Tree, of the University of California at Santa Cruz, recently announced her discovery of evidence that most of the time when people use the "thee" pronunciation, a "speech suspension" follows: they don't know what they're going to say next, beyond "uh" or "um."

Valet

After friends ridiculed me for sounding the t *in* valet *(as in* valet *parkers) instead of saying "vaLAY," I consulted four dictionaries. All say that the first pronunciation is "VALit," the second is "VALay," and "vaLAY" is a poor third. Shall I continue according to the dictionary and be laughed at—or what?"*

You raise a difficult issue. I don't believe that I have ever heard any American pronounce the *t* in *valet*—although many people from the land of Jeeves and *The Remains of the Day* do. Nonetheless, that *t* appears in the first pronunciations in five of six American dictionaries and one Australian one that I consulted for you. (The exception is *The Random House Unabridged.*)

No matter how one pronounces words with conspicuously foreign origins, some people will make fun. A person is more likely to be ridiculed, though, for doing the opposite of what you did: for, that is, gargling and snorting in an attempt to articulate *au gratin.* In a case like that, I would gently explain to the speaker that many English words are borrowed from other tongues, and that most of them quickly become Americanized—as is evidenced by the all-American first pronunciations given in our dictionaries.

What dictionaries declare nearly unanimously is nearly ipso facto correct. And so you may hold your head high as you say "VALit"—and keep it high throughout the exchange that will inevitably follow, while you perhaps also pull a couple of dictionaries out of your bag and show them around to prove your point. You might prefer, though, to consign "VALit" to a category with "It is I" as an answer to "Who's there?" We all know that it's correct, but we may still choose to be wrong, out of a wish not to seem to be flaunting our superior knowledge.

After that exchange appeared in the column, some-one wrote in to declare:

Regardless of the dictionary references, I will park my own car rather than concede.

Double or Nothing

Now, I do understand that people write me wanting to make a point or to find something out; rarely is it their primary aim to charm me. All the same, they do not charm me when they write letters that begin, "In your recent column why did you use the redundant [or 'wasteful'] expression ————," go on to hawk up some very ordinary turn of phrase, and conclude by telling me I ought to be ashamed of myself. An uncharming glint comes into my own eye when I notice in some of these letters that they contain what a person eager to find fault with such things would regard as redundancies or wastes of words of their own.

A component of speaking and writing well is the minor art of knowing when the expenditure of a few extra words to say something will yield a more polished or dramatic result and when it will strike others as foolish or prodigal. The analogies with spending money and living well are obvious. Many excesses do not enhance a person's life or standing but, rather, earn him or her contempt. And so writing guides give advice like "Use no more words than are necessary to do the job" (*The Complete Plain Words,* by Sir Ernest Gowers) and "No unnecessary idea, phrase or word should be included in a sentence" (*The Reader Over Your Shoulder,* by Robert Graves and Alan Hodge) and—practicing what it preaches—"Omit needless words" (Strunk and White's *Elements of Style*).

That said, it is also true that pleonasm, or the use of more words than are strictly required to express an idea, was long considered a rhetorical device, rather than necessarily a misuse. Now as ever, words that neither add information to a sentence nor are required by grammar can benefit emphasis or tone. Objections to these words are like a complaint against the pepper in a sauce because it adds no nutritional value to the food, or against some lucky couple's sailboat because they don't need it for transportation to work.

With all this in mind, let's look at some specific complaints about redundancies and wastes of words. Indeed, there are many redundancies to complain of. But I hope to show you that there's much more of what is generally called redundancy in our language than has probably ever come to your attention, and that a good deal of it is harmless or better.

Acronyms and Initialisms

Possibly the worst common redundancy is PIN *number—literally, "personal identification number number." Yet to simply say "Please give me your* PIN*" seems incomplete.*

A neat feature of English etymology is that it serves as a mnemonic device: once we know the context, *personal identification number* is pretty much self-explanatory. Acronyms and initialisms (strictly speaking, "acronyms" are pronounced as words and "initialisms" are spelled aloud) are derived in a less helpful way, and so it's natural—though you're right that it's bad form—to give a little assistance to any we are unsure of or imagine that others might be. Hence that extra *number* with PIN. Hence, too, *ATM machine* and *GPS system* and *AC current* and *HIV virus*. The proper way to give assistance, at least in writing, is with the likes of "PIN (personal identification number)" or "automated teller machine (ATM)." If it were up to me, though, I'd have people stop coining or using TLAs ("three-letter acronyms," an, um, initialism that I didn't coin) and go back to giving new things actual names.

Actually

See Emphasis words.

Apparatus

I thought I would lose my mind this evening when the television reporter covering the women's gymnastic

*Olympic trials kept referring to the balance beam, un-
even bars, and other gymnastic equipment each as a
"piece of apparatus." This is not a controversy, and I
do not need a dispute settled. I just felt like sharing
this annoying phrase with someone.*

Thanks. In fact, people don't even need to appear on
television to make fools of themselves if they use
words without really knowing what they mean.

Both

Overheard on a news broadcast: "And both *sides are
still* far apart *on the issues." Gee, I thought only one
side was far apart. Doesn't* both *suggest separate action? If you hear "They're* both *getting married,"
don't you picture two ceremonies?*

Well, yes. The classic redundancy for *both* is with
same, as in "*Both* of them decided to use the *same*
last name after they were married." But similar mistakes are possible with a number of expressions in
which the idea of "two" or, at any rate, "more than
one" already lurks somewhere. Examples are "*Both*
of them have a last name *in common*" (which would
be better said "The two of them..." or "They...")
"They share one name *between both* of them"
("...between them"), and "*Both* have *agreed* to use
one last name" ("The two of them..." or "They...").

*I wrote to you only yesterday, and I think I made the
kind of error I was referring to—misuse of a common
word. It's so embarrassing to have written "overheard
on a news broadcast." If you should use my letter in
your column, I would be most grateful if you would
change the offending word to the more appropriate*

heard. *I will leave you with this gem I heard on the BBC World Service:* "*...was accused of 'activities incompatible with diplomatic status,' often* shorthand *for 'spying.'* "

Concede

Please resolve an ongoing dispute with two friends, Angela and Edwin. To Angela, I had written (after a different dispute), "I concede defeat." Choosing to kick me while I was down, she commented that my admission of defeat was linguistically incorrect, since the word concede *already indicates defeat. What follows is the haughty opinion of Edwin, who majored in English at Harvard: "Angela is right. You should have said, 'I concede.' Concede defeat is redundant, like revert back."*

You can never win with Angela, can you? Are she and Edwin correct, or am I?

Concede, intransitive (that is, when it's not followed by an object), means "yield," so in fact you could have made your point with two words rather than three. But there's also a transitive version, which can mean either "yield [something]" or "admit [something]." *Concede* in this last sense is perfectly suitable to your purpose, so do hold your head up. Perhaps in your three words you went on a little longer than was necessary about Angela's having gotten the better of you, but since when do most people mind that?

Destroy

I know that English is a changing language. My old college professor drilled that fact into my brain. But it

*has changed so much that network news anchors now
go on the air and redundantly report that a tornado
totally destroyed a house. I hear local television news
reporters and anchors use the phrase (along with
completely destroyed) so frequently that I fear I may
have been gone from the college classroom too long
and that redundancy is now grammatically correct,
especially when striving for the sensational. Please
advise.*

Your question highlights a property that many verbs
quietly possess, the same one for which the adjective
unique is famous—namely, these words don't occur
by degrees. One doesn't, for instance, *partly,* or *totally*
or *completely, fire* a gun; one just *fires* it. The bullet
either *hits* something or *misses* the target, and it either
kills someone or fails to; in each case, there are no
three ways about it. And if the bullet hits the cuckoo
clock on the wall it certainly might *destroy* the clock,
but can the bullet be said to *totally destroy* it, or
partly destroy it?

There are verbs that do occur by degrees: someone
might, for example, *have completely forgotten* how to
use a gun, not *fully understand* how dangerous it is to
keep one sitting around loaded, and just manage to
partly conceal it when a police officer happens by his
house, selling tickets to the annual ball.

Then again, many verbs don't ordinarily occur by
degrees but may do so under special circumstances.
The man and the policeman might be said to *converse*;
they might be said to *argue*; they might be said to
partly converse and *partly argue*. To gain control of
the gun, they might *box* with each other; they might
wrestle; they might *partly box* and *partly wrestle*.

But, again, what we want to know is, If the gun goes off by mistake, will it *totally destroy* the cuckoo clock or just *destroy* it? The usage panel for the *Harper Dictionary of Contemporary Usage* was almost evenly split between those who found degrees appropriate to *destroy* and those who saw them as redundant, as you do. Some who had no objection to *completely destroyed* saw it as emphatic, rather than as suggesting that gradations of destruction are possible. But others insisted that of course there are gradations: "If a fire devastates part of a city," the author Isaac Asimov argued, "the city is *'partially destroyed.'* "

The American Heritage Dictionary doesn't come down firmly on one or the other side of the question, either. In two of its six definitions of *destroy*, it uses the word *completely*, indicating that the idea of completeness is built into the word in those senses. And two of the other definitions are "to do away with; put an end to" and "to kill." To that extent, the dictionary seems to agree with you that the word doesn't generally admit of gradations. But it goes on to say that synonyms for the word can be found under *ruin*—and there one learns that *ruin* itself "implies irretrievable harm but not necessarily *total destruction*."

Hmm. It seems to me that we are being led toward the fascinating possibility that gradations exist within the idea of gradations. Although some people perceive *totally destroy* and certain comparable constructions (say, "The policeman's lawsuit *completely bankrupted* him") as emphatic and are untroubled by the hint of gradation they contain, surely no one would see other, formally similar sentences ("If the bird in that clock

had been a real one, it would have been *completely
killed*") as anything but hopelessly silly.

Dunes

It has been contended that the use of sand dunes *is redundant and that only the word* dunes *should be
used. Would you please give me guidance?*

Dictionaries will tend to tell you that *dunes* are made
of sand, but you'll notice that not even a prescriptive
dictionary, like the *American Heritage,* or the major
usage guides warn against using the two words together. What's more, America's public lands include a
Great *Sand Dunes* National Monument—and also a
White Sands National Monument, known for its
gypsum-crystal dunes. I think the number of words
you should expend when referring to peaked formations of grains of disintegrated rock is up to you.

Emphasis words

The improper or superfluous use of actually *has been
driving me up a wall ever since I detected its continual
conversational misuse six months ago. I was helping
my sister with apartment hunting in Seattle when a
potential landlord asked her what she did for a living.
She replied, "Actually, I'm a consultant in the medical
field." From that moment on I have been keeping
track of this word as it has appeared in my own
(thankfully, less and less) and others' speech patterns.
Am I the only one who is besieged by this?*

Probably not, but let me introduce you to a few
people who are bothered by other things.

*Could you tell me—does anyone know—why sud-
denly everyone is compelled to use the word* indeed? *I
seem to hear it from the 6:00* A.M. *exercise girl on TV
straight through the evening news reports. Perhaps it
sounds educated, a device to impress. I instantly catalogue the user as a failure—someone whose grass is in
desperate need of cutting.*

*A phrase in common usage today that always trips
me up is* of course. *By my lights, this is a "word
whisker": something superfluous that improves sentence flow when shaved off.*

 The definition of of course *is instructive: "1. In
the natural or expected order of things; naturally.
2. Without any doubt; certainly." If* indeed *(my God!*
indeed *means "of course") the idea expressed in the
sentence is natural, expected, or certain, why interject*
of course? *I await your sage counsel on this matter.
You may, of course, edit this as you see fit.*

*I do enjoy your column. What I do not enjoy is seeing
comments from readers who are simply wrong. Now,
what did the word* simply *add to the previous sentence? Not much, I would imagine. Neither did a correspondent of yours have much to add when he used
the phrase "simply and more clearly." I think I can
justify* more clearly, *but what is simpler than* clear?

And much the same goes for *naturally, obviously, really, what's more, in fact, merely, just,* and quite a
large number of other words—among them *quite.*
And the *ever* in *ever since.* And what about *in the
past?* In a sentence like "*In the past* this was not a

problem," doesn't the past tense of the verb make the point? Similarly, "all that *remains today*" is redundant, and the *several* in "for *several* years" adds nothing in particular. Isn't the *No.* in *No. 1* redundant? And in "by photographing the sculpture from four *different* angles," what difference does *different* make? Out with the *first* in "when I *first* had this idea"! And on and on and on.

Or, at least, so someone who likes clean and, um, simple language could argue. There are writing styles that shun all the little words, like the ones above, nudging others' minds toward the speaker's or writer's vantage point. Ernest Hemingway, a winner of the Nobel Prize for Literature, wrote, "Prose is architecture, not interior decoration, and the Baroque is over." And yet it's not as if the only alternative to Baroque linguistic architecture were brutalism. Moreover, prose can be interior decoration instead of architecture—or it can be both things. That the writing of Saul Bellow, Isaac Bashevis Singer, Gabriel García Márquez, Toni Morrison, Seamus Heaney, and Wislawa Szymborska—all of whom won Nobel Prizes in the last quarter of the twentieth century—arises from ambitious blueprints and explores important themes does not mean that it is uniformly unadorned.

Or, to return to the little figure of speech that was invoked at the beginning of this section, no more than we should waste money should we want to waste words. But surely our linguistic pockets are deep enough for us to spend a few words frivolously, on things beyond the bare necessities—because these things may bring our listeners or our readers closer to us, or simply because it pleases us to spend them.

Exception

In today's New York Times, *I saw: "Bucknell has pro-duced few truly famous names. The writer Philip Roth is one* exception.*" The correct way of stating this, in my opinion: "Bucknell has produced few truly famous names. The writer Philip Roth is one."*

Right you are! Thanks.

Free gift

Eventually, I have found opportunity to ask a ques-tion that has been nagging me since the time I came to the USA as an immigrant. The expression free gift *sounded for me absurdly. Here is a definition of* gift *from* The American Heritage Dictionary: *"Something that is bestowed voluntarily and without compensa-tion." What will you think of this?*

As you become a more seasoned observer of the American scene, you will learn that a *free gift* stands in the same relation to an ordinary gift as a *Super Sale Spectacular!* stands to charging what traffic will bear for shopworn merchandise. Indeed, the element of hype built into this tautology always makes me sus-pect that any *free gift* coming to me will be worth ex-actly what I paid for it.

Have got

"How much money have *you* got?*" "I've* got *to get a haircut." What has happened to plain old* have? *Is frequent usage making this redundancy correct?*

Early in the twentieth century H. L. Mencken, in his *The American Language*, wrote, "The common American tendency to overwork a favorite verb has been often noted by English observers.... In our own time *to get* has done the heaviest service." Across the pond H. W. Fowler wrote, "*Have got* for *possess* or *have* is good colloquial but not good literary English."

Get is perennially called into question, and with *have,* it's perennially informal. The combination is not especially wasteful, though. Without *get,* in order to sound natural your first example sentence would need to be emended to "How much money *do* you *have*?" and what has been elided in your second would need to be put back ("I *have* to get a haircut"). The result in each case would be a sentence with just as many syllables as the original.

Indeed

See Emphasis words.

Obviate

Why do I always see in the print media obviates the need to *instead of simply* obviates? *I have been astonished at the frequency of this. For example, from an article in my local paper about a trial: "Reynolds' appearance on his own behalf—and denial that he had sex with Heard—obviated the need to call his wife, who could have made a strong impression on jurors...." The irony, of course, is that the word* obviate *obviates* the need to.

There are two points of view on *obviate*. According to the one you subscribe to, which most recent dictionaries support, the word means "make unnecessary"— and who would ever say *made unnecessary the need*

to...? According to the other, more traditional point
of view, which older dictionaries and the *Oxford
English Dictionary* support, the word has to do with
clearing away potential obstacles, and means something more like "do away with." In your example the
obstacle would be the need, not the calling, and "did
away with the need to call his wife" would be more
nearly what was meant than "did away with calling
his wife," so in this view *obviated the need to* is
what's needed after all.

These possibilities have little common ground.
Anyone who tries to fulfill both at once will end up
with the idea of making obstacles unnecessary—not
an idea that arises often. Come to think of it, there's a
third possible point of view on *obviate*: that it, like so
many other words, has two meanings.

Of course

See Emphasis words.

Own

*We sometimes hear "Harry owns his own clothing
business." Could he own anyone else's? Hardly possible. To correct this redundancy, I'd say, "Harry
owns a clothing business."*

I'm not fond of the repetition of *own* in your initial example, but "Harry *has* his *own* business" strikes me as
nothing more nefarious than a way of stressing that the
man is in business for himself. Your revision puts more
stress on the type of business that Harry owns.

Pre-

I recently saw a plastic bag of salad ingredients labeled pre-washed *and* pre-torn, *and wonder how this is different from their having been just* washed *and* torn? *I wonder if this insidious, redundant use of* pre- *has been sneaked into the language of hyperbole and marketing, to add a scientific-sounding ring to otherwise cold and mundane acts. Don't* pre-shrunk, pre-cooked, *and* pre-glazed *sound a bit more official than they would otherwise?*

Good question—and one that my colleague Cullen Murphy considered at length in an article called "Anticipation," in the November, 1998, *Atlantic Monthly.* He observed:

I wear pre-washed jeans. I have outstanding loans for which I was pre-qualified and which I hope to pre-pay, and hold credit cards for which I was pre-selected and pre-approved. I make pre-retirement deductions from my pre-tax earnings. I pre-medicate before going to the dentist, because of a pre-existing condition....

This is an age best seen, the argument goes, not as anything in itself but as 'post' something else: 'postmodern' (even 'post-postmodern'), to cite the most common example, not to mention post-industrial, post-Freudian, post-feminist, post-literate, post-human, post-grunge, or post-God. No doubt there is something to this argument. As a practical matter, though, we may be more beholden to what we're pre- than to what we're post-. And 'pre-' will only proliferate as anticipatory tools—genetic assays, medical diagnostics, environmental-impact analyses, demo-

graphic forecasting, economic modeling, market re-
search—further ease the path of its preferment.

Reason...because

The other day I heard my usually well-spoken son say
"The reason was because..." I said, "Oh, no. The
reason was that..." Since then I have heard and seen
"The reason was because..." in many places: on TV
and even in an English mystery novel. But it does not
seem correct to me and I was happy, recently, to hear
Alan Greenspan say "The reason was that..."

> *Perhaps I am living in the past (I am ninety-three),*
> *and am not au courant with modern colloquialisms.*

"The *reason* is *because*" is a notorious little waste of
words, no purpose being served by using both *reason*
and *because* to explain oneself. It's not so much a colloquialism as an oversight. The *reason* people so often
say this is *that* they don't think back to what they've
already said. Or perhaps they say it *because* they
don't think ahead?

Reason why

I was dismayed to see "the reason why" in your
column. I was taught that it is redundant. Any
comment?

Your letter was one of the more polite among many
written to, ahem, inquire about my sentence "Tradition...is *the* only *reason why*..." There's no doubt
that, for example, "Tell me *the reason why* you cried,
and *the reason why* you lied to me" would be better
the way the Beatles sang it—with four fewer words.

And yet *the reason why* is no more redundant than
the person who or *the place where.* In sentences,
therefore, that one is tempted to "correct" by simply
substituting *that* for *why,* why bother? Whether *the
reason why* is a waste of words is always worth thinking about, but sometimes the answer is no.

Refer back

*One of the responses in your latest column employed
five instances of "refer [or referring] back." For example, you wrote, "Which, a relative pronoun, ought
to be* referring back *to an antecedent noun, which in
this case doesn't exist." For as long as I've known, the*
back *in* refer back *has been a solecism, or redundancy.
My* Harper Dictionary of Contemporary Usage *(second edition) supports me by declaring, "Since the prefix 're-' means 'back,' a second 'back' is superfluous."
Is it now possible to* refer forward *to someone or
something? Could one say "The subject at the front of
the sentence* refers forward *to the predicate noun"? Or
might I say "If you didn't care for today's lackluster
performance, I* refer *you to tomorrow's expected
effort"?*

Perhaps you noticed that under "refer back" the
Harper Dictionary also refers the reader to "redundancy." But there *refer back* is not mentioned—
though *revert back* is. Certainly, *revert back* is
redundant, and *refer back* is sometimes said to be. Is
it really, though? Not according to some reputable
sources, including *Merriam-Webster's Dictionary of
English Usage.* Their idea is that, for example, you
could have referred this question to a third party but
instead you *referred* it *back* to me. And the phrase

where I originally used it was meant to make clear that a pronoun's antecedent will, preferably, antecede and the pronoun will indeed refer *back*.

Relation, Relationship

I am a member (perhaps the only member) of a group out to eliminate the use of the word relationship. Relation *has the same meaning but four fewer characters. Efficiency and economy being such wonderful things, I think we should always use the shorter of two words, especially when they have exactly the same meaning. Does anyone want to join the club?*

What would you do with a sentence like "He and she discovered they were blood *relations,* and so they thought they'd better call off their *relationship"?*

-self

When, not long ago, the U.S. Food and Drug Administration promulgated new guidelines for the use of the word *healthy* on food labels, *The Atlantic*'s Almanac department published an item about it. In response, a letter came in to Word Court about *healthy* versus *healthful,* which I published, in turn. (You can find the exchange in Chapter Four.) Trying to keep things simple, and because *The Atlantic* had merely quoted the FDA, I edited out the references to the Almanac item. But I was mindful of it when I wrote, "*I myself* like to observe the distinction you make." A number of letters arrived like the one that follows.

I find it amusing that some of the people contributing esoteric fine points on grammatical usage employ phrases such as "I myself." I don't know whether or not these are grammatically incorrect, but they sure are redundant. Phrases such as I personally *for "I" seem to indicate a lack of confidence in the writer. If your not sure about what your saying throw in an extra word here and there to reinforce it.*

Hey, come on. *Myself*—along with *yourself* and *himself* and *herself* and *yourselves* and *themselves,* and, for that matter, most other words—exists for a reason. As I used *myself* there, it distinguished between *I* the individual and *I* the representative of my magazine.

P.S. Has it ever occurred to you that there might be such a thing as being *over*confident?

Simply

See Emphasis words.

Surround

I may be a minority of one about the word surround. *To me,* completely surround *is a redundancy, and* surrounded on three sides *is a misuse. I realize that* Webster's New World Dictionary, Third College Edition, *defines* peninsula *as "a land area* almost entirely surrounded *by water..." To me, "a land area* almost surrounded *by water..." would be better.* Entirely *seems redundant here.* Webster's *also shows* surround *as a synonym for* enclose. *Am I being pedantic?*

No, not really. As *Webster's* itself says about *surround,* the word's meanings include "enclose on all sides: envelop" and "extend around the margin or edge of: encircle." Other dictionaries agree. What seems to get people into trouble is the fruitless search for one word that means "partly surround." *Encircle, enclose, encompass, gird,* and so on all mean "go all the way around," as *surround* does, and *abut, adjoin, border, neighbor,* and so on don't convey much more than "touch on." Your *almost surround* is as close as our language comes to what people have in mind.

Think to myself

The entry for this phrase could just as well have appeared in the "Unquestioned Answers" section, above, because no one has asked me about *think to myself.* But as I have often *said* to myself, the phrase is a silly—and common—redundancy. And so here it is in the section about things of that kind.

This past

I often see sentences like this: "This past winter *I went to twenty movies."* Or "This past autumn *I attended the theater ten times."* This past *looks to me like an oxymoron. What's wrong with saying (in February)* "This winter I went to twenty movies"? *Or (in February again)* "Last autumn I attended the theater ten times"?

Except that in February winter is far from over, nothing is wrong with saying either of those things. But what's wrong with keeping our options open? Since *this winter* means the present one or one in the near future, *this past winter* is a perfectly natural way to make the distinction.

Too

The New York Times *has just reported that some voters are rejecting a certain political candidate because*

they believe that "his views are too extreme." Does
this mean they might vote for him if he were per-
ceived as moderately extreme?

Definition one in my Webster's *for* extreme *is "the*
utmost...the farthest reaches," a denotation that
would preclude too extreme *as redundant. On the*
other hand, definition five indicates that extreme *can*
mean "drastic."

This *is* a sort of redundancy, but the problem isn't the
word *extreme.* At least, nothing is solved by changing
extreme to *drastic,* for being drastic to an appropriate
degree is no easier than being appropriately extreme.
The problem is *too,* which in combination with any
value-laden word can wind up declaring something
too foolish to say—to give you another example.
(What degree of foolishness would be all right?) *Too*
carries pejorative force, and in combination with a
pejorative word like *extreme* it can be too, too
much.

Heaping up any two kinds of disapproval in a
single sentence can cause a problem of the same kind:
"His views are *more extreme than centrist voters*
like," "His views *overemphasize* the *racist* elements in
his party's message," and "His views are *inappropri-*
ately offensive," for instance, are all just a little bit
too foolish to say.

Tragedy

I often hear the media, along with politicians and
police and fire officials, refer to an event as a
terrible tragedy. *This unnecessary use of the adjective*
is irritating—all tragedies are terrible. Any
comments?

I know what you mean, but I'm going to save my indignation for mentions of *wonderful tragedies.*

Whether or not

> *Why did you recently start a paragraph in Word Court with the redundant "whether or not"? It encourages sloppy thinking, which leads to sentences like "I don't know whether or not we are going or not."*

Just plain *whether* seems so abrupt in places, and the sentence you are writing about ("*Whether or not* you should use the word depends on your audience") struck me as one such place. What's more, *or not* tends to even out the balance between the alternatives: "*Whether* you should..." would give more weight to the idea that you might than that you might not.

Sometimes the *or not* is actually needed. Think of "I'll buy it *whether* my husband approves." As Theodore M. Bernstein explains in his *The Careful Writer* (you'll recall that I quoted this paragraph of his in Chapter Two of this book), wherever substituting *if* for *whether* would change the meaning ("I'll buy it *if* my husband approves"—hmm), the *or not* is de rigueur. Like it or not (and surely you wouldn't have me say just *Like it*), that's the rule.

I'm certainly in agreement with that last correspondent, nonetheless, that sloppy thinking is the problem underlying the redundancies that bear worrying about. Along with the example he devised, I'd call sloppy "...*looks visually* enticing," which I recently saw in catalogue copy; "have your travel agent secure an *advance reservation,*" in a travel newsletter; "a great-*tasting fla-*

vor," in an ad; "you will find *bargain* items at *low prices,*" in a guidebook; and a politician's comment, reported on NPR, that the moment was *"way too premature"* to consider a certain step. Nonce redundancies like these are the ones to beware of. Alas, unlike *whether or not*s, *actually*s, and *concessions of defeat*, they can't be rooted out by rote.

CHAPTER SIX

∾

Wise to the Words

The writing of good English is…a moral matter, as the Romans held that the writing of good Latin was.
—ROBERT GRAVES AND ALAN HODGE

WORD COURT
   The Importance of being a COMMA.
   You are in the position to confirm what the Supreme Court has already stated in U.S.v.s. Cruikshank 92 U.S. 542553. Namely that the 2ⁿᵈ· Amendment does NOT give persons the right to keep and bear arms without regulations within a well regulated Militia.
   "A well regulated Militia, being necessary to the security of a free State , the right of the people to keep and bear Arms. shall not be infringed."
   The comma after the word State is for the stated purpose, according to Webster's Encyclopidic Dictionary, as a punctuation mark denoting the shortest pause in reading, and separates a sentence into divisions.
   A comma is clearly NOT a period and cannot be used to separate and construct two sentences.
   Am I right or is the N.R.A. right?

P.S. Feel free to correct any errors in punctuation or structure. But NOT in content!

Several years ago, when the United States Constitution was having its bicentennial, National Public Radio decided to cover the Constitution from every angle anyone there could think of, including some loopy ones. A producer asked me to copy-edit it and its amendments, and tell *Morning Edition*'s listeners about the changes I thought should be made. That experience brought home to me how differently the Founders used punctuation from the way that I use it, or any contemporary writer does.

In the late 1700s the norms of comma placement had more to do with suggesting where pauses might occur in speech than they have today, and less to do with demarcating grammatical structure. Neither the commas nor even all of the words in the Constitution mean quite what they would if the document had just been drafted. Historical research, not grammatical inquiry, is the way to tell what the Founders had in mind—and what exactly the Second Amendment means.

That we need to conduct historical research in order to understand our own Constitution, a document of supreme patriotic and practical significance, is a good reminder that the more our language changes, the less of the past it can effortlessly convey to us, and the less of the present it can convey into the future.

The letter that began this chapter leaves me wanting to know something else, though. Does its author believe, as his postscript suggests, that punctuation and structure are trifles and his meaning will be clear even if what he writes is riddled with errors? (And, of course, he has made a few errors, including—despite his insistence that a comma is not a period—putting a period instead of a comma after "Arms.") Or does he believe his general point, that something as small as a comma can be all-important, in which case any imprecisions in his punctuation and structure may well make his letter as hard to interpret as the Second Amendment?

The truth about punctilios and meaning, I'm sure, is somewhere in the middle. On the one hand, it *is* hard to know what that letter means in every particular, just as the Second Amendment is notoriously open to interpretation. On the other hand, when we read either the letter or the Second Amendment, we get the idea. The amendment, further, is in force; people protest it, others militantly support it, and their disagreement is no more than peripherally concerned with commas. The Constitution and the Bill of Rights overall are widely admired, and not for their freedom from solecisms and the excellence of their punctuation. (All the same, my correspondents do enjoy complaining about the phrase *"more perfect* Union" in the Preamble, inasmuch as perfection is supposed to be incomparable.) Not for Shakespeare's rigorous adherence to the rules of contemporary standard English do we marvel at *Hamlet* and *As You Like It*. The point is: cultivate beautiful ideas and say them or write them down as best you can, and you will have editors like me as your acolytes.

Sometimes—often—that phrase *as best you can* is a euphemism for trying just hard enough to avoid embarrassing oneself, but here it means what it says. And we can almost always try a little harder to express ourselves a little more nearly perfectly. *As best you can* has many aspects, including some that this book has scarcely hinted at.

Oddly enough, a refinement on observing the punctilios—putting the commas where they belong, remembering that *perfect* is incomparable, and all the other hundreds of sparkly little facets of higher English we've considered—is forbearance from observing the punctilios inobservantly. For example: What's *between* two things is not supposed to include them, and so when the news on National Public Radio recently mentioned in an item about a railroad disaster that "these trains were built *between* 1991 *and* 1993," either that was put wrong or it was an awfully convoluted way of saying "trains built *in* 1992." I myself have corrected whole boxcar-loads of phrases like "presidential debates held *between* 1960 *and* 1980"—a phrase that in context was certainly meant to include the debates of 1960 and 1980. But not long ago I came upon a rate that "fluctuated *between* 33 *and* 45 percent." Hmmm. "Fluctuated *from* 33 *to* 45 percent," right? No doubt the rate did hit 33 percent and 45 percent. But the *fluctuation* occurred *between* the two points, making *between* the better choice here. Whenever I begin to think that I can make a minor distinction like that one with my eyes closed, some new, eye-opening variant of it turns up.

Besides using language that says what it means, we may decide to use language that fails to do that, the better to say what *we* mean. English contains words whose entire point, as we discussed in the "Double or Nothing" section of Chapter Five, is their effect on tone. It contains ordinary expressions with undevious reputations which mean the opposite of what they say. "*No doubt* it will be sunny this afternoon," for example, is a shade more doubtful than "It will be sunny this afternoon," and "*Surely* we won't need umbrellas" means only that that's one person's guess.

Whole realms of our language, in fact, are only tenuously related to what the words mean outright. Coded messages may lurk in what speakers and writers are avoiding saying. For example, "She has such a pretty face" in certain contexts means that her shape leaves something to be desired, and "She has a good figure" means that her face is not pretty. "Mistakes were made" not only means what it says but also hints that we won't be hearing the speaker take responsibility for the mistakes.

Further, there are the unintended consequences of what has and hasn't been said. We can hear the smug reproach or disparagement in "She has such a pretty face," and we may well take the remark as a declaration that the person making it is a prig. "Mistakes were made," as the listener hears it, sounds a lot like "I am a weasel." Variations on "I am not to blame" often come out of the mouths of politicians, but, strangely, by the time these reach the ears of listeners, they have all turned into "I am a weasel." A person who listens carefully can often hear advocacy journalists announcing "I am incapable of being fair-minded on this issue," and lifestyle journalists announcing "I am dippy," and many other people telling truths of which they're unaware.

Besides what isn't said, another kind of coded message is overstatement, and another example of unintended consequences is the effect that overstatement can have. As I learned one recent morning from another radio newsbreak, the union in a current and seemingly ordinary labor negotiation had the day before issued a press release likening the company to "a bloody-handed criminal blaming his victim after the fact." Good grief! No doubt this figure of speech was meant to convey the depth of the union's belief in its own cause. But it actually made me feel that things couldn't be as bad as all that, and that what the union said couldn't be accepted at face value. Ironically, the more passionate the overstatement, the likelier it is to arouse suspicion. When we feel so strongly about something that we'll say anything to make our point, we may be better off saying nothing.

Other examples exist of words performing different jobs from the ones for which they superficially seem intended, but here I will set that idea aside. Tone of language has a number of less convoluted tools at its disposal as well, among them how personal or reserved, how vulgar or dignified or prissy, how erudite, how funny, how hip, how righteous, or how considerate a speaker or writer is trying to be, and how ineptly or cleverly he or she is managing to try. Any one of these qualities which is present to any degree may have its own unintended consequences: hearers or readers may be put off to learn intimate details from that confiding stranger, or they may fail to be engaged by the reserved one, finding him stuffy.

On and on goes the list of qualities that can affect the impression language makes. What language describes can be all over the map, and yet language itself is relentlessly linear: words must be expressed, and understood, one at a time. Anyone trying to tell a complicated story, in which various things happen at once, or make a complicated argument, in which there are multiple relationships among ideas to be explored, has to wrestle the words into some sequence or other. And language can be as detailed or as loftily distant as we please: I can lead you in a slow, meticulous, attentive sweep of a given patch of conceptual territory, examining and analyzing many of its particulars as we go, or together we can skim over it, noting little more than its boundaries.

Speakers and writers who devote a great deal of attention to matters such as these—to schematizing their thoughts—and are not subtle about it tend to seem obsessive and pedantic (as in "Now let us consider three results of this fact, the first of which has two significant aspects"). But people who devote no attention at all to such matters can be annoying in their own way. If they're telling a joke, they never manage to put the punch line last, and serious and humorous subjects alike come out like shaggy-dog stories. In effect, these people are asking their readers or hearers to do much of their work for them.

Some part of any verbal communication may be, as well, sheer inept, random noise, such as the ambiguity that can result from typos and bad grammar and ideas that the speaker or writer hasn't thought through and would never express if he or she had. The louder this noise is, the more the listener or reader should beware. As Robert Graves and Alan Hodge warn in *The Reader Over Your Shoulder,* "When people have to write from a point of view which is not really their own, they are apt to betray this by hedging, blustering, an uneasy choice of words, a syntactical looseness." Or, in the words of an anonymous diplomat quoted in *The Complete Plain Words,* by Sir Ernest Gowers, "What appears to be a sloppy or meaningless use of words may well be a completely correct use of words to express sloppy or meaningless ideas."

Although we may sympathize with those who just say things or write them the way the things come into their heads, it is obvious that to do so is to ask to be misunderstood. Too bad, but getting the tone and the sequence right, as well as the information, can be a lot of work. This is true not just for high-flown rhetoric and literature meant to have enduring value but also for communication of the most humdrum sort.

Witless of me though it is to plunge into the humdrum at this rhetorically exalted moment, I'd like you to have an example of how much trouble one may need to go to in order to get something simple right. I know someone we'll call Barbara, to disguise her identity, whose neighbor employs a private garbage-collection service. As the garbage truck turns into or out of the neighbor's driveway, it often veers off the pavement onto Barbara's grass, gouging ruts as it goes. After the seventh or eighth time Barbara had smoothed out her lawn, she began to be annoyed. I offered to compose a letter for her.

> Dear ———,
> I hope you are well. I am writing now to call your attention to a small matter that perhaps has hitherto escaped your notice. By this I mean the irregularities in the surface of the portion of our property that lies nearest your home. These irregularities have been accumulating over the past number of months. Considering them unattractive, I have been investigating their origins. I am sorry to report...

Um, no. That won't do. I'm trying to be suave, but what I'm actually doing is droning on.

Dear ———,
Your garbage truck is digging ruts in my land. This
must stop.

Droning this is not, but now I seem hostile and
abrupt—as if I were a drafting a ransom note.

Dear ———,
I'm sure that *I* would want to know if we were upsetting our neighbors, including you, in any way. And so,
reluctantly, I must put pen to paper to extend to you
the same courtesy—namely,...

With this one, don't you picture me pausing every
few words to wring my hands?

Dear ———,
I'm writing about the ruts on my property along the
road running past our houses. It seems that your
garbage-collection service's truck is digging them
when it turns wide to enter your driveway. Smooth
them out though I do, they keep reappearing. I'd like
for the roadside to look nice. Can you help?

Ah. *There* we are.
I don't mean to present this version as a paragon. It
didn't work: my friend sent it, the truck kept gouging
ruts, and neither an apology nor any effort to repair the
damage was forthcoming. Sometimes not even *as best
we can* achieves the goal desired. All the same, we've got
to keep trying. Just now, too, I had a specific goal in
mind: to illustrate what varied impressions one person
can make even while conveying a single, simple message.
This book is, of course, practically a textbook on
what varied impressions different people can make. I'm

sure you've gotten mental pictures of many of my correspondents. The great majority of them seem like excellent company, don't they? But perhaps you've felt that a few of them drone on, a few are hostile and abrupt, and a few are on the verge of a nervous breakdown. No doubt the people gave these impressions in spite of themselves. They probably intended to demonstrate their suavity, or admirable directness, or sensitivity, but they lacked the command of language that would enable others to enter into their state of mind. If not that, then they were deluding themselves about the fine personal qualities they hoped to express.

I don't mean to present myself and my personal qualities, either, as any paragon. All the same, I believe that the highest purpose of language is to allow us to exhibit ourselves as the noble creatures we perceive ourselves to be. With our words—particularly our written words, or words that we have written down before we say them—we can be our best selves, and even selves better than our actual best. Our words, outside ourselves, can be objects for us to reflect on, objects to perfect, evidence for us to study if we want to know whether we're as kind or as clever as we like to think we are—and then they can be tools to help us be that kind or clever if we can just use them skillfully and patiently.

It is impossible for us to see ourselves minute by minute as others see us, or as they would see us if they were present; it is impossible to be continually our best selves. But we can demand of words serving as permanent representations of us that they be their best: judicious, lively, sympathetic, wise—or what qualities would you hope for?

The anthropologist Clifford Geertz wrote, in the introduction to *Local Knowledge*:

To see others as sharing a nature with ourselves is the merest decency. But it is from the far more difficult achievement of seeing ourselves amongst others, as a local example of the forms human life has locally taken, a case among cases, a world among worlds, that the largeness of mind, without which objectivity is self-congratulation and tolerance a sham, comes.

Then again, the philosopher E. M. Cioran wrote, in *The Trouble With Being Born*:

If we could see ourselves as others see us, we would vanish on the spot.

And though I wish to but know I cannot, so I shall.

Index